Sabine Damir-Geilsdorf, Ulrike Lindner, Gesine Müller,
Oliver Tappe, Michael Zeuske (eds.)
Bonded Labour

Sabine Damir-Geilsdorf, Ulrike Lindner, Gesine Müller,
Oliver Tappe, Michael Zeuske (eds.)

Bonded Labour
Global and Comparative Perspectives (18th–21st Century)

[transcript]

Bibliographic information published by the Deutsche Nationalbibliothek
The Deutsche Nationalbibliothek lists this publication in the Deutsche Nationalbibliografie; detailed bibliographic data are available in the Internet at http://dnb.d-nb.de

© 2016 transcript Verlag, Bielefeld

All rights reserved. No part of this book may be reprinted or reproduced or utilized in any form or by any electronic, mechanical, or other means, now known or hereafter invented, including photocopying and recording, or in any information storage or retrieval system, without permission in writing from the publisher.

Cover layout: Kordula Röckenhaus, Bielefeld
Cover illustration: Coolies in the West Indies, ca. 1890 (Houghton Library, Harvard University).
Back Cover: Labour Migrants in Dubai, 2014 (photo by Sabine Damir-Geilsdorf).
Printed in Germany
Print-ISBN 978-3-8376-3733-5
PDF-ISBN 978-3-8394-3733-9

Contents

Introduction: Global Variants of Bonded Labour
Oliver Tappe and Ulrike Lindner | 9

Coolies – Asiáticos and Chinos:
Global Dimensions of Second Slavery
Michael Zeuske | 35

Indentured Labour in Sub-Saharan Africa (1880-1918):
Circulation of Concepts between Imperial Powers
Ulrike Lindner | 59

Coolie Transformations – Uncovering the Changing Meaning and Labour Relations of Coolie Labour in the Dutch Empire (18th and 19th Century)
Matthias van Rossum | 83

Variants of Bonded Labour in Precolonial and Colonial Southeast Asia
Oliver Tappe | 103

"His Original Name Is . . ."
REMAPping the Slave Experience in Saudi Arabia
Alaine S. Hutson | 133

Contract Labour and Debt Bondage in the Arab Gulf States.
Policies and Practices within the *Kafala* System
Sabine Damir-Geilsdorf | 163

Re-presenting and Narrating Labour: Coolie Migration in the Caribbean
Liliana Gómez-Popescu | 191

Cultural Forms of Representation of 'Coolies': Khal Torabully and his Concept of Coolitude
Gesine Müller and Johanna Abel | 219

Authors | 229

Acknowledgements

This edited volume consists of papers presented at the workshop 'Forms of Bonded Labour', organized by the research group 'From Slave to Coolie' at the Global South Studies Center, University of Cologne (23-24 June 2014). At the international workshop 'Coolies, Forced Work, Migration and Transculturation', hosted by the Casa Fernando Ortiz (University of Havana/Cuba, 2-4 March 2015), the members of the GSSC research group deepened the discussion on the 'coolie variant' of global labour migration, as reflected in the introduction to this volume. We would like to express our gratitude to the Global South Studies Center for the financial and institutional support in organizing these workshops and the present publication. Special thanks are reserved for Sergio Vilaboy and his Cuban colleagues for the inspiring discussions and generous hospitality in Havana. Andrew Gardner, Vincent Houben, Marcel van der Linden, and Alexander Keese kindly shared their ideas on questions of global labour relations with us. Finally, we would like to thank our student assistants Bebero Lehmann and Fabian Heerbaart, cartographer Monika Feinen, and language editor Pax for supporting the production of this volume.

Introduction: Global Variants of Bonded Labour

OLIVER TAPPE AND ULRIKE LINDNER

INTRODUCTION

When in 1874 the Chinese Commission to Cuba investigated the bad reputation of coolie labour as a kind of semi-slavery, many Chinese labourers in Cuba and other colonies handed in written testimonies and petitions to report their terrible living conditions (Yun 2008: 34; cf. Ng 2014). In Cuba, Chinese coolies lived next to slaves from Africa, and their 'voluntary' contract did not spare them from being treated as chattels. As one coolie testified:

"We were all naked when we were inspected by buyers. We never saw people being humiliated in such a terrible way. We were sold to sugar plantations and treated worse than dogs and oxen. Foreign overseers rode on horses, with cowhide whips and guns in their hands. Regardless of our speed or quality, they lashed us from a distance; they hit us with clubs within reach. Some of us had bones broken and some spat blood right away. People with cracked head and broken legs still had to work instead of being sent into a ward. Countless people died of injury within eight years." (Quoted in Yun 2008: 120)

The same holds true for Indian coolies in Mauritius, who in 1839 – two years after the official beginning of Indian coolie migration to the island of Mauritius and six years after the official end of slavery in the British Empire – were already complaining about abuse, mistreatment and withheld wages.[1] Here, a

---

1 Report of the Committee appointed by the Supreme Government of India to enquire into the abuses alleged to exist in exporting from Bengal Hill Coolies and Indian

commission was appointed to investigate the problems – but still, after a short moratorium the coolie trade from India to Mauritius continued. Even if such reports became an embarrassment for the 'civilized' world and some flows of coolie migration were stopped, the coolie trade continued long into the 20th century.

Apparently, colonial systems of indentured labour in many respects still resembled the slavery that they allegedly replaced. With the signing of the contract, colonial coolies – like South Asian contract workers in the Arab Gulf States and Malaysia today – gave up basic rights and physical integrity. Even if payment, duration of contracts, and food provisions were usually guaranteed by certain bureaucratic regulations, the workers were extremely vulnerable, subject to arbitrary violence, and in danger of indebtedness. These specific kinds of bonded labour relations were marked by manifold ambiguities that render a free/unfree labour dichotomy analytically questionable.

FORMS OF BONDED LABOUR

This volume addresses historically and regionally different cases of bonded labour as examples of unfree labour relations, covering the period from the 18th century until today. While aspects of slavery and servitude, of debt, violence, and precarity, certainly play a significant role for the understanding of bonded labour in general, the authors in this collection also acknowledge the aspirations and agency of indentured labourers, thus aiming to illuminate the grey area between the poles of chattel slavery and 'free' wage labour. We try to avoid the dichotomy of free and unfree labour in order to focus more appropriately on diverse empirical cases (in accordance with the arguments of other recent studies of bonded labour relations; cf. Lerche 2011; Derks 2010; Coté 2014; Chalhoub 2011; Zeuske 2015; Houben/Lindblad 1999; Breman 2012, Chalcraft 2009).[2]

In order to achieve a truly global and comparative perspective, we present case studies from different world regions in both historical and contemporary perspectives (18th-21st century). In addition, this volume constitutes a transdisciplinary endeavour by bringing together case studies from history, social sciences, anthropology, and cultural studies. All contributions explore the econo-

---

Labourers of various classes to other countries (1839), Calcutta: G.H. Huttmann, Bengal Military Orphan Press.

2   For the ongoing, huge debate on free and unfree labour, see e.g. Brass/van der Linden 1997.

mic mechanisms, historical contradictions, and sociocultural dimensions of historical variants of bonded labour, especially what we call the coolie variant.

Bonded labour in a global historical perspective – including indentured and coolie labour – constitutes the common issue of the various studies. Being an interdisciplinary endeavour, the collection benefits from the productive exchange of ideas, concepts and approaches across disciplinary boundaries. The various chapters investigate forms of contract labour, debt bondage and indentured labour in various regions of the world – the Caribbean, Africa, Southeast Asia, and the Middle East – thus also aiming at a global understanding of the topic. Consequently, we deal with a huge variety of labour situations, in most cases strongly connected with migration movements.

We have chosen the term 'bonded labour' as the title for the edited volume as it seems to incorporate a broad range of labour relations between free and unfree labour, as Annuska Derks has argued in the introduction of a recent special issue on bonded labour in Asia (Derks 2010). We also try to link our volume to earlier research by Emmer, Boogaart, Klein, and Twaddle (Emmer/Boogaart 1986, Twaddle 1993, Klein 1993) who have already called attention to the variety of unfree labour situations in different regions of the world and who have addressed the blurred boundaries between slavery, bonded labour and various forms of coerced and contract labour.

However, there are certain specificities one would find in most of the case studies in the volume. Most investigate the problem of unfree labour, unequal power relations, various kinds of exploitation, graded rights and racial exclusion. The authors consider colonial coolies and modern neo-bondage as embodiments of global inequalities and human states of exception: Labourers are confronted with risky choices and temporary suspensions of basic human rights.[3] We look at forms of labour that are not free, but also not always forced labour. We investigate labour arrangements shaped by contracts that often bind the workers for several years to certain locations, with considerable legal or practical constraints on leaving the contract, and with restrictions of personal freedom and mobility. The forms of labour we are addressing are often shaped by debt relations, as indebtedness forces people to enter such labour contracts, and accumulated debts often prevent people from quitting a coercive contract and, instead, force them to sign another contract (cf. Breman 2008).

---

3 Severe long-term relations of labour bondage still exist today, as numerous case studies from South Asia demonstrate (cf. Breman/Guérin 2009; De Neve 2005; thanks to our colleague Michael Hoffmann for this clarification).

These forms of work organization and migration can be found up until today. Accordingly, in a report of 2013, the ILO tried to break down legal definitions of unfree labour into 'operational indicators', which can be summarized in the following three dimensions:

1) "Unfree recruitment", which means, in the description of the ILO, coercive as well as deceptive recruitment;
2) "Life and work under duress", with indications such as limited freedom, withholding of wages, forced overtime or task, and the retention of identity papers;
3) "Impossibility of leaving the employer." (Harroff-Tavel/Alix 2013: 37)

The first aspect seems to be of particular interest for our approach. Often, forms of bonded labour or contract labour are referred to as labour situations with a voluntary entry. However, in practice, the boundaries between compulsory/ coerced and voluntary entry are blurred.

In this volume, we investigate the tension between the allegedly 'voluntary' entry into the contract and the real social, economic, and political conditions that generate the forced entry and non-exit-ability of the contract. Indentured and contract labourers often agree to the initial terms of their contract, but are not able to end or alter the duration of the contract once it begins (cf. Allen 2013). Often forms of coercion, such as poverty, debt, or impending imprisonment, are necessary to bring people to agree to this form of contract. The chapters also deal with the ensuing migration flows created by forms of bonded labour. They explore the blurred boundaries of forced and voluntary labour migration, and the precarious conditions of workers under various systems of bonded labour. Other common topics are the ambiguous relationship between (in/voluntary) displacement and subsequent immobilization, and the transformations of social relations during and after periods of bonded labour (ibid.). Moreover, the single case studies consider regimes and bureaucracies of labour organization – in a way, the infrastructures of bonded labour. We also address the inherent violence of unfree labour, and forms of control over the working body.

Many of the chapters concentrate explicitly on indentured labour as a certain type of bonded labour. Indentured work migration was one of the biggest migration movements worldwide after the end of the slave trade and the eventual abolition of slavery in the British Empire in 1833. Other means of capitalist exploitation had to satisfy the needs of colonial economic interests, particularly in plantation economies and in sugar production. Planters refused or were not able to cope with free labour, and demanded 'reliable' workers in compounds after abolition.

Thus, since the 1830s, Asian workers, mostly from India and China and generally addressed as coolies, were brought to colonial environments to work in plantations and mines in various parts of the world in schemes of unfree labour (cf. Tinker 1974; Northrup 1995; Meagher 2008; Allen 2014; Zeuske 2016a). The British, Americans, French, Spanish and Portuguese were all strongly involved in the export of Asian labour (Yun 2008: 38-39) The colonial mechanisms of *corvée* and coolie labour served the economic and administrative interests of the colonial state (cf. Northrup 1995; Laviña/Zeuske 2014). Coolies became another form of disposable labour, caught in a precarious interplay between contract security and exploitation, debt and economic opportunity.

Map: Global coolie migration

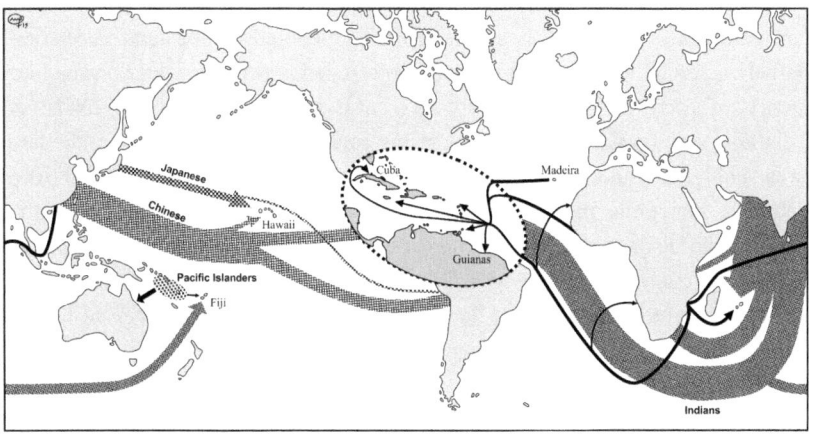

Revised map based on Northrup (1995: 3).

As a kind of "voluntary slavery" (Angleviel 2001), coolie labour was simultaneously both voluntary and coerced (notably by generally precarious socioeconomic conditions), perhaps including aspects of the conditions of both precolonial servitude and postcolonial 'voluntary' wage labour. Even if it was officially a voluntary negotiation process, often kidnapping, decoy, and fraud were involved. Conditions in the depots where the labourers were stored awaiting shipment and on the vessels on which they sailed were cramped and inhumane, resulting in sickness, misery, and death. Neither the Western colonial governments nor the Chinese and Indian government made more than a very slight attempt to correct the abuses. As Mazumdar (2007: 129) puts it: "[...] where Asian migrants came in as indentured workers on the heels of slavery, they faced conditions directly inherited from those of slavery".

European indentured labour to the Americas was, on the one hand, the precedent of the colonial coolie system, with migrants working under contracts, mainly in agricultural production. On the other hand, we should not ignore the significance of contracts in traditional forms of bonded labour, especially in China. Asian coolies in colonial times – contracted under penal sanctions – arguably faced more constraints, such as everyday violence and racism, forced immobilization in the workplace, and other elements of non-freedom (Bahadur 2014). The indenture system became not only a key pillar of colonial economy but also a means of control and discipline (cf. van der Linden 2011; Slocomb 2007). In the 1920/30s, the organized system of colonial indenture was coming to an end, even if similar forms of indenture persisted until the 1970s (Martinez 2005) and can also be found today.

The millions of Asian workers that migrated through the indenture system are commonly addressed as coolies. Before colonialism, the term *coolie* was largely reserved for casual day-labourers in Asian port cities, which formed key nodes of early global trade networks (Masashi 2009; Manning 2004). As Matthias van Rossum demonstrates in his contribution to this volume, the term was ambiguous and included a broad range of casual and/or seasonal wage labour – sometimes parallel to slave labour or even performed by slaves, thus making the distinction between coerced and free labour problematic. The term *coolie* obviously stems from two different sources, the Tamil word for a certain payment for menial work, and the Gujarati word for a person from an inferior class or group of society. As Breman and Daniel argue, the English term *coolie* brought together the two words for person and payment, creating a new "category of proto-proletarian individuals devoid of their personhood" (Breman/Daniel 1992: 270; cf. Hayot 2014; Tappe, this volume). In China, the menial worker in Canton and other port cities – usually a man without master or family, recruited under a contract with (very low) day-to-day payment – became the emblematic figure of the coolie.

Moving away from ideal types of the coolie, Balachandran in her research thinks of a coolie

"as a social relationship rather than merely a figure, person, or term, even perhaps as a characteristic relationship between labour and capital outside a relatively small part of the West. As a labouring subject, stabilized, nominally unlike apprenticeship and indenture contracts, by coercive mechanisms of indefinite duration that were produced and configured during the very decades of 'slave emancipation' and the emergence of a free-standing working class, the 'coolie' serves also to interrupt narratives of progress from slavery to free labour [...]." (Balachandran 2011: 289)

Coolie labourers can also be viewed through the lens of subalternity and hybridity since they often constituted suppressed and alienated communities in ecologically and culturally foreign settings. Colonial – more or less coerced – labour migration implied new sociocultural configurations, emergent processes of creolization, and both the opportunities and the constraints of subaltern agency (cf. Prabhu 2005). Social and cultural change through coolie migration is definitely an important vector of the analysis of translocal labour migration under colonialism – next to the economic relevance of coolie work for colonial and postcolonial societies and economies.

The experience of various forms of exclusion and violence – "life and work under duress" in the words of ILO's 1930 definition of forced labour[4] – implied specific cultural representations of the coolie communities. Coolies often suffered strong racial discrimination. As Banivanua-Mar (2007) shows in her study of Pacific Islanders working as so-called *kanaka* labourers in Queensland/Australia, these indentured workers were ambiguously situated between white settlers and the black aborigines, but were nonetheless a target of racial discrimination and outright violence. Subject to racial stereotypes and limited self-determination, the coolies found themselves excluded from the discourse that forged certain post-abolitionist ideas of contract labour in the colonies. How were the coolies represented by their employers, and how did they represent themselves? (Yun 2008; Bahadur 2014; Gómez-Popescu, this volume).

Considering cultural aspects is crucial for a deeper understanding of coolie history. Coolie migration resulted in radically altered sociocultural and demographic configurations in both home and host societies. Coolies formed temporary communities with exceptional gender and age ratios, often next to culturally and linguistically different societies (cf. Vertovec 1992; Mohapatra 2006). As in the case of slavery before, coolie migration triggered processes of creolization in the labour-receiving countries (even if one assumes that a large proportion of the coolies returned after having finished their contracts).

The formation of plural societies, for example in the Caribbean, is only one aspect of the cultural dynamics of global coolie migration. The radical experiences and shifting world-views of returnees arguably affected the communities and families in the countries of origin. Moreover, the legacy of coolie existence lingers on in individual memories, debates of multi-culturalism, and contemporary literary works (Bragard 2008; Müller/Abel, this volume).

---

4   For the full text of the 1930 Forced Labour Convention see: http://www.ilo.org/dyn/normlex/en/f?p=NORMLEXPUB:12100:0::NO::P12100_ILO_CODE:C029

Therefore, investigating cultural representations in the context of coolie labour opens a new dimension in understanding the experience of this specific labour relation. In this volume, all authors shed light on coolie life-worlds across the globe and throughout time – including present-day forms of contract labour that strikingly resemble 19th-century labour arrangements. Historical and anthropological accounts of contract labour certainly benefit from models and approaches of cultural studies and postcolonialism that address the very representations of coolie existence.

The concept of *coolitude* (Torabully 1992; Carter/Torabully 2002) provides an alternative to notions of creolization, négritude, and hybridity, inspired from the experience of displacement and transculturation of coolie communities that formed culturally heterogenous diasporas abroad (see below). This approach is certainly useful for the history of insular contexts where numerous coolie families found a new home in a multi-ethnic society – without completely breaking the kinship and cultural ties with the homeland. The legacy of the ambiguous history of coolie communities as in the case of Mauritius (Allen 1999), or former penal colonies such as Nouvelle-Calédonie (de Deckker 1994), manifests itself in literary works and other artistic expression – shaped by past and present discourses of cultural difference and feelings of exclusion.

CONTENTS OF THE BOOK

The present volume can be divided into four main sections with different yet complementary perspectives on global variants of unfree labour:

1) The historical shift from slavery to coolie labour under colonialism in Africa and the Americas.
2) Historical variants of bonded labour in Southeast Asia.
3) Slavery and sponsorship-systems in the Arabian peninsula.
4) Coolie cultures, identity discourses and representations.

The four main sections of the book reflect different perspectives on specific historical and sociocultural configurations of bonded or unfree labour – from slaves on Caribbean sugar cane plantations to contract workers in the modern Arab Gulf States.

From Slave to Coolie

By discussing different patterns of coolie labour in the Americas and Africa in the 19th and early 20th century, and by focusing on Spanish, Portuguese and German examples we highlight the global reach of indentured labour. This phenomenon is reinforced by the growing knowledge exchange on indentured labour between colonial empires, as addressed in Lindner's chapter. Secondly, we illustrate the blurred boundaries between slavery and indentured labour, especially in the Spanish and Portuguese Empire, where slavery and indenture co-existed next to each other. As a third point, we address the strong connection between racist stereotypes and fears and the development of indentured Asian migration. The influx of growing groups of Asian labourers in colonial societies with strict demarcation lines between indigenous and European also produced new anxieties and regulations.

Thus we also aim to provide a lens through which to view present-day forms of unfree labour. As Marcel van der Linden (2001: 449-54) points out, labour was always a commodity in relations of slavery, sharecropping, and debt peonage, as well as in free wage-labour. While these systems coexisted under colonialism (and before), European expansion and later industrialization substantially depended on the exploitation of overseas unfree labour in the form of slaves and coolies (cf. Zeuske 2013). The global economy of the colonial empires of the 19th century – marked by labour-intensive resource extraction (cf. Tappe 2016) – used coolie labour to continue with forms of plantation economy during and after the abolition of slavery, to stabilize colonial economies with 'insufficient labour', to exploit new possibilities in the field of mining, and more generally, to disguise new forms of slavery.

This is particularly true when it comes to the exploitation of cheap, unskilled migrant labour under conditions of coercion and vulnerability. The *longue durée* of unfree labour includes forms of slavery, indentured labour, bonded servitude, and contemporary cases of neo-bondage, such as for example Asian contract labourers in the Arab Gulf States (see Damir-Geilsdorf, this volume). In the past as today, different modes of forced labour were compatible with free wage-labour and subsistence production (see van Rossum, this volume), and both today and in the past, capitalism does in fact include and has included many variants of unfree labour (Lucassen 2008; Mann 2011; Brass 2014). The exploitation of labour has always taken advantage of global inequalities and corresponding migration patterns.

As already mentioned, the global coolie trade sent mainly Chinese and Indian labourers to the vast plantations in the New World, to Africa, the Indian

Ocean and South East Asia, and brought about a new dimension of global labour migration during the 19th century – when slavery was gradually abolished by the colonial powers and came to be considered morally corrupt (Northrup 1995). Beginning in the 1820s, the coolie trade became one of the most important factors of global migration in world history (Hoerder 2012), as in the case of the vast plantation enclaves in the Caribbean (Gómez-Popescu, this volume).

As Michael Zeuske alerts us, patterns of slavery did not necessarily cease to exist after abolition (cf. Keese 2014 for forced labour in Africa); indeed, they persisted in two ways: Firstly, the massive transfer of coolies by sea and subsequent coercive labour relations are included as a global dimension in the so-called 'Second Slavery' – that is, persistent patterns of bonded and forced labour (migration) after the formal abolition of the Atlantic slave trade (1820 in Spain, 1836 in Portugal; cf. Tomich/Zeuske 2009; Laviña/Zeuske 2014). Secondly, Zeuske shows how collaboration between colonialists and indigenous entrepreneurs contributed to continual regimes of forced labour, and thus to the blurring of the slave/coolie binary. That this notion of a binary is difficult to uphold is also illustrated by notary protocols and testaments in which *asiáticos* (or *chinos*) appear as subjects. Zeuske provides valuable insights into the exploitative labour relations, precarious living conditions, and experiences of violence and death in the coolie settlements abroad (for the Caribbean context see as well Yun 2008; Hu-Dehart 1993).

In her contribution, Ulrike Lindner addresses the integration of colonial Africa in the worldwide system of indentured labour during the period of high imperialism. Indentured labour in the 19th and early 20th century is mainly seen as a phenomenon of Indian and Chinese contract workers replacing slaves in the plantation productions of the Caribbean, the Indian Ocean (especially Mauritius) and South East Asia. However, there were significant numbers of Indian and Chinese indentured labourers who worked not only in the plantations and mines of British South Africa but in various colonies of the European powers in sub-Saharan Africa, thus also forming part of the history of labour migration and bonded labour in colonial Africa. The chapter discusses some of these developments and investigates the circulation of knowledge between imperial powers regarding the issue of Asian indentured workers. The chapter first focusses on exchange between German and British colonies in Africa, and then deals with the discussions of indentured labour in the Institute Colonial International in Brussels. The institute, founded in 1894, had the explicit aim of facilitating knowledge transfer between colonial powers and was mainly influenced by French, Dutch, German and Belgian colonizers. The discussions were strongly shaped by racial stereotypes and fears of competition between white Europeans and Asians, especially when bringing Asian coolies to 'black Africa'.

Both Lindner and Zeuske indicate the importance of Asian coolies for the globalized economy of the nineteenth and early twentieth century and for the development of colonial empires.

Shifting Meanings of Bonded Labour: Slaves and Coolies in Southeast Asia

In Dutch and French colonial interpretations of coolie labour, we can identify a hybridization of different historically and culturally specific regimes of labour. Local labour arrangements were complemented with medieval and early modern European examples of *corvée* and other forms of servitude. When the French in 17th-century Quebec introduced the so-called *trente-six-mois* to organize European settlement in the new domains across the Atlantic, they adopted a feudal framework that inspired later colonial systems of indentured labour (Mauro 1986; Engerman 1986; Stanziani 2014). In French Indochina at the turn of the 20th century, such old labour regimes were emulated to form a coolie system that also took local traditions of tributary labour into account.

An aspect of the colonial tax system, compulsory labour – for example in road construction – was called *corvée*. While abolished in 1789 with the French Revolution, this concept re-emerged in the context of French colonial policy to organize labour relations and taxation in rural Indochina. Indigenous labourers came to be referred to by the English term *coolie* (Bunout 1936). Meanwhile, in the Dutch colonies (West Indies and Indonesian archipelago), different ideas of coolie (Dutch: *koelie*) labour included casual wage labour, slave labour, *corvée* labour, or indentured labour modelled after the British system (Houben/Lindblad 1999).

In his chapter, Matthias van Rossum recovers the different and changing meaning of the concept of coolie, focusing on 18th and 19th century case studies for the Indonesian Archipelago (Batavia and surroundings) and South Asia (mainly Ceylon). As van Rossum demonstrates, the term *koelie* (coolie) was an important, but not necessarily stable concept. The notion referred to labour relations, but could mean different things in different regions and times. In the 18th century, for example, there seemed to have been a strong regional difference between these two important regions within the empire of the VOC, varying from temporary wage labour to tributary labour relations. In the 19th century, the term *coolie* changed, as it also did in the Dutch empire, and became synonym for the (formally and informally bonded) contract labour (cf. Breman 1989).

Here we find striking parallels with the French colonial context described by Oliver Tappe. In Indochina, he identifies a parallel structure of a coolie system based on the *treinte-six-mois*, the British coolie system, and local arrangements of *corvée* labour where the labourers where also considered 'coolies'. By then, the term *coolie* had travelled from India to the islands in the Indian Ocean and the Asian port cities, finally ending up in the mountains of Indochina, and still carrying connotations of low-skilled and menial workers (Breman 2008). Where Asian port cities became important hubs of the globalized colonial economy – as in the case of Macao, Malacca and Batavia – local concepts of coolie labour became entangled with the emerging colonial labour regime based on indentured labour. Labour relations in Southeast Asia were thus characterized by parallel and anachronistic patterns of unfree labour, partly inspired by forced labour in precolonial Asian kingdoms.

There are both similarities and differences between precolonial variants of slavery and bonded servitude in Southeast Asia. Social responsibility that was largely absent in later coolie regimes often formed part of precolonial bonded labour relations, even though the idea of a 'benign' slavery (still articulated by nationalist historiography in Thailand; cf. Winichakul 1994; Bowie 1996) is difficult to uphold. The ambiguous Tai-Lao concept of *kha* (slave/serf), which not only refers to a socioeconomic category but also includes connotations of ethnic difference and racial discrimination, implied mutual social obligations as well as everyday forms of sociopolitical exclusion. Aspects of socioeconomic coercion, arbitrary violence, and indebtedness, however, characterized both precolonial and colonial regimes of bonded labour (cf. Bush 2000; Jennings 2011).

Models of contract labour in present-day Southeast Asia show striking parallels with the aforementioned variants of bonded labour (Derks 2010). In the case of the migration of Vietnamese and Indonesian domestic workers to Malaysia, the migrants face both economic opportunities and precarious living conditions (Huong 2010; Killias 2010). The work contract here implies both security and coercion, thus creating ambiguous spaces of labour relations that can hardly be described with the free/unfree labour binary. By taking a rather broad concept of bonded labour, our approach allows a comparative perspective on a completely different geographical and cultural context, such as the Arab World.

Case Studies from the Arabian Peninsula

The introduction of capitalism in Asia created new economic enclaves where migrant labourers found themselves "cast adrift into a category of proto-proletarian individuals" (see above; Breman/Daniel 1992: 270), with basic human rights and even personhood stripped off. As the contributions by Alaine S. Hutson and Sabine Damir-Geilsdorf in this volume demonstrate, this observation is definitely true for different forms of bonded labour in Saudi Arabia and the Gulf States as well. At present, the fate of South Asian contract workers on the proliferating construction sites in the Gulf States is perhaps the most prominent example of different degrees of labour bondage (cf. Gardner 2012).

The chapter by Alaine S. Hutson examines the lives of enslaved Africans in 20th-century Saudi Arabia, on the basis of records of the British Legation in Jeddah from 1926 to 1938. By then, the British were liberating and repatriating runaway slaves as stipulated in Article 7 of the 1927 treaty of Jeddah. Her analysis of these records[5] shows the inadequacies of the established scholarly paradigm of a 'benign Islamic slavery' and a more oppressive slavery in the Atlantic World. Hutson's case studies illustrate that slaves in Saudi Arabia experienced patterns of subordination and humiliation similar to those experienced by the slaves in the Americas while doing similar work: for example, owners' naming practices, owners' assignments of labour based on a slave's country of origin, and Saudi Arabia's drafting of fugitive slave laws and treaties in response to slaves' seeking of British manumission and help in repatriation.

Furthermore, her contribution shows that after the end of manumission in 1936, the Saudi slave regulations were not widely known or followed by the Saudi police. One of her case studies for instance documents the example of a Sudanese domestic who had been enslaved while on *hajj* in 1908 at the age of twenty-six, and who after escaping was liberated and repatriated to Sudan in 1927. When he returned to Saudi Arabia in 1937 as a free man and an employee of the British government in Sudan – holding a legitimate Sudanese passport in order to perform the *hajj* – he was identified by his old owner and seized by the Saudi police.

---

5   These records are archived by Alaine Hutson in her online database for researchers: Runaways Enslaved and Manumitted on the Arabian Peninsula (REMAP); www.REMAPdatabase.org.

In her chapter on the Arab context, Sabine Damir-Geilsdorf analyzes current forms of bonded labour in the Arab Gulf States where both the migrant workers' residency and employment are regulated by a specific sponsorship system (*kafala*). Certain provisions in this kind of guest-worker scheme for temporary contract labourers differ from country to country, but substantial portions of the responsibility for controlling the migrant workers' entry and exit, as well as workers' mobility during their stay, are delegated to nationals and their proxies. Focusing on the examination of legal frameworks, recruitment policies and practices, and findings from fieldwork in Dubai and Qatar, Damir-Geilsdorf demonstrates that the high dependance of migrant workers on their national sponsors, mirrored in requirements such as an exit permit from the sponsor in order to leave the country, or his 'no objection certificate' (NOC) to change employers in order to avoid being categorized in official rethoric as an 'absconder' or 'runaway', subject to immediate detention and/or deportation, clearly violates workers' freedom of mobility (cf. Khan/Harroff-Tavel 2011).

At the same time, migrant workers' experiences in the Arab Gulf States show a high variability. While some of them are able to save substantial sums during their stay, low-income Asian labour migrants often end up in situations of debt-bondage, and in employment situations for which they did not voluntarily sign up at home. This is particularly the case when they fall victim to deceptive recruitment, contract frauds or illegal visa trading in which – not only in the Arab Gulf States but also in the sending countries – a chain of recruitment agencies, labour supply agencies, brokers, contractors, and sub-contractors and other intermediaries is involved (cf. Longva 1997; Kamrava/Babar 2012).

Taking into account these restrictions on personal freedom and mobility; the fact that migrant workers are criminalized and labelled 'absconders' or 'runaways' when they leave their employers before the termination of their work contract; and requirements such as 'exit permits' and 'NOC's from employers, accompanied by exploitative, squalid working conditions, some aspects of contract work under the *kafala* system can be considered contemporary forms of bonded labour. Working arrangements are often defined by an involuntary entry into the relation (Barrientos/Kothari/Philipps 2013: 1038-1039), whereas contemporary forms of non-freedom also arise from the inability to exit from working relations (Brass 2014: 575). These characteristics do not directly apply to contract labour in the GCC countries, since migrant workers come voluntarily, and at least theoretically have the option of cancelling their contracts.

The highly precarious situations of migrant workers are not an unequivocal result of the *kafala* system, though. Rather, they are a result of widespread labour-law violations and illegal practices by sponsors, companies, recruitment agencies, sub-contractors etc., and the lack of control or enforcement of regulations also contributes to the precariousness (as in the case of contract labour arrangements in Southeast Asia today). Especially low-skilled Asian migrant workers often face contract fraud, such as the substitution of their contracts when arriving at the airport, the withholding of wages, the confiscation of passports, or the requirement to work much longer hours than stated in the contract.[6]

Cultural Aspects and *Coolitude*

The system of indenture – as an aspect of colonial exploitation in general – has left durable traces on the material environment as well as on people's bodies and minds (see Stoler 2008). Structures such as the Aapravasi Ghat on Mauritius, the remnants of an immigration depot built in 1849 – today a Unesco World Heritage Site – function as *lieux de mémoire* (Nora 1989) of the colonial legacy. With its labour intensive sugar economy one of the first sites of the coolie experiment after the abolishment of slavery in 1833, Mauritius became the destination – and transit zone – for half a million indentured labourers, mainly from India (cf. Allen 1999; 2003).

The social and cultural dimensions of this global mass migration are still relatively poorly understood in comparison to the colonial economic strategies, bureaucratic regulations, and demographic effects. As already indicated, exploring cultural representations in the context of coolie labour opens a new dimension in our understanding of the experience of this form of migrant labour – a specific labour relation which implies precariousness and duress. Postcolonial and cultural studies aim to explore the interplay of re-configuration of the postcolonial self.

In her visual approach, Liliana Gómez-Popescu (this volume), examines a series of photographs (mainly taken by the United Fruit Company) that bear witness to the Chinese and Indian Coolie migration in the Caribbean at the turn of the twentieth century. She tackles the problem of cultural representation of coolie labour through the following questions: What exactly do such images visibilize? How do visual and textual documents re-present and narrate labour? How do they register the Coolie experience? Besides discussing the 'image' of the coolie, Gómez-Popescu also pays attention to the present-day vestiges –

---

6 Cf. Frantz (2013) for an insightful study of state complicity with regard to bonded labour relations in the case of Sri Lankan domestic workers in Jordan.

environmental degradation, ecological ruins – of colonial economic 'modernization'. The coolie system has imprinted itself on landscapes and bodies, forming part of imagined modernities, global migration, and the dispersal of working bodies, and has shaped both internal and external worlds.

Following Breman and Daniel (1992: 268) coolie-identity "is as much the product of self-perception as it is the construction of a category by those who did not belong to it". We have access to many sources with which to trace back colonial stereotypes and the emergence of the coolie concept as epithet for indentured labour. In contrast, we know considerably less about how the coolies perceived themselves and their predicament as bonded labourers, of how people responded to the feeling of being "mislabeled and degraded, unable to name themselves" (Bahadur 2014: xxi).

Authors such as Yun (2008) and Bahadur (2014) let 'the coolie speak', and engage with the silences of colonial history (see as well Roopnarine 2011; Singh 2012). More directed to the present repercussions of the ambivalent experiences involved in being a coolie, the poet Khal Torabully devoted himself to embracing the heritage of global scattering and everyday experiences of the former coolie communities that today shape the creole societies of the Caribbean and the Indian Ocean (Torabully 1992; Carter/Torabully 2002). As Gesine Müller and Johanna Abel show in their chapter, Torabully's visionary work implies a sense of shared beginnings and a revison of both historical and current globalization processes by including those who have been historically excluded. The poet desires to give speech to all those living subjects who, due to their miserable circumstances, have been forced to hire themselves out as wage and contract labourers.

Torabully's inclusion of the ethnic complexity of post-abolitionist societies in the Caribbean and in the Indian Ocean allows one to grasp the process of creolization in a less essentializing manner. With his concept of coolitude he advances Franco-Caribbean models of archipelagic creoleness, such as Négritude, Créolité, Antillanité and creolization, as well as the concepts of Indianité and Indienocéanisme. The concept of coolitude is not predicated by geographical affiliation or ethnic origin, but by the economic and legal situation of the coolies – contract labourers who made their way not only from India and China, but also from Europe and Africa to various archipelagic regions like the Caribbean, the Indian Ocean, and the Pacific. With his mosaic model of combined identities, Torabully introduces social status as a theoretically crucial factor in creolization. While former coolie migrants in many parts of the world – not to mention 'free' migrant workers that were lumped into that category as well (see Balachandran 2011 for the example of Indian seafarers on British vessels) – had rejected the term *coolie* as pejorative and insulting, Torabully aims to promote a more self-conscious and affirmative stance towards this historically laden concept.

We understand coolitude as a certain ethos stemming from the experience of hard work, displacement, exclusion, humiliation, resistance, and solidarity. How this resonates in artistic works of coolies or their descendants provides another lens through which to focus upon the coolie experience as cultural phenomenon (cf. Daniel 2008). This would also open new perspectives to the understanding of the everyday experience of contemporary contract labourers moving around the globe, and their cultural representations and intra-group dynamics in foreign and precarious environments.

OUTLOOK

On 31 March 2016, the German newspaper *Die Zeit* reported on North Korean contract labourers working on tomato farms in Poland – isolated in camps, with up to 90 per cent of their salaries claimed by the Korean government (Köckritz/Petrulewicz 2016). In another scandalous case a few months earlier, *The Guardian* uncovered the fate of Burmese migrants working under slave-like conditions in Thailand's booming shrimp industry (Mason et al. 2015). Similar examples of unfree labour haunt contemporary Africa, where human trafficking and forced labour proliferate, from domestic slaves to sex workers (van den Anker 2004).

Such contemporary cases of unfree labour fuelled the expansion of the somewhat misleading catch phrases of 'new' or 'modern slavery' (ibid.; Bales 2004; Miers 2003). They invoke ideas of a historically new phenomenon in an old guise. In our understanding, relations of unfree labour are, rather, an ongoing class-based phenomenon linked to broader conditions of global inequality – in colonial times as well as today. The idea of modern slavery, especially with regard to sexual exploitation, is still less concerned with ideas of global inequality than with 'victims' of human trafficking (Andrijasevic 2007; Molland 2012).

As some case studies in this volume suggest, the term 'new coolies' might be more appropriate. Such labour relations are characterized by different degrees of bondedness, coercion, and voluntariness, with graded rights, as well as with incentives and constraints on entry and exit of contract – while lacking key aspects of formal slavery such as the idea of property. However, postulating 'new' coolies (as in the case of the 'new' slaves) assumes a false historical break that would ignore the continuities of global relations of capitalist exploitation and ongoing global inequalities. In addition, the various coercive and precarious factors of past and present variants of bonded labour intersect, and blur rigid categories of slavery, coolie labour and 'free' wage work.

An alternative approach would be Michael Zeuske's idea of a historical continuity of slavery – what he frames as intersecting plateaus of slavery (Zeuske 2016b). From this perspective, abolition appears only as a minor hiatus in a long history of labour exploitation. Post-abolitionist regimes (and persistent local variants) of bonded labour are merely expressions of global inequalities and labour exploitation – or, rather, of capitalist relations in general. Consequently, also the ILO campaigns against indentured and forced labour were not able to address the underlying socioeconomic conditions of labour exploitation. As Lebaron and Ayers (2013) argue, neoliberal tendencies of global capitalism entailed more subtle forms of coerced labour.

Indeed, the boundaries between historical forms of bonded labour and the so-called free wage labour are difficult to uphold today – such labour regimes indeed overlapped in the past as well (see van Rossum, this volume; cf. Chalhoub 2011). Historical and present-day examples of 'coolie' contract labour epitomize disposable labour in a borderless capitalist world. This idea is today increasingly associated with neoliberal discourse (Ong 2006; Lebaron/Ayers 2013) and with notions of unbound mobility along global capitalist relations and value chains. Such labour relations imply an ambiguous interplay between opportunity and precariousness, freedom and forced immobilization, agency and vulnerability.

We are talking about the exploitation of labour under global capitalism, with some aspects of extremely unfree labour in fact anchored in arguably 'free' labour relations, intersecting and corresponding with outright unfree/forced labour. The historical example of the coolie as the colonial prototype of disposable labour still provides a useful model with which to understand variants of bonded labour in past and present configurations of (global) capitalist relations. It reveals the contingent nature of capital's emancipative claims and "it affords us a possibility to view the social relations of capital in a common frame unified across space, time, and social forms [...]" (Balachandran 2011: 289-90).

Studying the everyday lifes of Thai migrants in Singapore, Pattana Kitiarsa (2014) reveals the Agambenian 'bare life' of contract labourers, their vulnerable and precarious situation. His observation of migrant workers "stripped bare" and "economically and socially naked" (Kitiarsa 2014: 4) is also true for colonial coolies suffering sociocultural uprootedness, arbitrary violence, and economic duress. The 'coolie' appears emblematic of present-day global labour relations and unveils the ambiguities of present-day 'free' and 'flexible' labour arrangements (cf. Balachandran 2011).

Important aspects of contract labour are regional and global networks of labour recruitment (as in the case of the 'jobber' in the Indian construction industry, cf. Picherit 2009; and the global domestic labour economy with its peculiar mixture of state and non-state actors, cf. Killias 2010; Mills 1999; Nguyen 2015). Poverty, the desire for modernity, false promises, and indebtedness contribute to massive – allegedly 'voluntary' – labour mobilization. Yet today as in the past of the colonial coolie system, the aim of mobilizing the global poor results in re-immobilizing it "by tying it to the enclaves of capitalist production" (Breman/Daniel 1992: 271). In these very enclaves the workers often face racism, and have to endure sanctions from arbitrary violence to more subtle forms of legal coercion.

While it remains important to consider the precariousness/duress experienced by coolies, there is still need for more empirical research on the workers' agency and the sociocultural dynamics within coolie communities (cf. Roopnarine 2016 for an excellent case study of the West Indies). How did coolies cope with exploitation and uncertainty? How did gender relations shift and transform, and what new forms of social relations and self-empowerment emerged? How did the displaced workers express selfhood and belonging through artistic means? Khal Torabully's work inspires us to reflect on such aspects of the coolie experience.

To conclude, the treatment of colonial coolies reflected the "limits of liberalism" (Young 2015) under colonialism, while global market capitalism in the 21st century seems to bring forward new forms of unfree labour. For the duration of the contract, the workers – both in colonial times and the present – faced a temporary suspension of basic rights, and thus experienced vulnerability and distress. The contributions in this volume provide a vantage point from which to gain a better understanding of the history of unfree labour relations and, hopefully, also offer an opportunity to let the coolies speak.

REFERENCES

Allen, Richard B. (2014): "Slaves, Convicts, Abolitionism and the Global Origins of the Post-Emancipation Indentured Labor System." In: Slavery & Abolition 35/2, pp. 328–348.

—— (2013): "Slave Trading, Abolitionism, and "New Systems of Slavery" in the Nineteenth-Century Indian Ocean World." In: Robert Harms/Bernard K.

Freamon/David W. Blight (eds.), Indian Ocean slavery in the age of abolition, New Haven: Yale University Press, pp. 183-199.

—— (2003): "The Mascarene Slave-Trade and Labour Migration in the Indian Ocean during the Eighteenth and Nineteenth Centuries." In: Slavery & Abolition 24/2, pp. 33-50.

—— (1999): Slaves, Freedmen, and Indentured Laborers in Colonial Mauritius, Cambridge/New York: Cambridge University Press.

Andrijasevic, Rutvica (2007): "Beautiful Dead Bodies: Gender, migration and representation in anti-trafficking campaigns." In: Feminist Review 86/1, pp. 24-44.

Angleviel, Frédéric (2001): "De l'engagement comme, esclavage volontaire. Le cas des Océaniens, Kanaks et Asiatiques en Nouvelle-Calédonie (1853-1963)." In: Journal de la Société des océanistes 110, pp. 65-81.

Bahadur, Gaiutra (2014): Coolie Woman: The Odyssey of Indenture, Chicago: University of Chicago Press.

Balachandran, Gopalan (2011): "Making Coolies, (Un)making Workers: "Globalizing" Labour in the Late-19th and Early-20th Centuries." In: Journal of Historical Sociology 24/3, pp. 266-296.

Bales, Kevin (2004 [2000]): New Slavery: A Reference Handbook. 2nd edition, Santa Barbara: ABC-CLIO inc.

Banivanua-Mar, Tracey (2007): Violence and Colonial Dialogue: The Australian-Pacific Indentured Labor Trade, Honolulu: University of Hawai'i Press.

Barrientos, Stephanie/Kothari, Umar/Phillips, Nicola (2013): "Dynamics of unfree labour in the contemporary global economy." In: The Journal of Development Studies 49, pp. 1037-1041.

Bowie, Katherine A. (1996): "Slavery in nineteenth century northern Thailand." In: Edward Paul Durrenberger (ed.) State power and culture in Thailand, New Haven: Yale University Press, pp. 100–138.

Brass, Tom (2014): "Debating Capitalist Dynamics and Unfree Labor: A Missing Link." In: The Journal of Development Studies 50/4, pp. 570-584.

—— /van der Linden, Marcel (eds.) (1997): Free and Unfree Labor: The Debate Continues, Bern: Peter Lang.

Breman, Jan (2012): Outcast labour in Asia: circulation and informalization of the workforce at the bottom of the economy, New Delhi: Oxford University Press.

—— /Guérin, Isabelle (2009): "Introduction: On bondage: Old and New." In: Jan Breman/Isabelle Guérin/Aseem Prakash (eds.), India's unfree workforce: of bondage old and new, New Delhi: Oxford University Press, pp. i-xii.

—— (2008): "On Labour Bondage, Old and New." In: The Indian Journal of Labour Economics 51/1, pp. 83-90.
—— /Daniel, Valentine E. (1992): "Conclusion: The making of a Coolie." In: Journal of Peasant studies 19/3, pp. 268-296.
—— (1989): Taming the Coolie Beast: Plantation Society and the Colonial order in Southest Asia, Delhi: Oxford University Press.
Bunout, René (1936): La main-d'œuvre et la législation du travail en Indochine, Bordeaux: Imprimerie-Librairie Delmas.
Bush, Michael L. (2000): Servitude in Modern Times, Cambridge: Polity Press.
Carter, Marina/Torabully, Khal (2002): Coolitude. An Anthology of the Indian Labour Diaspora, London: Anthem Press.
Chalcraft, John (2009): The invisible cage: Syrian migrant workers in Lebanon Stanford studies in Middle Eastern and Islamic societies and cultures, Stanford: Stanford University Press.
Chalhoub, Sidney (2011): "The Precariousness of Freedom in a Slave Society. Brazil in the Nineteenth Century." In: International Review of Social History 56/3, pp. 405-439.
Coté, Joost (2004): "Slaves, Coolies, and Garrison Whores. A Colonial Discourse of "Unfreedom" in the Dutch East Indies." In: Gwyn Campbell/Elizabeth Elbourne (eds.), Sex, Power, and Slavery, Athens: Ohio University Press, pp. 561-582.
Daniel, E. Valentine (2008): "The Coolie." In: Cultural Anthropology 23/2, pp. 254–278.
de Deckker, Paul (ed.) (1994): Le peuplement du Pacifique et de la Nouvelle-Calédonie au XIXe siècle: Condamnés, Colons, Convicts, Coolies, Chân Dang, Paris: L'Harmattan.
de Neve, Gert (2005): The Everyday Politics of Labour Working lives in India's Informal Economy, Delhi: Social Science Press.
Derks, Annuska (2010): "Bonded Labour in Southeast Asia: Introduction." In: Asian Journal of Social Science 38, pp. 839-852.
Emmer, Peter Cornelis/van den Boogaart, Ernst (eds.) (1986): Colonialism and Migration: Indentured Labour Before and After Slavery, Dordrecht: Martinus Nijhoff Publishers.
Engerman, Stanley L. (1986): "Servants to Slaves to Servants: Contract Labour and European Expansion." In: Peter Cornelis Emmer/Ernst van den Boogart (eds.), Colonialism and Migration: Indentured Labour Before and After Slavery, Dordrecht: Martinus Nijhoff Publishers, pp. 263-295.

Frantz, Elizabeth (2013): "Jordan's Unfree Worksforce: State-Sponsored Bonded Labour in the Arab Region." In: Journal of Development Studies 49/8, pp. 1072-1087.

Gardner, Andrew (2012): "Rumour and Myth in the Labour Camps of Qatar." In: Anthropology Today 28/6, pp. 25-28.

Harroff-Tavel, Hélène/Nasri, Alix (2013): Tricked and trapped: human trafficking in the Middle East, Beirut: International Labour Organization.

Hoerder, Dirk (2012): "Migrations and Belongings," In: Emily S. Rosenberg (ed.), A World Connecting: 1870-1945, Cambridge/London: Belknap Press of Harvard University Press, pp. 435-592.

Houben, Vincent/Lindblad, J. Thomas (eds.) (1999): Coolie Labour in Colonial Indonesia. A Study of Labour Relations in the Outer Islands, c. 1900-1940, Wiesbaden: Harrassowitz.

Hu-Dehart, Evelyn (1993): "Chinese Coolie Labour in Cuba in the Nineteenth Century: Free Labour or Neo-Slavery?" In: Slavery & Abolition 14/1, pp. 67-86.

Huong, Lê Thu (2010): "A New Portrait of Indentured Labour: Vietnamese Labour Migration to Malaysia." In: Asian Journal of Social Science 38, pp. 880-896.

Hayot, Eric (2014): "Coolie." In: Rachel Lee (ed.), The Routledge Companion to Asian American and Pacific Islander Literature, New York: Routledge, pp. 81-90.

Jennings, Eric T. (2011): Imperial Heights: Dalat and the Making and Undoing of French Indochina, Berkeley: University of California Press.

Jiménez Pastrana, Juan (1983): Los chinos en la historia de Cuba, 1847–1930, La Habana: Ciencias Sociales.

Kamrava, Mehran/Babar, Zahra (eds.) (2012): Migrant Labor in the Persian Gulf, London: Hurst and Company.

Keese, Alexander (2014): "The Slow Abolition within the Colonial Mind: British and French debates about 'vagrancy', 'African laziness', and forced labour in West Central and South Central Africa, 1945–1965'." In: International Review of Social History 59/3, pp. 377–407.

Khan, Azfar/Harroff-Tavel, Hélène (2011): "Reforming the Kafala: Challenges and Opportunities in Moving Forward." In: Asia and Pacific Migration Journal 20/3-4, pp. 293-313.

Killias, Olivia (2010): "'Illegal' Migration as Resistance: Legality, Morality and Coercion in Indonesian Domestic Worker Migration to Malaysia." In: Asian Journal of Social Science 38, pp. 897-914.

Kitiarsa, Pattana (2014): The "Bare Life" of Thai Migrant Workmen in Singapore, Chiang Mai: Silkworm.
Klein, Martin A. (1993): "Introduction: Modern European Expansion and Traditional Servitude in Africa and Asia." In: Martin A. Klein (ed.), Breaking the Chains: Slavery, Bondage, and Emancipation in Modern Africa and Asia, Madison: University of Wisconsin Press, pp. 3-36.
Köckritz, Angela/Petrulewicz, Barbara (2016): "Schuften für den Führer." In: Die Zeit 13/2016; http://www.zeit.de/2016/13/nordkorea-zwangsarbeiter-ausland-polen.
Laviña, Javier/Zeuske, Michael (eds.) (2014): The Second Slavery: Mass Slaveries and Modernity in the Americas and in the Atlantic Basin, Münster: Lit.
Lebaron, Genevieve/Ayers, Alison J. (2013): "The Rise of a 'New Slavery'? Understanding African unfree labour through neoliberalism." In: Third World Quarterly 34/5, pp. 873-892.
Lerche, Jens (2011): The Unfree Labour Category and Unfree Estimates: A Continuum within Low-End Labour Relations, Manchester: Manchester Papers in Political Economy, CSPE.
—— (2007): "A Global Alliance against Forced Labour? Unfree Labour, Neo-Liberal Globalization and the International Labour Organization." In: Journal of Agrarian Change 7/4, pp. 424-52.
Longva, Anh Nga (1997): Walls Built on Sand: Migration, Exclusion, and Society in Kuwait, Boulder: Westview Press.
Lucassen, Jan (2008): Global Labour History: a state of the art, Bern: Peter Lang.
Mann, Michael (2011): Sahibs, Sklaven und Soldaten. Geschichte des Menschenhandels rund um den Indischen Ozean, Mainz: Philipp von Zabern.
Manning, Patrick (2004): Migration in World History, London/New York: Routledge.
Martinez, Julia (2005): "The End of Indenture? Asian Workers in the Australian Pearling Industry, 1901-1972." In: International Labour and Working-Class History 67, pp. 125-147.
Masashi, Haneda (2009): Asian Port Cities, 1600-1800: Local and Foreign Cultural Interactions, Singapore: NUS Publishing.
Mason, Margie et al. (2015): "Shrimps sold by global supermarkets is peeled by slave labourers in Thailand." In: The Guardian, 14 Dec 2015; http://www.theguardian.com/global-development/2015/dec/14/shrimp-sold-by-global-supermarkets-is-peeled-by-slave-labourers-in-thailand.

Mauro, Frédéric (1986): "French indentured servants for America, 1500-1800." In: Piet C. Emmer (ed.), Colonialism and Migration: Indentured Labour Before and After Slavery, Dordrecht: Martinus Nijhoff, pp. 83-104.

Mazumdar, Sucheta (2007): "Localities of the Global: Asian Migrations between Slavery and Citizenship." In: International Review of Social History 52/1, pp. 124-133.

Meagher, Arnold J. (2008): The Coolie Trade: The Traffic in Chinese Laborers to Latin America 1847-1874, Philadelphia: Xlibris Corporation.

Miers, Suzanne (2003): Slavery in the twentieth century: the evolution of a global problem, Lanham: AltaMira Press.

Mills, Mary Beth (1999): Thai Women in the Global Labor Force: Consuming Desires, Contested Selves, New Brunswick: Rutgers University Press.

Mohapatra, Prabhu P. (2006): "'Following Custom?' Representations of Community among Indian Immigrant Labour in the West Indies, 1880–1920." In: International Review of Social History 51/S14, pp. 173-202.

Molland, Sverre (2012): "Safe Migration, Dilettante Brokers and the Appropriation of Legality: Lao-Thai 'trafficking' in the context of regulating labour migration." In: Pacific Affairs 85/1, pp. 117–136.

Ng, Robert (2014): "The Chinese Commission to Cuba (1874): Reexamining International Relations in the Nineteenth Century from a Transcultural Perspective." In: Transcultural Studies 2, pp. 39-62 (online: http://heiup.uni-heidelberg.de/journals/index.php/transcultural/article/view/13009/11493).

Nguyen, Minh (2015): Vietnam's socialist servants: Domesticity, class, gender, and identity, London/New York: Routledge.

Nora, Pierre (1989): "Between memory and history: les lieux de memoire." In: Representations 26, pp. 7-24.

Northrup, David (1995): Indentured Labor in the Age of Imperialism, 1834-1922, New York: Cambridge University Press.

Ong, Aiwa (2006): Neoliberalism as Exception: Mutations in Citizenship and Sovereignty, Durham/London: Duke University Press.

Picherit, David (2009): "'Workers, trust us!': Labour middlemen and the rise of the lower castes in Andhra Pradesh." In: Jan Breman/Isabelle Guérin/Aseem Prakash (eds.), India's Unfree Workforce. Of Bondage Old and New, New Delhi: Oxford University Press, pp. 259-283.

Prabhu, Anjali (2005): "Interrogating Hybridity: Subaltern Agency and Totality in Postcolonial Theory." In: Diacritics 35/2, pp. 76-92.

Roopnarine, Lomarsh (2016): Indian Indenture in the Danish West Indies, 1863-1873, London: Palgrave Macmillan.

—— (2011): "Indian migration during indentured servitude in British Guiana and Trinidad, 1850–1920." In: Labor History 52/ 2, pp. 173-191.
Singh, Sujala (2012): "Alienated coolie-boy/alien language: Reading the subaltern adolescent in Mulk Raj Anand's *Coolie.*" In: Contemporary South Asia 20/4, pp. 511-523
Slocomb, Margaret (2007): Colons and Coolies: The Development of Cambodia's Rubber Plantations, Bangkok: White Lotus Press.
Stanziani, Alessandro (2014): Bondage: Labor and Rights in Eurasia from the Sixteenth to the Early Twentieth Centuries, New York: Berghahn.
Stoler, Ann Laura (2008): "Imperial Debris: Reflections on Ruins and Ruination." In: Cultural Anthropology 23/2, pp. 191–219.
Tappe, Oliver (forthc. 2016): "Coolie Chains: Global Commodities, Colonialism, and the Question of Labour." In: DIE ERDE – Journal of the Geographical Society of Berlin.
Tinker, Hugh (1974): A New System of Slavery: The Export of Indian Labour Overseas, 1830-1920, London/Oxford: Oxford University Press.
Tomich, Dale W./Zeuske, Michael (eds.) (2009): The Second Slavery: Mass Slavery, World-Economy, and Comparative Microhistories, Binghamton: Binghamton University.
Torabully, Khal (1992): Cale d'étoiles, Coolitude, Sainte-Marie, Réunion: Azalées.
Twaddle, Michael (1993): "Visible and Invisible Hands." In: Michael Twaddle (ed.), The Wages of Slavery: From Chattel Slavery to Wage Labour in Africa, the Caribbean and England, London: Frank Cass, pp.1-12.
van den Anker, Christien (ed.) (2004): The Political Economy of New Slavery, London: Palgrave Macmillan.
van der Linden, Marcel (ed.) (2011): Humanitarian Intervention and Changing Labor Relations. Long-Term Consequences of the Abolition of the Slave Trade, Leiden/Boston: Brill.
—— (2001): "Global Labour History and 'the Modern World-System'." In: International Review of Social History 46, pp. 423–459.
Vertovec, Steven (1992): Hindu Trinidad: Religion, Ethnicity and Socio-Economic Change, Basingstoke: Macmillan.
Winichakul, Thongchai (1994): Siam Mapped: A History of the Geo-Body of a Nation, Honolulu: University of Hawai'i Press.
Young, Elliott (2015): "Chinese Coolies, Universal Rights and the Limits of Liberalism in an Age of Empire." In: Past and Present 227/1, pp. 121-149.
Yun, Lisa (2008): The Coolie Speaks. Chinese Indentured Laborers and African Slaves in Cuba, Philadelphia: Temple University Press.

Zeuske, Michael (forthc. 2016a): Welt- und Globalgeschichte der Sklaverei, Stuttgart: Reclam.
—— (forthc. 2016b): Andere Imperien, andere Sklavereien: China in globaler Perspektive, Münster: Lit.
—— (2015): Sklavenhändler, Negreros und Atlantikkreolen. Eine Weltgeschichte des Sklavenhandels im atlantischen Raum, Berlin/Boston: De Gruyter.
—— (2013): Handbuch Geschichte der Sklaverei: Eine Globalgeschichte von den Anfängen bis heute, Berlin/Boston: De Gruyter.

Coolies – Asiáticos and Chinos: Global Dimensions of Second Slavery

MICHAEL ZEUSKE

> "A los chinos les gustaba mucho el opio [The Chinese very much enjoyed opium]."[1]
> BARNET 1966: 71

A particular dimension of Spanish-Portuguese cooperation in the 19th century runs under the label coolies become slaves (Spanish: *culíes*) – and not coolies instead of slaves![2] After severe disputes in the 15th century, Portugal and Castile had closely cooperated in the Atlantic slave trade between 1520 and 1640 (from 1580 until 1640, Portugal was controlled by Castile/Spain). After the so-called uprising of Portugal in 1640, the country formed an alliance with Great Britain and became an enemy of Spain. Other slave trade powers supplied slaves to the Spanish colonial empire in America (Borucki/Eltis 2015, Ribeiro da Silva 2015). After the abolition of the Atlantic slave trade in the British Empire in 1808, new local alliances were formed between Portuguese-Brazilian and Spanish-Cuban (Iberian) slave traders - in particular in West Africa and in Pacific Asia. From a territorial aspect, the deportation of coolies included China, the Pacific, and the

---

1   I would like to thank the Global South Studies Center (GSSC, Cologne, Germany) for financing a research visit in Madrid and Lisbon (August 2014).
2   Cf. Luzón (1989-1990); Naranjo/Balboa Navarro (1999); Balboa Navarro (2000). Tinker's (1993 [1974]) empirical foundation is British colonialism; however, his concept of the "new system of slavery" can be perfectly applied to the Iberian sphere as well (cf. Allen 2013, 2014; Behal/van der Linden 2006; López 2013; Zeuske 2014, 2015a, 2015b).

Indian Ocean in Atlantic slavery and its last period, being Second Slavery. Today, the term Second Slavery refers to various forms of bonded labour and describes the interconnection between the slavery economies and the modern era of the 19th century, in particular in the South of the USA, in the South of Brazil, Puerto Rico, Suriname, and in Western Cuba (Cuba grande), but also in the Sokoto Caliphate, Morocco, Egypt, Indonesia, Mauritius and other islands of the Indian Ocean (Zeuske 2015a).[3] All those who profited from the human body as an asset have been looking for alternative sources of muscle labour around the entire world since the crisis of slave labour in the 1840s (the British since 1806). The prices for deported people from Africa increased due to slave ships being chased by British cruisers – particularly in areas outside Africa (Clarence-Smith 1984, Miers 2003: 3-4, 30-31). Prices increased in the Americas, while prices dropped in Africa. Alternative workers consisted mainly of coolies and *emancipados*, i.e. deported people from the slave trade ships who were freed by British war vessels or other war vessels.

Regarding the *emancipados* (liberated slaves/emancipated slaves or recaptives), Rodolfo Sarracino has written as early as 1988 that legally, they were "no eran ni libertos ni esclavos [neither libertos nor slaves]" (1988: 67). Around the year 1850, it became apparent that the chinos were also quickly assimilated and – as I put it – transculturalised as slaves into an "estructura social esclavista [a social structure of slavery]" (ibid.: 67).

The slave traders and enslavers did not favour any ethnic or other groups. Some of them did not even favour humans. They would equally have used animals as 'slaves'. Mules, donkeys, or oxen were taken into consideration; however, they could not be used everywhere. In addition, the slave traders thought and operated in the same way as the protagonists of Jules Verne's novels: in a global and cosmopolitan way. They experimented with Mayas from Yucatán, Apache from northern Mexico, Lebanese or Syrian Christians and Arabs from the Ottoman Empire, with Catholic Germans from the Black Forest of the German Empire, Spaniards from Galicia and the Canary Islands, 'free' Africans who were in debt from Fernando Po, and Portuguese from the Cape Verde Islands, Azores, or Madeira.

In addition, in the Eastern Hemisphere, transport, trade (*blackbirding*), and contract slavery of Melanesians and Polynesians (*kanaka*) to Australia, to French

---

3   On Second Slavery as the foundation of an autonomous modern era (and not as an opposition to the modern era of industrialism or as part of it), see Tomich (1988, 2004), Tomich/Zeuske (2009), and Laviña/Zeuske (2014).

and German colonies in the Pacific, and to Peru and Guatemala played a role.[4] Little is known as to what extent the Spanish and the elites from Spanish colonies were involved (the battle against the Iranun raid warriors in the Zulu Sea around the middle of the 19th century indicates that the Spanish were involved, with 'Portuguese' from Timor, Flores, and Solor also involved (Warren 1977; 2002).

After the crises of 1830-1835 and 1844-1848, the demand of the Cuban sugar industry for workers again grew to such large dimensions that the Atlantic was no longer a sufficient recruiting area; especially since aggressive British policy increasingly unsettled the West African slave trade (Klein 1999). As of 1844, in addition to the enormous deportation of slaves from Calabar, West Central Africa, and East Africa, the *hacendados* (planters) and *negreros* (slavers/ traders/traffickers) started to contemplate purchasing Chinese coolies from Chinese harbours that were controlled by the British and Portuguese (the Spanish initially preferred the city of Amoy (Xiamen) (Yun 2008). As of 1847, slave traders such as Zulueta shipped Chinese coolies (*culíes*) from the south of the Chinese Empire via the China Sea and the Atlantic (sometimes via the Pacific) to Cuba.[5] Some Chinese also arrived in the Portuguese harbours of Africa (such as the island of Moçambique, Luanda, Cacheu, or Bissau (Estácio/Havik 2011). Coolies mainly arrived via two cities in the Pearl River Delta (*Rio das Pérolas*), which were a little over 100km away from each other: The city of Canton (Guangzhou – from 1757 to 1842 the only Chinese city with permission for foreigners to trade) and Macao, which had permission for 'Portuguese' and 'Spanish' to trade.[6] In the first Opium War (1839-1842), Great Britain won foreign trade permission in five other cities in China (Canton (Guangzhou), Fuzhou, Amoy (Xiamen), Ningbo, Shanghai).

---

4 Cf. Maude 1981; Docker 1981; Moore 1985; Campbell 1989; Munro 1990; Horne 2007; Brown 2007. On the debate on slavery and contract slavery types in general: Tinker 1993 [1974]; Baak 1999.

5 Cf. Pérez de la Riva 1974: 213, 217, 219-223; Corbitt 1971; Clarence-Smith 1984: 25-33; Hu-DeHart 1993; Rodríguez 1997; Naranjo Orovio/Balboa Navarro 1999; Schottenhammer 2004; Fernández de Pinedo Echevarría 2002; Marrero Cruz 2006; López 2008; The Cuba Commission Report. A Hidden History of the Chinese in Cuba. The Original English-Language Text (Johns Hopkins Studies in Atlantic History and Culture), introd. by Helly, Denise (1993) Baltimore and London: The Johns Hopkins University Press.

6 Strictly spoken, Macao was not a colony but rather a leasing territory. Portugal paid an annual rate to China (cf. Clarence-Smith 1985: 28).

Overall, between 1847 and 1874, Chinese contract workers, who were almost exclusively men and mostly Chinese from Canton, travelled around half the world to Cuba through European hands (mainly on the route across the Indian Ocean and the Atlantic). Evelyn Hu-DeHart (2007) has written about the traders who promoted the project *coolies become slaves*. The members of the Zulueta Clan mentioned above (Julián Zulueta y Amondo on Cuba, in Spain, and in the USA; his uncle Pedro José de Zulueta y Madariaga in London and his uncle José Fernando Zulueta), at the head of their enterprises, represented what today would be called a multinational or transnational company:

"global capitalists closely linked to the world financial markets, importing and exporting a variety of products around the world. So, for them to initiate the coolie trade from China to the Americas constituted a normal expansion of their global economic activities. Sometime in 1846, an agreement was sealed between Zulueta and Company in London and the British in the [early] treaty port of Amoy. On June 3, 1847, the Spanish ship Oquendo docked in Havana with 206 Chinese on board after 131 days at sea." (Ibid.: 167)[7]

Around 1840, Amoy was a harbour outside the control of the Chinese Empire, where Spanish players in the export and trade of opium established themselves (often in alliances with English businesses that were in the same trade in Hong Kong and Singapore).[8]

As nearly always in the global history of labour, contract workers, in this case the Chinese coolies in Cuba, were often in an even less favourable position than *emancipados* and slaves.[9] They were basically slaves of the state, as were the *emancipados*. The state (precisely: *Junta de Fomento* – an economic committee consisting of planters and big merchants), kept them in *depósitos* (*barracones*/barracoons – a type of prison), supervised them, and punished them. In addition, this state also circulated them and offered them on labour markets, or used them for public works (Yun 2008; López 2013). One of the young men

---

7   Cf. Marrero Cruz 2006: 55-56.
8   Cf. Fradera 1999. On Portuguese attempts to stimulate the Malwa opium production and on Portuguese opium trade (particularly via Damão, Diu, and Surat) see: Clarence-Smith 1985: 25-29. The Portuguese opium trade had important global historic consequences. Since the British were unable to get Portuguese exports into China under control, it became one of the reasons for the first Opium War 1840-1842 (see: ibid.: 26); see also: Permanyer-Ugartemendia 2014.
9   Cf. Palmer 1998; van der Linden 2003, 2007, 2008; Zeuske 2014.

who was entrapped by the 'canvassers' in China, described the status of the Chinese in Cuba like this: "No matter what status one had in China, one will become a slave [in Cuba]" (Yun 2008: 243).

The alliance between 'Spaniards' and 'Portuguese' worked best in this new slave trade too, next to the initially relatively good cooperation between the 'Spanish' (such as the Zuluetas) and the 'British' in Hong Kong and in the financial centre London (Zeuske 2015a), and again, as of the 1850s, with the 'Portuguese' in Macao/China, in the Pearl River Delta. Macao was a free port as of 1845, and increasingly under Portuguese control as of 1847.[10]

This is also part of a forgotten chapter of the European colonial history, namely Spain in East Asia and on the Pacific. The 'Portuguese' and 'Spanish', together with their alliance partners in Spain and Cuba, organized "a de facto Chinese slave trade to Cuba" (Clarence-Smith 1984: 29). The Iberians often had serious conflicts with the British in India (due to the opium trade, amongst other things). However, sometimes they closely cooperated, in particular regarding the transport of coolies (Tinker 1993 [1974]; Yun 2008). At times, Macao was Portugal's most profitable colony. Between 1847 and 1874, 140,000 Chinese were transported to Cuba; out of these, 125,000 arrived in Cuba alive. After 1880, about 35,000 Chinese arrived again, mostly from California; see above for global figures.[11] Between one sixth and one quarter of them travelled through Macao (1850-1875) (Teixeira 1976; Dias 2001). In addition, around 100,000 coolies were deported to Peru, where they were mostly deployed on plantations in coastal areas (in total, roughly 225,000 people arrived in Cuba and Peru as 'new' coolie slaves).[12]

In the 1850s, a Chinese coolie cost two thirds of an African *pieza* (the contract between 400 and 500 dollar[13]) even though the transport costs from

---

10 On the history of Macao from about 1550, see: Schleich 1988.
11 Cf. Naranjo Orovio/Balboa Navarro 1999; Luzón 1989-1990; Schottenhammer 2004.
12 Cf. Hu-DeHart 2005: 169. These 225,000 people from China are part of the approximately 2.5 million migrants mentioned by Adam McKeown (2004: 157) who came from South Asia and East Asia to the Americas (half of these 2.5 million came to the Americas before 1885 and the other half afterwards (ibid.). See also: McKeown 2010.
13 Cf. López 2013: 27. "Pieza" or "Pieza de India" (English: Piece of the West-Indies) is a unit of measure used for the evaluation of enslaved people. A healthy man with a complete set of teeth and "without a flaw", or a woman meeting the same criteria between the age of fifteen and thirty, was regarded as a full Pieza. Younger, older, or deported people with flaws were valuated as half a Pieza or a two-third Pieza in relation to a full Pieza.

China to Cuba were much higher. On this, the *negreros* said: "'Chinese [are] weaker and less productive than Africans'" (Clarence-Smith 1984: 29). Legally, the contracts of the Chinese were sold and not their bodies, as was the case for the deported people from Africa. However, in reality, they were treated in the same way as Africans.

The situation in South East China strongly contributed to the emergence and development of this de facto slave trade. Here, a pool of people who could be enslaved had emerged due to severe conflicts between Cantonese people and immigrating Hakka (one of the eight Han Chinese groups), extensive clan wars, and the heavy fighting of the Taiping civil war. The authorities of the Empire emptied the overcrowded prisons by selling men to the slave traders. The main ports were Swatow, Canton, Amoy, Huangpu (Whampao), Hong Kong (before and while it had the status of a British colony), and first of all, Macao.[14] In addition, there was 'raid slavery', carried out by pirate communities especially who plagued and raided the marine and river coasts (mostly in the provinces Guangdong and Fujian). Parents in distress sold their children. Many people in debt, often addicted to gambling and/or drugs due to the opium that the British forced onto the market,[15] were sold or sold themselves. In addition to these directly enslaved people ("straight slaves"; Clarence-Smith 1984: 29), there were some free men who fell for false promises or small amounts of money that were given to them in advance.

This list of social groups that were generally renamed later as coolies, is problematic. In late Qing China, people who were called culiés/coolies after passing through Canton and later through Macao, were not called like this before. The labels, categories, and legal status of these men in China are known only rudimentary from the investigations of the *Cuba Commission Report* (1874; cf. Ng 2014). As almost always in history, Western categories stopped at the gates of China, that is – in this case – the southern ports (Canton, Macao, Amoy, Shanghai, etc.). The most important large social and legal group that later became known as coolies outside China, were called in China probably *gugong / gugongren*, that is people who could not even sell themselves into more or less formal slavery (by contract) because of high debts, and who had to rent their bodies and labor case by case (also by contract).

---

14 Cf. Hu-DeHart 2007: 168; Van Dyke 2005; López 2013.

15 As of ca. 1815, the Spanish, under protagonism of a radical liberal, did the same for Manila (and certainly for Latin America as well); cf. Fradera 1999.

Figure 1: China's southern provinces Guangdong and Fujian.

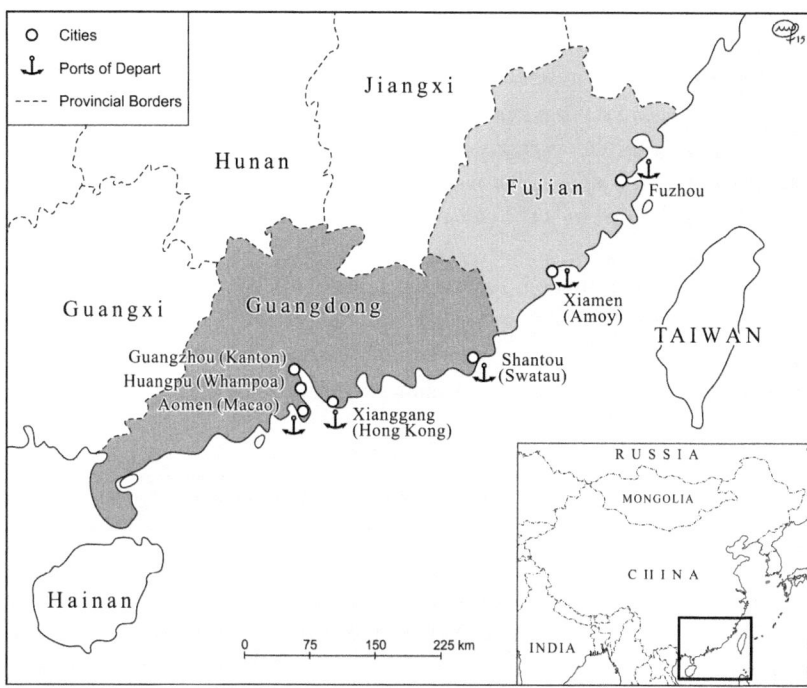

Source: Revised map; private archive Michael Zeuske (Leipzig/Köln).

The liberal elites of Portugal created the formal prerequisites for the boom of their colony Macao. Regarding the legislation, the Portuguese copied the example of Great Britain in India. Slaves were no longer called slaves:

"a escravidão em Macau se pode hoje considerar de facto extinta, e que aos poucos indivíduos ali registrados como escravos e libertos mal pode dar-se esse nome [Slavery in Macao can be considered as de facto eradicated today. The few persons registered as slaves and libertos here [the owners did not register most of their house slaves and enslaved children [transl. MZ]] can hardly be labelled under this name]." (Silva 2013: 187)[16]

---

16 For laws and documents regarding abolition in the Portuguese Empire, refer to: "Apêndice Documental." In: Silva 2013: 133-207.

Full of false humanity, it was claimed:

"se podria declarar de direito, assim como já felizmente o é de facto, extinta a escravidão na Cidade de Macau, adquirindo assim a honra de ser a primeira das Possessões portuguesas onde fosse proclamado este grande acto de civilização [slavery has fortunately de facto been extinguished in the city of Macao; this fact could even be declared by law, thus the city would receive the honour of being the first of the Portuguese territories where this great act of civilization has been proclaimed [transl. MZ]]." (Ibid.)

Slaves without an institution, such as the numerous people who had been stolen, fled, or had been deported from South China, no longer had to be called slaves or *gugongren* – they became coolies. The law was one of the prerequisites for the massive upswing of the diaspora of Chinese coolies in Cuba and in Peru, as well as Panama, as of 1857.

How much Portuguese Macao benefited from uprisings and civil wars in China, is shown in a letter of governor Isidoro Francisco Guimarães from Macao:

"Macao continua tranquillo tiramdo muito partido do actual estado de coisas que lhe permitte fazer um negocio extraordinario. Todo esta carissimo mas todos ganam proporcionalmente excepto os que vivem do Governo ... O numero de lorchas augmenta, e acham-se todas empregadas no commercio entre Cantaõ e Macao que hoje se faz todo em embarcações estrangeiras por que os rebeldes que ocupam o rio não permetten a passagem das embarcações chinas [Macao is very calm while it enormously benefits from the current state of affairs, allowing Macao to make extraordinary profits. Everything is very expensive, but everyone gains proportionally, apart from those who live off the government [as does the letters' author [MZ]] [...] The number of lorchas [ship that has a hull of European design and Chinese rigging [MZ]] increases, and all of them are involved in the trade [including human trafficking [MZ]] between Canton and Macao, for which altogether foreign vessels are used today [those from Portuguese Macao were regarded as foreign ships [MZ]] since the rebels who occupy the river do not allow Chinese vessels to pass [transl. MZ]]."[17]

Like a horseman of the apocalypse, pestilence follows close behind wars, smuggling, and human trafficking. The governor reports: "dysenterias, garri-

---

17 Letter by governor Isidoro Francisco Guimarães from Macao, 12 de fevereiro 1855 (No. 281) to the Ministro e Secretario d'Estado dos Negocios da Marinha e Ultramar, in: AHU Lisboa, Macau Timor, ACL-SEMU-DGU-005, Cx. 0021, 1854-1855.

tilhas, e febres [dysentery, garritilhas [untranslatable to me but sounds severe – MZ], and fevers [plural]]".[18] In addition, there were foreign military operations (e.g. Spanish fleet operations against pirates), precursors of the Second Opium War (1856-1860), and battles between 'rebels' and *imperialistas* (imperial troops) (Dias 2001).

In the 1850s, the trade of contract workers as the 'new' slavery was exposed in the British media. Up to then, the masses of deported people had been trafficked through Hong Kong. The British passed the *Passenger Act* (1855), which cut off the legal transport channel for coolies on British ships. Since then, the trade primarily operated via Macao; most of the coolies were transported on French ships (Legoy 1982). To emphasize the Iberian alliance again: 'Portuguese' from Macao specialized in procurement, as it were, at the initial point of enslavement. Their partners, 'Spaniards' and 'French', specialized in the de facto slave trade to Latin America, particularly to Peru (Pacific route) and Cuba (Pacific and Atlantic route). British and US American ships, as well as a few Dutch ships, also brought coolies to Portuguese colonies in Africa (especially to Moçambique) (Clarence-Smith 1984: 29; Yun 2008). 'Portuguese' and Creole agents organized the formation of larger groups of coolies in the barracoons (prison-like barracks) of Macao. On Chinese soil, Chinese were exclusively active as recruiters (*runners/corretores*). However, the *colonos* were brought to Macao on "lorchas portuguezas" (river boats with Chinese rigging) – this means the 'Portuguese' were active here, too. The governor of Macao often had to deal with what he called "abuse": "abusos que se commetiam em Whampoa no engajamento de culis que se embarcavam em Lorchas portuguezas [abuses [i.e. deportations] that occurred in Whampoa during the recruitment of Chinese who embarked on Portuguese lorchas [transl. MZ]]".[19]

Some Cuban, Peruvian, and Spanish entrepreneurs sent their own agents and staff to Macao; however, most of the business was done by the 'Portuguese', Creole middlemen, and the colony's administration. One of the three most important coolie transport enterprises on Cuba was also managed by a Portuguese. However, the Portuguese played a minor role in sea transport using ships to Cuba and Peru.

---

18 Report by Isidoro Francisco Guimarães from Macao, 12 de março de 1855 (No. 285) to the Ministro e Secretario d'Estado dos Negocios da Marinha e Ultramar, in: AHU Lisboa, Macau Timor, ACL-SEMU-DGU-005, Cx. 0021, 1854-1855.

19 "Report No. 85", Macaó 25 de septembro de 1859, Isidoro Guimarães to the Ministro e Secretario d'Estado dos Negocios da Marinha e Ultramar, in: AHU, Macau Timor-ACL-SEMU-DGU-005, Cx. 0025.

Practically all of the official correspondence and reports on coolies first of all stressed the "contract" as opposed to the "detestable slavery". On the contracts, Evelyn Hu-DeHart writes:

"Portuguese authorities in Macau oversaw the loading process and legalized the documents. The contract was supposed to be read to the coolie in the appropriate Chinese language, so that he fully understood its terms, and signing it signified acceptance and agreement. He was also given a copy in Chinese to keep, while a Spanish version was issued to the planter in Cuba or Peru who bought his contract [...]. Throughout the years of the trade, some of the basic terms remained constant, such as the eight years of servitude and the pay of one peso a week, or four a month. In addition to a salary, coolies were paid in food and clothing, which usually consisted of some specified amount of rice, meat or fish, yam or vegetables, as well as two changes of garment, one jacket and one blanket a year. Housing was also provided without rent. The contract specified three days off during the New Year, and usually Sundays as well, although this was rarely honored even when stipulated. Furthermore, the contract provided for medical attention, although it also stipulated the circumstances under which the planter could withhold wages until the coolie's recovery from illness or injury. The planter was also assured a full eight years' service, so that the coolie was obligated to make up for lost days of work by extending his service beyond the eight calendar years. In addition, he was given an advanced payment of eight to 14 pesos, to be used for passage and a new change of clothing at the time of departure, which constituted a debt to the planter to be repaid by deductions from his salary at the rate of one peso per month." (Hu-DeHart 2005: 171)[20]

There were several new forms of contracts in Cuba and Peru, most of them in Spanish (Yun 2008; see figure 2). This contract work became a main path for the transition to 'new' slaveries and thus for the safeguarding of workforce and capital during Second Slavery. It remains open for discussion whether this contract work can be regarded as a path to 'free' labour at all. To demonstrate the dimensions, I would like to repeat: This affected around 2.5 million people between 1806/1838 and 1940 – primarily from British-India and China up to the formal end of slavery in the Americas in the second half of the 19th century, and also from the Dutch East Indies afterwards.[21]

---

20 Cf. Jiménez Pastrana 1983.
21 Cf. Tinker 1993 [1974]; McKeown 2004; Houben/Seibert 2013; Houben/Lindblad 1999.

Figure 2: Contract of a Chinese man called Hung Sang to emigrate and work (for eight years) in Cuba (1866).

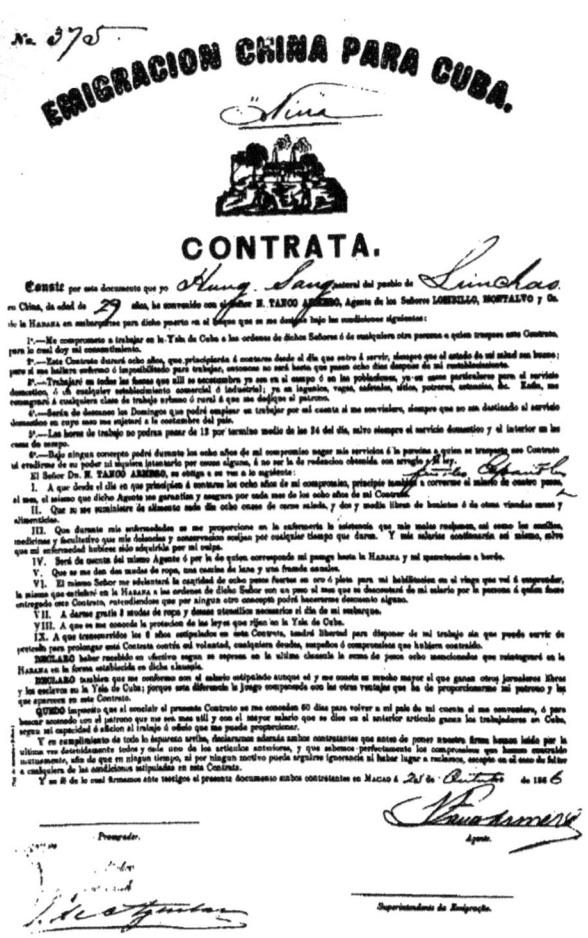

Source: Archivo Nacional de Cuba (ANC), Donativos y Remisiones, legajo 547, número 28 (1866): "Documento que contiene Contrata de trabajadores chinos con destino a Cuba. Fecha Macao, 25 de octubre de 1866" (Original).

Francisco Diago y Tato was one of the first hacendados who purchased people deported from China in a prototype transport from the *Junta de Fomento* in 1847. He purchased them to employ them for the cultivation of his modern ingenios (plantations) in the plains of Cárdenas (Pérez de la Riva 1974: 217, 219-223). After an interruption from 1848 to 1852, the trade with Chinese, which took place via Macao since 1855, gained momentum. The transport and treatment of the asíaticos or chinos were similar, and at times even worse, to those of people who were deported as part of the slave trade. The Chinese coolies were considered as 'free workers' who had decided to travel to Cuba themselves and had signed a contract. Trade with the Chinese was barely controlled (López 2008).

Figure 3: Liberated Africans on Deck of Bark "Wildfire" 1860.

Source: Bark Wildfire 1860, en route to Cuba, under: "Slaves", available online: http://www.slavevoyages.org/tast/resources/images-list.faces.

Chinos and Mayas arrived in such large numbers that the *Real Consulado* (professional association of the planters and big merchants) felt the need to pass a Reglamento (code), similar to that for African slaves, in 1849 (*Reglamento para el manejo y trato de los colonos asiáticos e indios en la isla de Cuba. 10 de abril de 1849*).[22] Coolie slaves, deported children from Africa (such as the boys, of the *Wildfire* 1860; see figure 3), as well as *emancipados*, prevented mass production of sugar from breaking down in the 30 years between 1857 and 1886. Thus, they also secured the capital value of enslaved human bodies. With the forced immigration of new types of slaves such as the *emancipados* and coolies, the 'normal' slaves, who were sporadically smuggled in higher or lesser numbers due to the Atlantic slave trade being prosecuted, also increased in value. The prices of slaves, which fell towards the end of the 1840s, increased again considerably when the Atlantic slave trade to Brazil broke down and the crisis of 1857 ended (Klein 1999: 190; Tornero 2002). The large production of sugar in Cuba could be expanded and their product prices could be lowered. The intermediate step of state slavery and global deportation of coolies, for which primarily the British bore responsibility on a global level, also revived the human trafficking by the 'Spanish' *negreros* of Cuba. Thus, after a temporary high from 1850 to 1854, the Atlantic slave trade and the human trafficking of coolies experienced another upturn as of 1856, which lasted until 1874.[23] When the Confederates of the USA were beaten in the American Civil War, the smuggling of human slaves slowly ended.

The following figures show the large impact of the Chinese intermezzo on the general development of human trafficking and the slave trade.[24]

Table 1: Table of deportations to Cuba (1853-1874)

Year	People deported from Africa	People deported from China
1853	12 500	4 307
1854	11 400	1 711
1855	6 408	2 985

---

22 Printed in: Rodríguez Piña 1990: 187-191.
23 The Crown passed several orders against the "trata"; see: ANC, GSC, leg. 1035, no. 35897 (1861): "Contra los importadores de la trata en la Isla, armadores y complices".
24 For the most detailed and complete list of departures from Chinese harbours (141515), sales in Havana (124793), and casualties of the passage (16578), refer to: "Chinese Landing in the Port of Havana, 1847-1874", cf. López 2013: 23.

1856	7 304	4 968
1857	10 436	8 547
1858	19 992	13 385
1859	30 473	7 204
1860	24 895	6 193
1861	23 964	6 973
1862	11 254	344
1863	7 507	952
1864	6 807	2 153
1865	145	6 400
1866	1 443	12 391
1867	?	14 263
1868	?	7 368
1869	?	5 660
1870	?	1 227
1871	?	1 448
1872	?	8 160
1873	?	5 093
1874	?	2 490
Total for all years	174 528	124 242

Source: Hu-DeHart 1993: 71.

The transition from slavery to the 'free' work on sugar plantations, which was in no way less hard work, monotonous, and poorly paid, rested on the shoulders of former slaves, Chinese (many of whom did not live to see 'freedom' as of 1886), female slaves, and *patrocinados* (as of 1880, the Spanish government had passed the *patronato*, a type of *apprenticeship* for slaves similar to that in British colonies in 1834-38), and – as of ca. 1880 – on the shoulders of destitute Spanish farmworkers.

As mentioned above, the Chinese on Cuba, *asiáticos*, were often treated even worse than slaves. The transport operators of the large shipping companies made a distinction between slaves and contract workers; however, intellectually and in reality, the Chinese were treated in the same racist and violent way as *emancipados* and African slaves (Hu-DeHart 1993; Hu-DeHart 1999). Often, the *asiáticos* were not even granted the same right to ransom themselves as was granted to the deported people from Africa (Pérez de la Riva 1974). In addition, due to unfamiliarity and the lack of women in the Chinese populations in America (this was even more noticeable in Peru than in Cuba), their lives were worse than those of slaves. Even for *chinos*, there was a life *beyond the plantation* – however, it was rarely better than on the plantations. Coolies worked in warehouses and in the harbour, mainly doing hard dock work and handling; on *potreros* (ranches), in railway construction, often on urban construction sites, and a few also worked in sales. A number of foreign visitors also witnessed coolies, often together with punished slaves, doing convict labour (López 2013).

William Clarence-Smith (1984: 29) clearly records: "In spite of an elaborate legal rigmarola [i.e.: confused talks] of 'indentured labour', there can be no doubt that the Chinese in Cuba were effectively in the position of slave". He cites the following reasons: *Asiáticos* were not only subject to a contract in Cuba; in addition, as described above, they were also forced into many subsequent contracts – in Spanish. None of the original contracts contained a "repatriation clause". The Chinese workers were openly sold under the legal fiction of "'endorsing' contracts" (Yun 2008: 132). Those who survived the eight years and did not continue to lead miserable lives as slaves due to deceptive contracts, were regarded as vagabonds (*vagrantes*) – this was punished by rigorous legislation in Cuba. 'Vagabonds' were forced to sign new contracts (*recontracting*), or they were sentenced to convict labour (Hu-DeHart 2005).

Legislation stipulating that at least one fifth of coolies were to be female was simply ignored.[25] Merchants called for the transport of female coolies to Cuba, and this was discussed by Portuguese authorities. However, they rejected this as "pure" slavery. In 1859, the governor of Macao wrote about the "embarque de mulheres chinas para Havana [(the) shipping of Chinese women to Havana [transl. MZ]]"[26] The Ministério in Lisboa ordered the following: "que se conceda á casa de D. Rafael R. Torrices a exportar mulheres chinas para a Havana. Ultimamente o agente daquella firma requereo para dar começo a expedição de Colonos do sexo feminino [that a concession may be given to the trading house of Don Rafael R. Torrices for exporting Chinese women to Havana [transl.

---

25 Of the 34,650 Chinese noted in the 1862 Cuban census, 25 were females. The Cuban census of 1872 noted 58,400 Chinese, of whom only 32 were females, two under contract and 30 free; cf. Hu-DeHart 2005: 170.

26 "Report No. 70", Macaó 21 de Agosto de 1859, Isidoro Guimarães to the Ministro e Secretario d'Estado dos Negocios da Marinha e Ultramar, in: AHU, Macau Timor-ACL-SEMU-DGU-005, Cx. 0025.

MZ]]".[27] The governor was against this: "taes carregações não seriam senão compostas de mulheres compradas, e que constituiria um negocio de pura escavatura [such cargo would be nothing else but made up of bought women and they would constitute a business of pure slavery [transl. MZ]]".[28]

Only a small number of former coolies who were able to allocate money returned to China. This money was mostly acquired through illegal activities such as the dealing of opium,[29] gambling, or small shops on the plantations or nearby. For the East Cuban region around Santiago de Cuba, one known returnee is documented: a cook who travelled on a coolie ship via England and Hong Kong to China (López 2013: 44-45). A similar small number became crew foremen or foremen of temporary workers in Cuba or in Peru. On this, Evelyn Hu-DeHart writes:

"Recontracting in turn quickly gave rise to the appearance of a group of ex-coolies who became in effect labor contractors (contratista or enganchador) taking on the task and responsibility of recruiting, managing and, very importantly, disciplining labor crews (cuadrillas) on plantations. In a role which can also be described as a middleman subcontractor, they did all the negotiating on behalf of their labor crews, collecting a 'salario colectivo [collective salary]' from the planter which they then distributed to the workers after taking a cut of about 10 percent." (Hu-DeHart 2005: 174)[30]

In conclusion, this chapter agrees with many authors, such as Kathleen López (2013: 50-53) or Franklin Knight, in the assumption that the lives of coolies had the nature of slavery: "Chinese labor in Cuba in the nineteenth century was slavery in every social aspect except the name" (Knight 1970: 119). Nancy Morejón speaks of "a 'new' coolie concept of slavery" (Yun/Larement 2001:

---

27 "Report No. 70", Macaó 21 de Agosto de 1859, Isidoro Guimarães to the Ministro e Secretario d'Estado dos Negocios da Marinha e Ultramar, in: AHU, Macau Timor-ACL-SEMU-DGU-005, Cx. 0025.

28 "Report No. 70", Macaó 21 de Agosto de 1859, Isidoro Guimarães to the Ministro e Secretario d'Estado dos Negocios da Marinha e Ultramar, in: AHU, Macau Timor-ACL-SEMU-DGU-005, Cx. 0025. A regulamento (coolie regulation) was enclosed with the report (published in: Boletim do Governo, Macau, sabbado, 7 de Junho 1856).

29 Cf. Hu-DeHart 2005: 170. On the broader background, cf. Fradera 1999; Barnet 1966.

30 On Cuadrillas under the leadership of chinos and on the competition with the "most profitable brokers of Chinese labor" (colonial officials, police), see López 2013: 62-64.

100). Very clearly, we see here the blurred boundaries between indentured labour and forms of slavery.

In 1872, there were 58,400 Chinese people in Cuba; 34,408 of these were still subject to a contract (59 percent). After the census of 1872, 14,046 Chinese were legally free (either naturalized (a type of citizenship) or as foreigners); 7,036 were regarded as escaped contract workers; 1,344 were detained as *cimarrones* in *depósitos* (where they worked); another 1,508 were also detained – because they waited for 're-contracting' or a sentence, or because they were convicted.[31] In the census of 1877, 25,226 chinos were still under contract and 21,890 had fulfilled their contracts (López 2013: 44).

Slavery in the form of coolie slavery has left deep marks in the history of Cuba, Peru, Panama, California, and the Caribbean plantation economies.

REFERENCES

Primary Sources

Arquivo Histórico Ultramarino (AHU, Lisboa), Macau Timor, ACL-SEMU-DGU-005: Letter by the governor Isidoro Francisco Guimarães from Macao, 12 de fevereiro 1855 (No. 281) to the Ministro e Secretario d'Estado dos Negocios da Marinha e Ultramar, Cx. 0021, 1854-1855 (without foliation).

AHU Lisboa, Macau Timor, ACL-SEMU-DGU-005, report by Isidoro Francisco Guimarães from Macao, 12 de março de 1855 (No. 285) to the Ministro e Secretario d'Estado dos Negocios da Marinha e Ultramar, Cx. 0021, 1854-1855 (without foliation).

AHU, Macau Timor-ACL-SEMU-DGU-005, "Report No. 70", Macaó 21 de Agosto de 1859, Isidoro Guimarães to the Ministro e Secretario d'Estado dos Negocios da Marinha e Ultramar, Cx. 0025 (without foliation).

AHU, Macau Timor-ACL-SEMU-DGU-005, "Report No. 85", Macaó 25 de septiembre de 1859, Isidoro Guimarães to the Ministro e Secretario d'Estado dos Negocios da Marinha e Ultramar, Cx. 0025 (without foliation).

Archivo Nacional de Cuba, La Habana, Donativos y Remisiones (ANC, DyR), legajo (leg.), 547, número (no.) 28 (1866): "Documento que contiene

---

31 Resumen por jurisdicciones del padrón general de asiáticos de la Isla, correspondiente al año de 1872 (23 de septiembre de 1873) In: Boletín de Colonización 1, no. 18 (15 de octubre de 1873), pp. 5.

Contrata de trabajadores chinos con destino a Cuba. Fecha Macao, 25 de octubre de 1866" (Original).

ANC, Gobierno Superior Civil (GSC), leg. 1035, no. 35897 (1861): "Contra los importadores de la trata en la Isla, armadores y complices".

Boletim do Governo, Macau, sabbado, 7 de Junho 1856.

The Cuba Commission Report. A Hidden History of the Chinese in Cuba. The Original English-Language Text (Johns Hopkins Studies in Atlantic History and Culture), introd. by Helly, Denise (1993) Baltimore/London: The Johns Hopkins University Press.

Liberated Africans on Deck of Bark "Wildfire" 1860, in: "Slaves", online under: (http://www.slavevoyages.org/tast/resources/images-list.faces).

Resumen por jurisdicciones del padrón general de asiáticos de la Isla, correspondiente al año de 1872 (23 de septiembre de 1873) In: Boletín de Colonización 1, no. 18 (15 de octubre de 1873), p. 5.

Secondary Sources

Allen, Richard B. (2013): "Slave Trading, Abolitionism, and "New Systems of Slavery" in the Nineteenth-Century Indian Ocean World." In: Robert Harms/Bernard K. Freamon/David W. Blight (eds.), Indian Ocean slavery in the age of abolition, New Haven: Yale University Press, pp. 183-199.

—— (2014): "Slaves, Convicts, Abolitionism and the Global Origins of the Post-Emancipation Indentured Labor System." In: Slavery & Abolition Vol. 35/2, pp. 328–348.

Baak, Paul (1999): "About Enslaved Ex-slaves, Uncaptured Contract Coolies and Unfreed Freedmen: Some Notes about 'Free' and 'Unfree' Labour in the Context of Plantation Development in Southwest India, Early Sixteenth Century – Mid 1990s." In: Modern Asian Studies 33/1, pp. 121-157.

Balboa Navarro, Imilcy (2000): "Colonos contratados: chinos e indios sudamericanos." In: Imilcy Balboa Navarro (ed.), Los brazos necesarios. Inmigración, colonización y trabajo libre en Cuba, 1878-1898, Valencia: Centro Francisco Tomás y Valiente UNED Alzira-Valencia/ Fundación Instituto de Historia Social, pp. 123-133.

Barnet, Miguel (1966): "La vida en los ingenious." In: Miguel Barnet (ed.), Biografía de un cimarrón, La Habana: Instituto de Etnología y Folklore, pp. 49-123.

Behal, Rana P./Linden, Marcel van der (eds.) (2006): Coolies, Capital, and Colonialism. Studies in Indian Labour History, Cambridge: Cambridge University Press.

Borucki, Alex/Eltis, David/Wheat, David (2015): "Atlantic History and the Slave Trade to Spanish America." In: The American Historical Review 120/2, pp. 433-461.

Brown, Laurence (2007): "A Most Irregular Traffic. The Oceanic Passages of the Melanesian Labor Trade." In: Emma Christopher/Cassandra Pybus/ Marcus Rediker (eds.), Many Middle Passages. Forced Migration and the Making of the Modern World, Berkeley: University of California Press, pp. 184-203.

Campbell, Ian C. (1989): "Sandalwood and 'Blackbirding'." In: Ian C. Campbell (ed.), A History of the Pacific Islands, Berkeley: University of California Press, pp. 101-115.

Clarence-Smith, William Gervase (1984): "The Portuguese Contribution to the Cuban Slave Trade and Coolie Trade in the Nineteenth Century." In: Slavery & Abolition 5/1, pp. 25-33.

―――― (1985): "Illegitimate and legitimate commerce, 1820s-1850." In: William Gervase Clarence-Smith (ed.), Third Portuguese Empire: A Study in Economic Imperialism, 1825-1975, Manchester: Manchester University Press, pp. 22-60.

Corbitt, Duvon C. (1971): A Study of the Chinese in Cuba, 1847–1947, Wilmore: Asbury College.

Dias, Alfredo Gomes (2001): "Do tráfico de escravos à emigração dos cules." In: Revista Lusófona de Humanidades e Tecnologias 4/5, pp. 109-117.

―――― (2001): "Do tráfico de escravos à emigração dos cules", August 15, 2014. (http://revistas.ulusofona.pt/index.php/rhumanidades/article/view/1359/1109)

Docker, Edward W. (1981): The Blackbirders. A Brutal Story of the Kanaka Slave-Trade, London: Angus & Robertson.

Estácio, António/Havik, Philip J. (2011): "Recriar China na Guiné: os primeiros Chineses, os seus descendentes e a sua herança na Guiné Colonial." In: Africana Studia 17, pp. 211-235.

Fernández de Pinedo Echevarría, Nadia (2002): "Chinos y yucatecos." In: Nadia Fernández de Pinedo Echevarría (ed.), Comercio exterior y fiscalidad: Cuba 1794-1860, Bilbao: Servicio Editorial. Universidad del País Vasco/Euskal Herriko Unibertstatea, pp. 222-224.

Fradera, Josep María (1999): "Opio y negocio, o las desaventuras de un español en China." In: Josep M. Fradera (ed.), Gobernar colonias, Barcelona: Ediciones Península, pp. 129-152.

Horne, Gerald (2007): The White Pacific: U.S. Imperialism and Black Slavery in the South Seas after the Civil War, Honolulu: University of Hawai'i Press.

Houben, Vincent/Seibert, Julia (2013): "(Un)freedom: Colonial Labour Relations in Belgian Congo and the Dutch East Indies Compared." In: Ewout Frankema/Frans Buelens (eds.), Colonial Exploitation and Economic Development. The Belgian Congo and the Netherlands Indies Compared, London/New York: Routledge, pp. 178-192.
—— /Lindblad, J. Thomas (eds.) (1999): Coolie Labour in Colonial Indonesia. A Study of Labour Relations in the Outer Islands, c. 1900-1940, Wiesbaden: Harrassowitz.
Hu-DeHart, Evelyn (1993): "Chinese Coolie Labour in Cuba in the Nineteenth Century: Free Labour or Neo-Slavery?" In: Slavery & Abolition 14/1, pp. 67-86.
—— (1999): "Race Construction and Race Relations: Chinese and Blacks in Nineteenth-Century Cuba." In: Roshni Rustomji-Kerns (ed.), Encounters: People of Asian Descent in the Americas, Lanham: Rowman, pp. 105-112.
—— (2005): "Opium and Social Control: Coolies on the Plantations of Peru and Cuba." In: Journal of Chinese Overseas 1/2, pp. 169-183.
—— (2007): "La Trata Amarilla. The "Yellow Trade" and the Middle Passage, 1847-1884." In: Emma Christopher/Cassandra Pybus/ Marcus Rediker (eds.), Many Middle Passages. Forced Migration and the Making of the Modern World, Berkeley: University of California Press, pp. 166-183.
Jiménez Pastrana, Juan (1983): Los chinos en la historia de Cuba, 1847–1930, La Habana: Ciencias Sociales.
Klein, Herbert S. (1999): "The End of the Slave Trade." In: Herbert S. Klein (ed.) The Atlantic Slave Trade, Cambridge: Cambridge University Press, pp. 183-206.
Knight, Franklin W. (1970): Slave Society in Cuba during the Nineteenth Century, Madison: University of Wisconsin Press.
Laviña, Javier/Zeuske, Michael (eds.) (2014): The Second Slavery. Mass Slaveries and Modernity in the Americas and in the Atlantic Basin, Berlin: LIT Verlag.
Legoy, Jean (1982): "Le Havre et le transport des coolies au milieu du XIXe siècle." In: Recueil de l'Association des Amis du Vieux Havre 39, pp. 1-17.
López, Kathleen (2008): "Afro-Asian: Marriage, Godparentage, and Social Status in Late-Nineteenth Cuba." In: Afro-Hispanic Review 27/1, pp. 59-72.
—— (2013): Chinese Cubans. A Transnational History, Chapel Hill: University of North Carolina Press.
Luzón, José Luis (1989-1990): "Chineros, diplomáticos y hacendados en la Habana colonial. Don Francisco Abella y Raldiris y su proyecto de inmi-

gración libre a Cuba (1874)." In: Boletín Americanista, Barcelona, año XXXI, 39-40, pp. 143-158.

Marrero Cruz, Eduardo (2006): "Traficante de esclavos y chinos." In: Eduardo Marrero Cruz/ Julián de Zulutea y Amondo (ed.), Promotor del capitalismo en Cuba, La Habana: Ediciones Unión, pp. 46-79

Maude, Henry Evans (1981): Slavers in Paradise. The Peruvian Labor Trade in Polynesia, 1862-1864, Stanford: Stanford University Press.

McKeown, Adam (2004): "Global Migration 1846-1940." In: Journal of World History 15/2, pp. 155-189.

—— (2010): "Chinese Emigration in Global Context, 1850-1940." In: Journal of Global History 5/1, pp. 95-124.

Miers, Suzanne (2003): Slavery in the twentieth century: the evolution of a global problem, Lanham: AltaMira Press.

Moore, Clive (1985): Kanaka: A History of Melanesian Mackay, Port Moresby: Institute of Papua New Guinea Studies and the University of Papua New Guinea.

Munro, Doug (1990): "The Origins of Labourers in the South Pacific: Commentary and Statistics." In: Clive Moore/Jacqueline Leckie/Doug Munro (eds.), Labour in the South Pacific, Townsville: James Cook University, pp. XXXIX-LI.

Naranjo Orovio, Consuelo/Balboa Navarro, Imilcy (1999): "Colonos asiáticos para una economía en expansión: Cuba, 1847-1880." In: Revista Mexicana del Caribe 8, Año IV, Chetumal, Quintana Roo, pp. 32-65.

Ng, Robert (2014): "The Chinese Commission to Cuba (1874): Reexamining International Relations in the Nineteenth Century from a Transcultural Perspective." In: Transcultural Studies 2, pp. 39-62 (online: http://heiup.uni-heidelberg.de/ journals/index.php/transcultural/article/view/13009/11493).

Palmer, Colin A. (ed.) (1998): The Worlds of Unfree Labour: From Indentured Servitude to Slavery, Brookfield: Variorum.

Pérez de la Riva, Juan (1974): "El viaje a Cuba de los culiés chinos." In: Pedro Deschamps/ Juan Pérez de la Riva (eds.), Contribución a la historia de gentes sin historia, La Habana: Editorial de Ciencias Sociales, pp. 191-213.

—— (1974): "El tráfico de culiés chinos." In: Pedro Deschamps/ Juan Pérez de la Riva (eds.), Contribución a la historia de gentes sin historia, La Habana: Editorial de Ciencias Sociales, pp. 215-232.

—— (1974): "Informe del señor D. Francisco Diago a la Real Junta de Fomento sobre el proyecto de inmigración china." In: Pedro Deschamps/ Juan Pérez de la Riva (eds.), Contribución a la historia de gentes sin historia, La Habana: Editorial de Ciencias Sociales, pp. 219-223.

—— (1974): "El chinito Pablo. Los primeros chinos que se liberaron." In: Pedro Deschamps/ Juan Pérez de la Riva (eds.), Contribución a la historia de gentes sin historia, La Habana: Editorial de Ciencias Sociales, pp. 233-249.

Permanyer-Ugartemendia, Ander (2014): "Opium after the Manila Galleon: The Spanish involvement in the opium economy in East Asia (1815-1830)." In: Investigaciones de Historia Económica - Economic History Research 10, pp. 155-164.

Ribeiro da Silva, Filipa (2015): "Between Iberia, the Dutch Republic and Western Africa: Portuguese Sephardic long- and short-term mobility in the seventeenth century." In: Jewish Culture and History 16/1, pp. 1-19.

Rodríguez Piña, Javier (1990): Guerra de castas: La venta de indios maya a Cuba, 1848-1861, México: Consejo Nacional para la Cultura y Artes.

Rodríguez, José Baltar (1997): Los chinos de Cuba. Apuntes etnográficos, La Habana: Fund. Fernando Ortiz.

Sarracino, Rodolfo (1988): "Interacción de las políticas británica e hispana de migraciones y el regreso de emancipados a África." In: Rodolfo Sarracino (ed.), Los que volvieron a Africa, La Habana: Editorial de Ciencias Sociales, pp. 65-130.

Schleich, Thomas (1988): "Die portugiesische Händlerkolonie auf Macao – von der stillschweigenden Duldung durch chinesische Provinzbehörden zur Bedrohung durch japanische Isolationspolitik und niederländische Konkurrenz." In: Piet C. Emmer et al. (eds.), Dokumente, Bd. IV: Wirtschaft und Handel der Kolonialreiche, München: Verlag C.H. Beck, pp. 202-205.

Schottenhammer, Angela (2004): "Slaves and Forms of Slavery in Late Imperial China (Seventeenth to Early Twentieth Centuries)." In: Gwyn Campbell (ed.), The Structure of Slavery in Indian Ocean Africa and Asia, London/Portland: Frank Cass, pp. 143-154.

Silva, Susana Paula Franco Serpa (2013): "Do Abolicionismo as novas formas de Escravatura. Portugal e os Açores no século XIX." In: Margarida Vaz do Rego Machado/Rute Dias Gregório/Susana Serpa Silva (eds.), Para a história da escravatura insular nos séculos XV a XIX, Ponta Delgada: Centro de História de Além-Mar, pp. 97-207.

Teixeira, Padre Manuel (1976): O comércio de escravos em Macau: The so-called Portuguese slave trade in Macao, Macau: Imprensa Nacional.

Tinker, Hugh (1993 [1974]): A New System of Slavery: The Export of Indian Labour Overseas, 1830-1920, London: Hansib.

Tomich, Dale W. (1988): "The 'Second Slavery': Bonded Labor and the Transformations of the Nineteenth-century World Economy." In: Francisco

O. Ramírez (ed.), Rethinking the Nineteenth Century: Contradictions and Movement, New York: Greenwood Press, pp. 103-117.
—— (2004): Through the Prism of Slavery. Labor, Capital, and World Economy, Boulder: Rowman & Littlefield Publishers, Inc.
—— /Zeuske, Michael (eds.) (2009): The Second Slavery: Mass Slavery, World-Economy, and Comparative Microhistories, 2 volumes, Binghamton: Binghamton University.
Tornero, Pablo (2002): "Azúcar, sociedad y precios de esclavos en las plantaciones cubanas (1784-1879)." In: José Antonio Piqueras (ed.), Azúcar y esclavitud en el final del trabajo forzado. Homenaje a M. Moreno Fraginals, México City: Fondo de Cultura Económica, pp.115-145.
van der Linden, Marcel (2003): Transnational Labour History: Explorations, Aldershot: Ashgate.
—— (2007): "Labour History: The Old, the New and the Global." In: African Studies 66/2/3, pp. 169-180.
—— (2008): Workers of the World. Essays toward a Global Labor History, Leiden: Brill.
van Dyke, Paul A. (2005): The Canton Trade. Life and Enterprise on the China Coast, 1700-1845, Hong Kong: Hong Kong University Press.
Warren, James F. (2002): Iranun and Balangingi: globalization, maritime raiding, and the birth of ethnicity, Singapore: Singapore University Press.
—— (1977): "Slave markets and exchange in the Malay world. The Sulu Sultanate, 1770-1878." In: Journal of Southeast Asian Studies 8, pp. 162-175.
Yun, Lisa (2008): The Coolie Speaks. Chinese Indentured Laborers and African Slaves in Cuba, Philadelphia: Temple University Press.
——/Laremont, René (2001): "Chinese Coolies and African Slaves in Cuba, 1847-74." In: Jounal of Asian and African Studies 4/2, pp. 99-122.
Zeuske, Michael (2014): "Versklavte und Sklavereien in Spanisch-Amerika. Gedanken zur 'Weltarbeiterklasse' in globaler Perspektive." In: Jahrbuch für Forschungen zur Geschichte der Arbeiterbewegung, pp. 5-36.
—— (2015a): Sklavenhändler, Negreros und Atlantikkreolen. Eine Weltgeschichte des Sklavenhandels im atlantischen Raum, Berlin/Boston: De Gruyter.
—— (2015b): "Atlantic Slavery und Wirtschaftskultur in welt- und globalhistorischer Perspektive." In: Geschichte in Wissenschaft und Unterricht 66/5/6, pp. 280-301.

Indentured Labour in Sub-Saharan Africa (1870-1918): Circulation of Concepts between Imperial Powers

ULRIKE LINDNER

INTRODUCTION

When German mining companies in the German colony of South West Africa pressed their government to recruit Chinese or Indian indentured workers for their enterprises in 1912, a discussion ensued in neighbouring South Africa. In the Transvaal, at that time already part of the Union of South Africa, tens of thousands of Chinese had been imported to work in the mines at the Witwatersrand between 1904 and 1907 (Richardson 1984). The advice of a Transvaal Newspaper to the German colonial minister was to keep German South West Africa as a "white colony" and to refrain from importing Asian coolies as it would endanger the racial order.[1] But German South West Africa proceeded with its endeavour to recruit Indian indentured workers, even though it was not successful, as the Indian government restricted indenture in general.

Almost at the same time, in 1910, a British government committee, the Sanderson committee, exploring the future use of Indian contract migrants in colonial environments, mentioned the "invaluable service" of Indian immigration in many colonies of the British Empire and proposed encouraging the introduction of indentured labourers in the future.[2] It also stated that it would be

---

1 National Archive of Namibia, ZBU 2076 W IV R1, (transcript, German Consulate, Johannesburg to Chancellor Bethmann-Hollweg, 16 August 1912).
2 Report of the Committee on Emigration from India to the Crown Colonies and Protectorates (Sanderson Committee), Cd. 5192, London HMSO 1910, p. 22.

advisable for British colonies in Africa to attract Indian immigrants, especially in Uganda, at the same time mentioning the growing difficulties that had developed between Indians and Europeans in African colonies with a considerable "white" settler population, such as in Natal and the East Africa Protectorate (Kenya).[3] Both examples firstly show how attractive Asian contract labour seemed to be for colonial governments and colonial entrepreneurs worldwide, including in Africa, and even at a time when the indenture system had already received much criticism due to the abuse and exploitation of indentured workers. It was receding in many parts of the world before WWI, with the final abolition of Indian indenture in 1920 (Tinker 1974: 364). Secondly, they show how contested the discussion about Asian immigrants in colonies with a "white" settler population and other indigenous ethnicities had become, and how the issue of race and of a racial order was developing into a central issue in many colonial societies at the end of the 19th century (Lake/Reynolds 2008).

Indentured labour in the 19th and early 20th century is mainly seen as a phenomenon characterized by Indian and Chinese contract workers, often called coolies, replacing slaves in the plantation productions of the Caribbean, the Indian Ocean (especially Mauritius), and South East Asia.[4] However, there were significant numbers of Indian and Chinese indentured labourers working not only in South Africa, but also in various colonies of the European powers in sub-Saharan Africa. They also formed part of the history of labour migration and of bonded labour in colonial Africa. In the period of high imperialism between 1880 and 1918, when the African colonies were increasingly integrated into a post-slavery global economy, demand for 'reliable' contract labour in plantations, mines, and infrastructure projects increased (Lindner 2011: 409, 437-438).

Not only in South Africa but also in other parts of the continent, the colonial powers tried to introduce Asian contract labour and experimented with forms of indenture. This chapter examines different manifestations of indentured labour in late imperial Africa. It will then address a concrete example of negotiation processes and knowledge transfer between imperial powers in Africa around the issue of indentured labour, and will analyze the discussions on the impact of indentured Asian labour on the racial colonial order. As a last point, the chapter will look at the Institut Colonial International, founded in 1894 by British, French, Dutch, and Belgian colonizers as an institution explicitly created for the transfer of colonial knowledge between colonial powers (Lindner 2015), and will

---

3   Ibid., pp. 12, 93-97.
4   For earlier forms of coolie labour, cf. van Rossum, this volume.

show how information about coolie/indentured labour was discussed and circulated between imperial powers via the institute's publications.

INDENTURED LABOUR IN COLONIAL EMPIRES OF THE 19TH CENTURY

Generally, the banning of the slave trade after 1806, and finally the abolition of slavery in the British Empire in 1834, triggered a new, highly regulated system of indentured labour. Asian indentured labourers were used worldwide by the British Empire and by other colonial powers to meet the demand for contract work on plantations (sugar, tea) and in mines – generally, in places where the employers were not willing to rely upon free labour and where slave labour was no longer available (Northrup 1995: 17-18). The move towards indentured labour was particularly dominant in sugar-producing colonies such as Mauritius and Guiana (cf. Adamson 1972). The indentured labour system became part of the new imperial economy of the 19th century and spread around the world. Indentured workers from India and China were transported to the Caribbean, the Americas, Africa, South East Asia, and Australia and formed a new labour force, mostly working in plantations and mines.

However, various forms and variations of indentured labour existed before the British Empire initiated regulated forms of colonial indenture, as van Rossum (this volume) has shown in his analysis of the situation in Dutch colonies at the end of the 18th and beginning of the 19th century. Furthermore, slavery and indenture were often used side-by-side, most prominently in Spanish Cuba, where slavery was abolished much later and where Chinese coolies lived amongst the slaves, with slavery and indenture forming a combined system of bonded labour (Hu-DeHart 1993). Marina Carter has addressed similar developments in Mauritius, where slave labour and the apprenticing of slaves overlapped with the introduction of indentured workers (Carter 1993). The big flows of indentured migration dwindled during and after WWI, as the Indian government stopped indenture to several British colonies after 1911 (Tinker 1974: 314-315). However, similar forms of labour allocation persisted through the next decades, in some industries until the 1970s, as Julia Martinez has shown in her research on pearl diving in Australia (Martinez 2005).

In this article, I use the term "indentured labour" because the phenomenon I am dealing with, a form of inter-colonial regulated work migration by Asian workers in the 19th and early 20th century, is commonly addressed as such, e.g. by Hugh Tinker and David Northrup, who wrote the two comprehensive histories of this form of work migration in the 19th century (Tinker 1974; Northrup 1995). Asian indentured migration was originally regulated by law in India as early as in 1837, three years after the abolition of slavery in the British Empire. According to these regulations, indentured workers from India should go for one or two five-year periods of service to Mauritius, and should have free passage there and back, as well as a certain monthly salary. Before departure, they should appear in front of an officer of the Government of India and an emigration agent, and should receive a written contract (Tinker 1974: 64). The system was first used to meet the needs of the sugar planters in the British colony of Mauritius, who had previously cultivated their plantations using slaves and Indian convicts (Meagher 2008: 29-30).

After the two Opium Wars (1839-42, 1856-60), Europeans were allowed to trade in the port cities of China, and used their rights immediately to recruit labour for French, British, and Spanish colonies. In the late 1850s, French and Spanish companies had begun to import Chinese indentured workers from several harbours in China, particularly from Canton, to their plantations and mines in the Caribbean and Latin America (Campbell 1923; López 2013). The British Empire also began to use Chinese labour for their colonies in the West Indies. Contracts comparable to the British regulations issued in India in 1837 were created in China from 1859 onwards in order to bring Chinese coolies to the British West Indies (Campbell 1923: 130). Whereas the British government tried to regulate and organize the recruitment of Chinese coolies, in the Spanish case private merchants controlled the trade with indentured workers (López 2013: 16). Not only did indentured Indian and Chinese labourers come to colonies of the British and Spanish Empires, but similar regimes were also used to bring indentured labourers to French, Dutch, and Portuguese colonies and to other colonial settings. The regulations differed to some degree between the different colonial empires, and changed over time; however, the basic system of indenture and the forms of the contracts remained similar for several decades.

From the beginning, the indenture system was extremely open to misuse (Mann 2003: 13). Regulations were insufficiently controlled, or not at all; indentured workers often did not receive correct contracts, and generally received poor pay – very rarely the promised salary. Furthermore, people were kidnapped and forced into indenture. Indentured workers mostly suffered under extremely harsh working and housing conditions. They had to endure horrible transport conditions in crowded ships, and suffered from racial prejudices (Tinker 1974: 161-163). The situation was well known amongst the colonial powers: As early as 1839, a committee appointed by the Government of India published a report on the situation of the coolies on Mauritius. The report clearly exposed the problems of indentured work and the exploitation and abuse of coolies.⁵ The accounts of Indian coolie witnesses were heard, who openly told the committee that they did not receive the promised food, that they were beaten, and that their masters withheld their salaries. They had no means to reinforce their claims, as the police in Mauritius supported the plantation owners. As a coolie woman, Bibee Zuhoorun, stated regarding her treatment by her master, Mr. Boileau, in 1838:

"There was two years and a half wages due to me, but I never did receive one pice [sic], the police did not see that I got any .... I had an allowance of rice served out to me – three small pots full for every seven days, every Sunday a little dholl [sic] and a little ghee, no fish, no turmeric, no tamarind, nothing that was put down in the agreement [...] Mr Boileau treats his coolies very ill. The three times I complained of Mr. Boileau at the Police he was summoned but did not attend [.] there was some communication between him and the police and I was sent back - the last time I said I would not work, I would get back to Calcutta, as I could not comply with what he wished me to do, I would not stay with him, and then I was put in the house of correction."⁶

The system of indenture was already being called a "new system of slavery" in British Parliament in 1840 (Twaddle 1993: 1). In Mauritius, the complaints about the abuse of indentured labour led to a moratorium on Indian immigration. However, in 1842, the importing of Indian coolies started again, because the sugar planters were able to use their influence and pressed for more contract labour (Maegher 2008). Generally, the indenture system of sugar production in Mauritius was seen as economically successful. Indentured work migration was allowed to spread to the sugar-producing colonies of the Caribbean. Successful sugar production remained of the greatest interest for the British colonial government, and mostly outweighed any concerns about the ill-treatment of coolies, as for example Adamson has shown in his study of indentured labour in British Guiana (Adamson 1972: 256). Consequently, the Marquess of Salisbury, Secretary of State for India, wrote to the Indian Government on indentured Indian labour in 1875:

---

5   Report of the Committee appointed by the Supreme Government of India to enquire into the abuses alleged to exist in exporting from Bengal Hill Coolies and Indian Labourers of various classes to other countries, 1839.

6   Ibid., p. 66.

"[...] we may also consider from an Imperial point of view, the great advantage which must result from peopling the warmer British possessions, which are rich in natural resources and only want population, by an intelligent and industrious race to whom the climate of these countries is well suited, and to whom the culture of the staples suited to the soil, and the modes of labour and settlement, are adapted. In this view, also, it seems proper to encourage emigration from India to Colonies well fitted for an Indian population."[7]

Despite the problems and misgivings, and despite the growing critique in the metropoles, as well as in India and other colonies, the indenture system was used during the next decades to bring hundreds of thousand workers to the plantations and mines of the British and other colonial empires. The official opinion, as also stated in the report of the Sanderson Committee from 1910, which was called to investigate the emigration from India to the crown colonies and protectorates, was that this form of emigration had a highly positive effect on the economy as well as on the development of these colonies in general:

"There can be no doubt that in this manner Indian indentured immigration has rendered invaluable service to those of your colonies in which, on the emancipation of the negro slaves, the sugar industry was threatened with ruin, or in which a supply of steady labour has been required for the development of the Colony by methods of work to which the native population is averse. The Indian immigration has had a twofold effect. It has admittedly supplied labour which could not be obtained in sufficient quantities from other sources. But we were also told by some competent witnesses that according to their observation, in British Guiana and the West Indies at all events, the thrifty and persevering habits of the Indian immigrant have had an educative effect, perceptible though gradual, on those among whom he has come to live and that his example and his competition have introduced new habits of industry and improved methods of agriculture."[8]

The report also stressed that Indians who remained in foreign colonies after indenture might be able to attain certain prosperity; this was judged as a positive effect of the whole system of indenture as well.[9]

In the late 19th century it had become common to send Asian working migrants around the globe, facilitated by the new steamships that could reach

---

7   Report of the Committee on Emigration from India to the Crown Colonies and Protectorates 1910, p. 7.
8   Ibid., pp. 21-22.
9   Ibid., p. 22.

distant destinations in far less time. Millions of Chinese and Indians were recruited as coolies (Emmer 1986). Aristide Zolberg (1997: 288) refers to one million Indian indentured labourers (in addition to many other migrants) who left the subcontinent between 1834 and 1916 and worked in Britain's Caribbean colonies; Thomas Metcalf (2007: 136) mentions a figure of 1.3 million. After the end of the Opium Wars, when the Chinese government was forced to lift barriers to emigration, a constantly growing network emerged, which shipped Chinese labourers to America, Africa, Australia, various South East Asian colonies, and South Africa.

The Chinese emigration was probably the largest non-European migration movement at the end of the 19th century. Although there are no precise figures, it is assumed that between 1860 and 1920, around 15 million Chinese migrated to South East Asia alone (Zolberg 1997: 289-291; Hoerder 2012: 435-439). It would certainly paint a biased picture if one were to consider only the European recruiters as actors. It has been argued that poverty and landlessness in parts of India and China created a pool of migrants who would undergo the conditions of indentured work and would be attracted into the colonial system of indenture (Klein 1993: 20; Northrup 1995: 65). However, there were also free migrants without working contracts who tried to use the opportunities migration might offer to them. Generally, one should stress the fact that forms of contract labour and free labour existed next to each other, being intertwined in many ways, as McKeown (2004) has argued for the Chinese migration in the 19th century. Still, the regulated indentured labour system, being part of the highly suppressive colonial economic order, created a huge migration flow within and between the colonial empires of the 19th century.

INDENTURED LABOUR AND COOLIES IN AFRICA

In Africa as well, due to shortages of labour in many colonies, the colonial powers were generally keen to employ Asian indentured workers, who were judged to be a cheap and reliable workforce. In all the African sub-Saharan colonies, European colonizers depended on the cheap labour of Africans and other ethnic groups, in the plantations of East and West Africa as well as the farms and mines of South Africa, and, in general, for all infrastructural projects such as building roads and railways. In addition to Africans from each colony, there was a strong inter-colonial migration, e.g. from the Portuguese colonies to the mines in British South Africa. The contracts and the forms of occupation in this case of work migration resemble indentured labour, as Legassick and de

Clerq have argued in their research (Legassick/de Clerq 1984). In the Gulf of Guinea in West Africa, on the Portuguese Islands of Principe and Sao Tome, forms of indentured labour were used to disguise slavery from the 1870s onwards. In that case, the workers were of African descent, not Asian migrants (Clarence-Smith 1993: 156-157).[10]

Asian indentured workers, mostly addressed as coolies,[11] were imported to regions in colonial Africa where there was a strong demand for cheap and readily available labour, i.e. mainly plantation economy and mining industries. Thousands of indentured workers came from Asian countries to Africa, altogether around 250,000 (Northrup 1995: 37), whose descendants still form significant cultures in South Africa. Here, Indian coolies came to the plantations of Natal, and Chinese workers to the mines of the Transvaal. Around 150,000 Indians arrived in the colony of Natal in South Africa between 1860 and 1911 to work in the tea and sugar plantations (Bhana 1991: 3-4). Indians also migrated to other African colonies. Particularly in East Africa, a long-standing exchange between India and the African coast dominated the commerce in the region and produced a continuing flow of migration. East Africa was even being addressed as the "America of the Hindu" by Sir Harry Johnston, Commissioner of British Central Africa and Special Commissioner in Uganda (1899-1901) (Metcalf 2007: 165). Additionally, around 39,000 Indian indentured workers were brought in for railway-building in British East Africa (Kenya) during the 1890s (Northrup 1995: 37). Chinese labourers also migrated to some sub-Saharan African destinations, most prominently to the Rand mines in the Transvaal between 1902 and 1910 (Bright 2013; Richardson 1984).

If we look at Southern Africa in more detail, the plantations and mining industry of British South Africa had always been based on itinerant and bonded labour. Africans from the whole southern part of the continent worked in the gold mines of Witwatersrand in the Republic of Transvaal, which stood under British suzerainty. In 1909 the mines near Johannesburg employed a total of about 150,000 workers (Legassick/de Clercq 1984: 141; Richardson 1984: 262). Consequently, Indian and Chinese indentured labour was employed in various regions of British South Africa. Indian coolies went to the colony of Natal as early as 1860 to work on the sugar plantations and later on the tea plantations

---

10 Similar forms of unfree labour were already being used at the beginning of the 19th century when freed African slaves – after the suppression of the slave trade by the British – were quickly indentured and had to stay on in unfree labour contracts (cf. Northrup 1995: 45).

11 For a discussion of the term "coolie", see the introduction of the volume.

(Metcalf 2007: 138). They had five- or ten-year contracts. In the meantime, regulations from India demanded that migrants should be able to stay on after their periods of servitude. Thus many of the immigrant Indians stayed in the British colony after their contracts came to an end. They often went on to work in other areas, including the coal and mining industries. Others became independent traders, or small farmers (Naicker 1971: 276-277).

The huge and growing number of free Indians who settled as traders was considered problematic. In 1882, the Times of Natal, a newspaper of the settlers and the white middle class, was alarmed about the growing number of Indian shops in the colony and asked the Legislative Council of Natal to improve legislation in order to prevent them competing against the white population (du Bois 2012: 46). On the other hand, the colony's tea, sugar, and coffee planters of course favoured the continuation of indentured labour in Natal. The Indian workers themselves had to endure very bad labour conditions under the indenture system in Natal. While some planters complied with the regulations, most planters routinely breached their obligations to provide suitable lodgings, food, and medical care. This was well known by the government of Natal. For example, a commission investigating mistreatment and withheld wages by a sugar planter, Henry Shire, heard 22 coolies and recorded their complaints in 1862. The commission stated: "that he [Shire] has extended the hours of Coolie labour – made unlawful deductions from their pay – placed some of them on half diet and administered flogging by means of Kafirs to others – all of which acts contrary to law."[12] However, the coolies finally had to return to Shire. He was only advised to obey the laws in the future. The Coolie Commission of 1872, enquiring into the discontent on the plantations, also found that illegal floggings, withheld wages, and sexual assault were common.[13] Still, indentured labour continued to be used in Natal because it served the interests of the planters best.

By 1893, the size of the Indian population was almost as high as the European population: 41,000 compared with 43,000 respectively. This was now viewed with growing alarm by most of the Europeans (du Bois 2012: 53). Finally, various laws were passed to restrict the rights of the Indian community after 1893, and moves were made to disenfranchise them. It is well known that

---

12 The Shire Commission Report, Durban, February 1862, as cited in Meer (1980: 99).

13 Report of the Coolie Commission, appointed to inquire into the condition of Indian immigrants in the colony of Natal and the mode in which they were employed; and also to inquire into the complaints made by returned immigrants to the protector of emigrants at Calcutta, Pietermaritzburg: P. Davis and Sons, Government Printers, 1872, as cited in Meer (1980: 118-169).

Gandhi, who came to Durban in 1893, opposed discrimination against Indians. In Natal, he organized protests against obligatory registration, which seriously restricted the freedom to move of all Asians, and was partly successful.[14] Gandhi also fought for the end of indenture in general during the first decade of the 20th century (Tinker 1974: 300).

Chinese indentured migration started considerably later. The South African gold industry had completely collapsed during the Second South African War (1899-1902), and reconstruction began quickly after peace was secured in 1902. The need for labour increased, and could not immediately be met by African workers. Between 1904 and 1907, therefore, about 63,000 Chinese indentured labourers were recruited for the goldmines in the British colony of Transvaal (Richardson 1984: 167). In the Transvaal, the "import" of Chinese labourers was controversially discussed. While the Chinese were judged to be hard workers and were preferred by some mining companies, European workers and traders in particular feared the competition of the Chinese, and were very doubtful about immigration.[15] The Chinese workers therefore had to submit to strict and cruel regulations. The Transvaal administration wanted at all costs to prevent groups of Chinese people from settling permanently in the colony, as had happened in Natal.[16]

Generally, there was a growing insecurity about the influence and impact of Asian labour in the African colonial setting, in which – in the eyes of most colonizers – there should be strict separation between Africans and Europeans. At the end of the 19th century racial segregation became a goal in itself, particularly in African colonies with a settler population. In the British East African Protectorate too, where Indians played an important role in trade, administration, and colony infrastructure, they were viewed with increasing distrust by the growing white settler population after 1900.

---

14 See for Gandhi in Natal e.g. Lake/Reynolds (2008: 114-133).
15 National Archive of Namibia, ZBU 2076, WIV R1 (transcript, German consulate Johannesburg to Chancellor Bethmann-Hollweg, 16 Aug. 1912), fo. 43.
16 Bundesarchiv Berlin-Lichterfelde R 1001/8747 (Schnee, Colonial Advisory Board London to German Foreign Office, Colonial Section, 26 Mar. 1906), fos. 142-143.

CIRCULATION OF KNOWLEDGE ABOUT INDENTURED LABOUR: THE EXAMPLE OF GERMAN AFRICAN COLONIES

Debates on indentured labour allocation and its consequences circulated through the increasingly globalized economy and through the different colonial administrations in the decades before WWI. Even the short-lived German colonial empire (1884-1918) became part of the global migration market. German entrepreneurs, as representatives of an aspiring colonial nation, were keen to be involved in recruiting indentured labour. Whenever there was a shortage of labour in the German colonies, voices were quick to call for coolies from India or China (Conrad 2006: 168-73). The most significant immigration of Chinese indentured workers can be observed in the German Pacific colonies New Guinea and Samoa. Here, a considerable number of Chinese coolies – altogether around 10,000 between 1889 and 1914 – were brought in to work in mines and on plantations (Steen 2014: 148).

In Africa as well, German colonial companies were keen to employ Asian coolies for mines and infrastructure projects, and on plantations. German agents attempted to bring Indian and Chinese coolies to African destinations for several years. The German East African Company (Deutsch-Ostafrikanische Gesellschaft) tried to negotiate the importing of Chinese workers in various Chinese Ports and in Singapore. Finally, around 500 Chinese coolies from Singapore came in the 1890s to work on plantations and in infrastructure projects. However, this experiment proved to be rather disastrous and the coolies returned only after two years, complaining about the bad treatment they had experienced under the Germans (Haschemi Yekani 2015: 63). There were further projects being developed to bring indentured Indians to German East Africa, but they failed after long negotiations (Lindner 2011: 438-439). The government of India had become more reluctant to send Indian indentured workers to non-British destinations during the 1880s (Tinker 1974: 274-278).

In German South-West Africa the discovery of diamonds in 1908 and the forced development of the railways from 1905 onwards meant that the needs of companies and businesses for easily accessible labour grew. Both mining and railway companies wanted to participate in the global labour market, and from 1910 onwards they attempted to recruit Indian and Chinese labour to import into the German colony (Lindner 2011: 410). German companies and mining associations were mainly influenced by conditions in neighbouring British South Africa. Particularly German mine owners and businessmen in the colony who knew about the influx of indentured labour in South Africa hoped that by importing Indians and Chinese they would get better and harder-working labourers than they thought they could find among the country's indigenous population.

Putting this plan into practice turned out to be difficult. Since 1910, the Lüderitz Bay Chamber of Mining (situated in Lüderitz Bay in the South of the colony) had been trying to persuade the government that increased immigration of indentured labourers was required to fill existing labour shortages.[17] However, the government of German South-West Africa imposed numerous conditions on the Chamber of Mining: indentured labourers were to be examined for illness at the place where they were recruited, and again before they landed in Africa; they were not permitted to move to the interior of the country; if they withdrew from their labour contracts, they had to be transported home at the Chamber of Mining's expense. The regulations were modelled closely on those that applied to Chinese indentured labourers in the Transvaal, and which were well known in German South West Africa via government reports and newspaper articles.[18] In this case, one can observe a concrete form of knowledge exchange between the two colonies on the topic of Asian labour, both with a rigid racial order and a white settler population.

The German mining companies tried to recruit Indians under such conditions, but the Indian colonial government refused to grant the German colonial government permission to recruit, as German South-West Africa demanded immediate repatriation of the coolies to India and the Indian government would not accept that.[19] The recruiting of Chinese workers seemed too problematic for the government of German South West Africa, as the Chinese government had forced the German colonies in the South Sea to treat the Chinese workers differently from the indigenous population and to grant them certain privileges, after long negotiations between German and Chinese officials (cf. Steen 2014). Since German South West Africa had enforced a rigid racial order after the end of the devastating Herero-and-Nama War (1904-1907), Chinese workers with certain privileges should not complicate the demarcation

---

17 National Archives of the Republic of South Africa, Pretoria NTS 201 3038/12/7473 (transcript, Consul Müller to Foreign Secretary, 23 April 1912).

18 National Archive of Namibia, BLU 30 (Governor of German South-West Africa to District Office Lüderitz Bay, 20 Apr. 1912). For similar regulations in Transvaal, of which the German Colonial Office took note, see Bundesarchiv Berlin-Lichterfelde R 1001/8747 (transcript, German Consulate General Shanghai to Chancellor von Bülow, 29 July 1904).

19 Bundesarchiv Berlin-Lichterfelde, R 1001/1232 (Crowe, Foreign Office, to Imperial German Embassy London, 25 Sept. 1912).

lines between "white" and "native", and the mining companies abstained from recruiting Chinese labour (Lindner 2011: 421).

The mine owners now attempted to hire Indians in Natal and the Cape Colony to work in the German colony. If Indians had stayed on in a colonial setting after their contract had ended, they were to some extent free to choose their new work.[20] A German company which had been mining copper and lead in Namibia since about 1900 employed around 200 Indian coolies as workers in the German colony in 1910. They had been recruited not in India, but in the Cape Colony, where the hiring of Indian workers whose contracts had expired was permitted. However, for the Indian workers contracts in the German colony were hardly attractive, and work recruitment was never successful: only around 300 Indians ever lived in the German colony as indentured workers.

Some general points can be highlighted through the example of German-British transfer of knowledge about indentured labour, and through the German discourse on coolies. In German African colonies as in many other colonies, business and mining associations were keen on Asian labour, trying to convince the administrations to facilitate the immigration of coolies. Here the stereotype of the reliable, strong, hard-working Asian coolie seemed to be the prevailing view.

However, there were different views from the side of the colonial administration and the settlers. These arguments can be found in German African and British African colonies with a white settler population who saw free Asian migrants as a threat and wanted the terms of indenture to be restricted. Generally, two main problems were addressed when dealing with indentured labour in the African setting: First, the possible competition between Asians and Europeans in colonies with some white settlement in Africa. Asian workers were increasingly regarded as competition by the European population. Even in German East Africa, with a small population of free Indians and hardly any indentured Indian workers, the so-called "Indian Question" was widely discussed in the settler-dominated East African press (Lindner 2011: 442-443). Most of the colonies that put up legal barriers to the immigration of Asians justified them in similar ways, namely that because of their modest needs and low standard of living by comparison with Europeans, Asians, and in particular Indians and Chinese, were superior to the "white race" in the ongoing competitive (Darwinian) struggle. Therefore they had to be regulated and their

---

20 National Archive of Namibia, ZBU 2076 W IV R2 (Lüderitz Bay Chamber of Mining to Consulate Durban, 12 June 1912), fo. 49.

rights to be restricted.[21] Administrations and white settlers wanted to prevent Asian workers from developing into competitors of the Europeans in the colony.

The argument of competition can be found not only for colonial Africa, but on a more general level as well: Even the Sanderson Report on Indian emigration from 1910, in general stressing the allegedly positive consequences of the system of indenture, conceded that the success of some of the Indian traders created jealousy amongst the European population in several colonies, including in British East Africa.[22] The British Anti-Slavery and Aborigines Protections Society, being highly critical of the system of indenture, particularly of the recruiting procedures, was also quite outspoken with regard to concerns about competition between Europeans and Asians:

"The conditions under which the coolies leave India, the terms of the indentures, the legislation of the Colonies, combine to wean the coolie from his Indian home: consequently the fittest not only survive but settle down to live in the colony, ultimately competing successfully with both the Whites and indigenous natives." (Harris 1910: 2)

Kay Saunders has explored similar conflicting interests in Queensland in Australia; here too, planters had sought to import Asian indentured labour from the Pacific islands, China, and India for sugar production. The immigration of Asian coolies collided with a developing "white-only" policy of the settler colony Australia and with the interests of the growing European unions, who wanted to dispense with Asian labourers as competitors during the last decade of the 19th century (Saunders 1984).

Secondly, and strongly connected with the issue of competition, was the discussion of the place of the Asian migrants in the racial order of the colony. To come back to the example of German South West Africa: The colonial government wanted at all costs to prevent indentured labourers from settling permanently in the colony. Despite being considered a threat to the white population, it was a major concern that they should not complicate racial structures by forming an additional group between the African and the European population. Racial categorization played a considerable role in the way the colonial government dealt with the immigrant groups of Indian and Chinese indentured workers. Indians and Chinese people were classified by most of the

---

21 Bundesarchiv Berlin-Lichterfelde, R 1001 /8731 (The Treatment of Asians in Foreign Colonies, 1912), fo. 1.

22 Report of the Committee on Emigration from India to the Crown Colonies and Protectorates 1910, p. 22.

racial categorizations in use during the age of high imperialism as occupying a median position between "white" and "black".[23] Contact with these ethnic groups represented a special challenge to the mostly dichotomic racial concepts of the European colonial administrations in Africa, as they had to deal with intermediate groups with certain rights between those of the Europeans and those of the indigenous population.

The racial constructs and stereotypes applied to Indians and Chinese were of course never definitive, but were constantly changed and challenged. In the German context, Chinese people had long been regarded as members of a nation with a highly developed civilization. It was not until the middle and end of the 19th century that, under the influence of new racial theories, they were classified as a lower "Mongolian race" that was clearly inferior to the "white Caucasian/ European race" (Leutner 1986: 409-11; Mühlhahn 2000).

Such racial categorization combined with social Darwinist thinking about competition between certain "races" developed a strong influence on the perception of indentured Asian labourers, particularly in colonial settings with a settler population. Clearly, the arguments about the advantages and disadvantages of indentured labour travelled between the colonies of different European empires. The dangers of the impact of Asian indentured workers on colonial societies were widely discussed, particularly in the African colonial setting with its mostly strict racial order, at least at the end of the 19th century. In the German case, the colonial administration in German South West Africa, lacking knowledge in such matters as the allocation of Asian workers, took the experiences of the colonial government in the South African British colonies Natal and Transvaal as a starting point for their own considerations and reactions to Asian immigration. However, one can observe the transfer of knowledge on a much wider scale.

CIRCULATING IMPERIAL KNOWLEDGE ABOUT INDENTURED LABOUR VIA THE METROPOLES – THE DISCUSSIONS IN THE INSTITUT COLONIAL INTERNATIONAL

As I have argued in my research, during the two decades before the outbreak of WWI, imperial cooperation and knowledge transfer reached a considerable scope, not only between neighbouring colonies, as shown here for Southern

---

23 Thieme, 'Die Halbweißen Frage in Samoa', *Berliner Tageblatt*, 26 Mar. 1914, p. 1, as cited in Gründer (1999: 295), cf. also Wareham (2002: 55).

Africa, but also on a more general inter-imperial level (Lindner 2011, Lindner 2015). One of the rather prominent examples of this development is the Institut Colonial International in Brussels (ICI), which was founded in 1894 in Brussels by Belgian, French, Dutch, and British colonial administrators and experts to promote the exchange of colonial knowledge between imperial powers (Daviron 2010, Lindner 2015, Wagner 2015). From the beginning, the ICI devoted a lot of time to the discussion of labour shortage, labour allocation, and labour management in colonial economies, including the use of indentured labour.

The small office of the ICI was situated in Brussels, and the yearly or biannual sessions of the institute took place either in Brussels or in the capital cities of other member states. The explicit aim of the institute was to share knowledge of colonial rule, as stated in the first session in 1894.[24] The philosophy of the institute was based on the new French concept of "colonisation comparée", developed by the economist and publicist Joseph Chailley in 1892, one of the founders of the Institute (Singaravelou 2012: 149). Soon after its foundation the institute invited members of many imperial nations who joined in the common endeavour to develop and share colonial knowledge. The following European empires with colonies in Africa had permanent delegates at the institute before WWI: Germany, Britain, Belgium, France and Portugal.

The institute was able to attract high-profile experts from different colonizing nations. In 1912/13, the institute had as presidents and vice-presidents Lord Reay, former governor of Bombay; Bernhard Dernburg, former German colonial secretary; and Joseph Chailley, director of the French Colonial Union. Among the members one would find e.g. Baron Descamps, one of the ministers in the Belgium government concerned with the Congo; and Prince August d'Arenberg, president of the Committee of French Africa, and president of the Suez-Canal Company.[25] The number of delegates grew from 70 in the beginning to 150 at the end of the 1920s (Daviron 2010: 482). The most active members before WWI were France, Belgium, Germany, and the Netherlands (Singaravélou 2012: 153), Great Britain was less prominent in the ICI. This was seen

---

24 Institut Colonial International, Compte Rendu (1894: 4): "De créer des relations internationales entre les personnes qui s'occupent d'une façon suivie de l'étude du droit et de l'administration des colonies, hommes politiques, administrateurs, savants, - et de faciliter l'échange des idées et des connaissances spéciales entre hommes compétents."

25 Institut Colonial International, Compte Rendu (1907:14); Institut Colonial International, Compte Rendu (1912: 21); Institut Colonial International, Compte Rendu (1921:15, 21).

as a grave problem by contemporary delegates, as Great Britain's expertise in colonial matters was still unequalled and a stronger engagement of British delegates was hoped for. However, Great Britain had less interest in forms of comparative colonization than the continental European imperial powers, and was very reluctant to participate in the undertakings of the institute (Lindner 2015: 68).

The institute organised yearly or biannual meetings in Belgium (Brussels, The Hague) or in the capital cities of other member states, dealing with topics of colonial administration, colonial law, colonial economy and, quite substantially, with the organization of labour in colonial settings. The ICI printed extensive reports of the meetings with elaborate and detailed expert studies (cf. Institute Colonial International, Compte Rendu 1895). Furthermore, the ICI published books in the series "La bibliotheque colonial international". In this context, too, the topic of labour was extensively covered, e.g. with three volumes collecting and interpreting labour contracts in German colonies, the Belgian Congo, and in French, British, and Dutch colonies, published from 1895 to 1898. The volumes also included various regulations of indentured labour in colonies of European imperial powers.[26]

Regarding the indentured labour of Asian coolies, the institute soon aimed to develop an international regulation that would allow all European colonial empires to recruit Asian labour. Already in the first session of the institute in The Hague in 1895 the problem of "insufficient" colonial labour was addressed (Institut Colonial International, Compte Rendu 1895: 221-223). Different African colonies with plantation economies were debated, and labour legislation in French, German, and Dutch colonies was discussed, for example in the German African colonies Togo and Kamerun with their cocoa and coffee plantations. Labour was addressed as a problem in colonies with an "insufficient" indigenous population, but also in colonies with local people who were – in the eyes of the experts of the ICI – unwilling to work. Such problems were identified in several African colonies of the delegates.

It was clear that indentured labour and the importing of Asian coolies was a favoured concept to overcome such problems, particularly in the German and French African colonies. The ICI, being mostly focused on the economic profit of the colonies, emphasised the advantages of indentured labour, contrary to colonial settler societies. In the discussion of the institute – similar to the German discourse – the stereotype of the hard-working Asian coolie was

---

26 Institut Colonial International (ed.) (1895-98): Bibliothèque Coloniale Internationale. La Main-d'oeuvre aux colonies. Vol. 1-3, Paris: A. Colin.

dominant (Institut Colonial International, Compte Rendu 1895: 141), following the interests of companies, businesses and plantation-owners worldwide.

However, it was also seen that misuse would bring strong criticism, especially from the broad abolitionist movements that had been criticizing indenture during the last decades as forms of disguised slavery. Thus, the ICI was keen to develop formal regulation that would allow several European empires to move workers more regularly between colonies, and which would generally facilitate indentured migration (Institut Colonial International, Compte Rendu 1895: 226-229). France was particularly engaged in that question, as the sugar plantations of French Reunion were far less successful than its neighbour, British Mauritius. Mauritius profited considerably from the enormous influx of Indian indentured labour (Daviron 2010: 484).

During the next meetings until 1900, the delegates of the ICI tried to develop a draft for an international treaty that would regulate the employment of Asian coolies in European colonies. The draft only focused on inter-colonial migration, not on countries "inhabited by savages still independent with no regular government and not submitting to the law of nation at it has been developed in European nations" (Institut Colonial International, Compte Rendu 1899: 43). China was seen as a huge problem when the ICI tried to prepare a treaty. China had a regular government and was not under colonial rule; however, the ICI members considered China unable to join in a treaty with European states, as China was not seen as an equal, according to the racial concepts prevalent during high imperialism.

During the meetings, in several sessions, the delegates addressed the consequences of immigration of Asian indentured workers on a broader level. Within the ICI too, the racial complications that followed the engagement of indentured labour were debated and seen as a problem. Racial stereotypes shaped the discussion of Indian, Chinese, and African workers. Indians were seen as effective but *"remuants et querelles"* (agitated and quarrelsome), while the Chinese were considered very hard workers, "almost like blacks" (Institut Colonial International, Compte Rendu 1895: 225-226). The perceived advantages and disadvantages of different ethnic groups were thoroughly addressed in the discussions of the ICI.

During the next meetings, the ICI tried to outline a treaty for the allocation of indentured labour between colonial empires; however, this was abandoned as not feasible in 1899 (Daviron 2010: 483). The delegates now developed a regulatory model that several European colonial empires should adopt. A draft for a possible inter-colonial regulation was drawn up, trying to standardize recruitment, work contracts, transport, arrival in the country of destination, and the control of contracts and working conditions in the colonies (Institut Colonial International, Compte Rendu 1899: 357-366).

Eventually however, the ICI never managed to implement an international regulation of Asian labour. The ICI, as a non-governmental, small international organization, was not in a position to negotiate a treaty. The main problem was that Great Britain, a major supplier of indentured labour, was not interested in such a treaty (Daviron 2010: 485). Furthermore, during the first decade of the 20th century, the Indian government restricted indentured migration considerably as an answer to growing nationalist agitation in India, as already discussed above. Neither the French nor the Germans had been successful in bringing new Indian coolies to their colonies (cf. Lindner 2011, Tinker 1974).

Already during the last years before the First World War, the discussions and publications of the ICI concentrated much more on how to recruit more local labour for plantations and mining in colonies with certain schemes, and how to employ certain constraints and contracts to retain the labourers in their workplaces.

What should be important here is that the ICI – institutionalizing colonial knowledge transfer and creating new forms of regular discussion and meetings between political and scientific experts – also served as a forum to circulate knowledge about indentured labour between imperial European powers. At least before WWI, indentured labour was still seen as a key issue by colonial empires to maximise the profit in their colonies, mainly to maintain the plantation economy in old colonial dependencies, but also as a possible way to create a plantation economy in new African protectorates. In the discussions of the institute one can also observe the decrease of formally regulated indentured labour, particularly from India since the 1910s, and the appearance of new forms of bonded labour, especially in Africa, now often locally recruited.

CONCLUSION

First of all, it is clear how closely the colonies of various empires were involved in the global streams of indentured labour migration. Even the short-lived German empire was part of the ongoing discussions and negotiations. It is also important to stress that Africa was an integral part of the indentured migration movements. Indentured labour was still seen as a solution for labour allocation in Africa shortly before WWI, as the discussions in the colonies, in the ICI, and the Sanderson report clearly indicate.

With the increasing scientific interest in colonization and with a further differentiation of colonial knowledge, the exchange of colonial knowledge reached new dimensions. The administrations of different colonial empires became more interested in their neighbours and tried to learn from one anothers' experiences with indentured labour, as we could observe in the German-British example and on a more general level in the discussions of the ICI. However, one should also emphasise that the ICI established and intensified ties between imperial powers in order to manage and exploit colonial labour. Seeing it from a postcolonial perspective it was an institution that served to institutionalize the construction of Eurocentric knowledge about colonized people – turning coolie labour into a commodity.

Furthermore, it is obvious that the immigration of Asian workers became a highly contested issue at the end of the 19th century, not only because of the mounting criticism regarding the abuse of indentured workers. It was also closely connected with discussions of racial demarcation and social Darwinist concepts. While European companies, planters, and many colonial experts – such as the ICI delegates – wanted to take advantage of the opportunities offered by globalized Asian migration, local colonial administrations and settlers often insisted on maintaining a strict policy of regulation, which was strongly associated with anxieties related to racial difference. In the period of high imperialism coolie labour thus stood at a point of intersection between many conflicting aims: those of maximizing the profit of colonial dependencies in an increasingly globalized economy, of suppressing the worst abuses of the system in order to prevent upheaval in the sending colonies, and at the same time that of strengthening racial demarcation and European superiority in colonial societies.

REFERENCES

Adamson, Alan (1972): Sugar Without Slaves: The Political Economy of British Guiana, 1838-1904, New Haven: Yale University Press.
Bhana, Surendra (1991): Indentured Indian Emigrants to Natal 1860-1902: A Study Based on Ship's Lists, New Delhi: Promilla & Co.
Bright, Rachel K. (2013): Chinese Labour in South Africa, 1902-1910: Race, Violence and Global Spectacle, Basingstoke et al.: Palgrave Macmillan.
Campbell, Persia Crawford (1923): Chinese Coolie Emigration to Countries within the British Empire, London: P.S. King & Son.
Carter, Marina (1993): "The Transition from Apprenticeship to Indentured Labour in Mauritius." In: Michael Twaddle (ed.), The Wages of Slavery:

From Chattel Slavery to Wage Labour in Africa, the Caribbean and England, London: Frank Cass, pp. 114-130.

Clarence-Smith, William Gervase (1993): "Cocoa Plantations and Coerced Labor in the Gulf of Guinea." In: Martin A. Klein (ed.), Breaking the Chains: Slavery, Bondage and Emancipation in Modern Africa and Asia, Madison: University of Wisconsin Press, pp. 150-170.

Conrad, Sebastian (2006): Globalisierung und Nation im Deutschen Kaiserreich, München: C. H. Beck.

Daviron, Benoit (2010): "Mobilizing Labour in African agriculture: The Role of the International Colonial Institute in the Elaboration of a Standard of Colonial Administration, 1895-1930." In: Journal of Global History 5/3, pp. 479-501.

Du Bois, Duncan (2012): "The 'coolie curse': The Evolution of White Colonial Attitudes towards the Indian Question, 1860-1900." In: Historia 57/2, pp. 31-67.

Emmer, Peter Cornelis (1986): "The Meek Hindu: The Recruitment of Indian indentured labourers for service overseas, 1870–1916." In: Peter Cornelis Emmer/Ernst van den Boogaart (eds.), Colonialism and Migration: Indentured Labour Before and After Slavery, Dordrecht: Martinus Nijhoff Publishers, pp. 187-207.

Gründer, Horst (1999): '... da und dort ein junges Deutschland zu gründen': Rassismus, Kolonien und kolonialer Gedanke vom 16. bis zum 20. Jahrhundert, München: Deutscher Taschenbuch Verlag.

Haschemi Jekani, Minu (2015): Die (Un-) Erwünschten. Rassismus, Arbeit und koloniale Ordnung an der Küste Tansanias, 1885-1914, Diss. phil., European University Institute Florence.

Harris, John H. (1910): Coolie Labour in the British Crown Colonies and Protectorates, London: Edward Hughes & Co.

Hoerder, Dirk (2012): "Migrations and Belongings." In: Emily S. Rosenberg (ed.), A World Connecting: 1870-1945, Cambridge/London: Belknap Press of Harvard University Press, pp. 435-592.

Hu-DeHart, Evelyn (1993): "Chinese Coolie Labour in Cuba in the Nineteenth Century: Free Labour or Neoslavery?" In: Slavery & Abolition 14, pp. 67-86.

Institut Colonial International (ed.) (1894): Compte Rendu des Séances tenues à Bruxelles les 28 et 29 Mai 1894, Brussels: Typographie-Lithographie Populaire.

—— (1895): Compte Rendu de la Session tenue à la Haye, les 9, 10, 11 et 12 Septembre 1895, Paris: Armand Clon et Cie.

—— (1899): Compte Rendu de la Session tenue à Bruxelles 5, 6, et 7 Avril 1899, Brussels: Ètablissements généraux d'Imprimerie.

—— (1907): Compte Rendu de la Session tenue à Bruxelles les 17, 18 et 19 Juin 1907, Brussels: Établissements généraux d'Imprimerie.

—— (1912): Compte Rendu de la Session tenue à Bruxelles les 29, 30 et 31 Juillet 1912, Brussels: Augustin Challamel.

—— (1921): Compte Rendu de la Session tenue à Paris les 17, 18 et 19 Mai 1921, Brussels: Établissements généraux d'Imprimerie.

—— (1895): Bibliothèque Coloniale Internationale. La Main-d'oeuvre aux colonies. Vol. 1: Documents officiels sur le contrat de travail et le louage d'ouvrage aux Colonies. Colonies allemandes. Etat indépendant du Congo. Colonies françaises. Indes orientales néerlandaises, Paris: A. Colin.

—— (1897): Bibliothèque Coloniale Internationale. La Main-d'oeuvre aux colonies. Vol. 2: Documents officiels sur le contrat de travail et le louage d'ouvrage aux Colonie. Indes anglaises, Colonies anglaises, Paris: A. Colin.

—— (1898): Bibliothèque Coloniale Internationale La Main-d'oeuvre aux colonies. Vol. 3: Documents officiels sur le contrat de travail et le louage d'ouvrage aux Colonie. Colonies Françaises, Surinam, Paris: A. Colin.

Klein, Martin A. (1993): "Introduction: Modern European Expansion and Traditional Servitude in Africa and Asia." In: Martin A. Klein (ed.), Breaking the Chains: Slavery, Bondage, and Emancipation in Modern Africa and Asia, Madison: University of Wisconsin Press, pp. 3-36.

Lake, Marilyn/Reynolds, Henry (2008): Drawing the Global Colour Line. White Men's Countries and the International Challenge of Racial Equality, Cambridge: Cambridge University Press.

Legassick, Martin/Clercq, Francine de (1984): "Capitalism and Migrant Labour in Southern Africa: The Origins and Nature of the System." In: Shula Marks/Peter Richardson (eds.), International Labour Migration: Historical Perspectives, Hounslow: Temple Smith, pp. 140-160.

Leutner, Mechthild (1986): "Deutsche Vorstellungen über China und Chinesen und über die Rolle der Deutschen in China 1890-1945." In: Heng-yue Kuo (ed.), Von der Kolonialpolitik zur Kooperation: Studien zur Geschichte der deutsch-chinesischen Beziehungen, München: Minerva-Publikation, pp. 401-443.

Lindner, Ulrike (2011): Koloniale Begegnungen: Deutschland und Großbritannien als Imperialmächte in Afrika 1880-1914, Frankfurt am Main: Campus.

—— (2015): "New Forms of Knowledge Exchange between Imperial Powers: The Development of the Institut Colonial International (ICI) since the End of the 19th Century." In: Volker Barth/Roland Czetowski (eds.), Encounters of

Empires: Interimperial Transfers and Imperial Manifestations, 1870-1950, London: Bloomsbury, pp. 57-78.

Lopez, Kathleen (2013): Chinese Cubans: A Transnational History, Chapel Hill: The University of North Carolina Press.

Mann, Michael (2003): "Die Mär von der freien Lohnarbeit: Menschenhandel und erzwungene Arbeit in der Neuzeit. Ein einleitender Essay." In: Comparativ 13/4, pp. 7-22.

Martinez, Julia (2005): "The End of Indenture? Asian Workers in the Australian Pearling Industry, 1901-1972." In: International Labor and Working-Class History 67, pp. 125-147.

McKeown, Adam (2004): "Global Migration 1846-1940." In: Journal of World History 15/2, pp. 155-189.

Meagher, Arnold J. (2008): The Coolie Trade: The Traffic in Chinese Laborers to Latin America 1847-1874, Philadelphia: Xlibris Corporation.

Meer, Y.S. (ed.) (1980): Documents of Indentured Labour: Natal 1851-1917, Durban: Institute of Black Research.

Metcalf, Thomas (2007): Imperial Connections: India in the Indian Ocean Arena, 1860-1920, Berkeley: University of California Press.

Mühlhahn, Klaus (2000): Herrschaft und Widerstand in der „Musterkolonie" Kiautschou, München: Oldenbourg 2000.

Naicker, N.P. (1971): "Indians in South Africa." In: Anirudha Gupta (ed.), Indians Abroad: Asia and Africa. Report of an International Seminar, New Delhi: Orient Longman, pp. 274-302.

Northrup, David (1995): Indentured Labor in the Age of Imperialism, 1834-1922, Cambridge: Cambridge University Press.

Report of the Committee appointed by the Supreme Government of India to enquire into the abuses alleged to exist in exporting from Bengal Hill Coolies and Indian Labourers of various classes to other countries (1839), Calcutta: G.H. Huttmann, Bengal Military Orphan Press.

Report of the Committee on Emigration from India to the Crown Colonies and Protectorates (Sanderson Committee) (1910), Cd. 5192, London: HMSO.

Report of the Committee on Emigration from India to the Crown Colonies and Protectorates (1910) Part II, Minutes and Evidence, Cd. 5193, London: HMSO.

Report of the Committee on Emigration from India to the Crown Colonies and Protectorates (1910) Part III, Papers laid before the committee, Cd. 5194 London: HMSO.

Richardson, Peter (1984): "Chinese Indentured Labour in the Transvaal Gold Mining Industry, 1904-1910." In: Kay Saunders (ed.), Indentured Labour in the British Empire, 1834-1920, London: Croom Helm, pp. 260-291.

—— (1984): "Coolies, Peasants and Proletarians: The Origins of Chinese Indentured Labour in South Africa, 1904-1907." In: Shula Marks/Peter Richardson (eds.), International Labour Migration: Historical Perspectives, Hounslow: Temple Smith, pp.167-185.

Saunders, Kay (1984): "The Workers' Paradox. Indentured Labour in the Queensland Sugar Industry to 1920." In: Kay Saunders (ed.), Indentured Labour in the British Empire, 1834-1920, London: Croom Helm, pp. 213-259.

Singaravélou, Pierre (2012): "Les stratégies d'internationalisation de la question coloniale et la construction transnationale d'une science de la colonisation à la fin du XIXe siècle." In: Monde(s) 1/1,pp. 135-157.

Steen, Andreas (2014): "Germany and the Chinese Coolie: Labour Resistance and the Struggle for Equality 1894-1914." In: Nina Berman/Klaus Mühlhahn/Alain Patrice Ngang (eds.), German Colonialism Revisited: African, Asian and Oceanic Experiences, Ann Arbor, Michigan: University of Michigan Press 2014, pp. 147-160.

Tinker, Hugh (1974): A New System of Slavery: Export of Indian Labour Overseas, 1830-1920, London: Oxford University Press.

Twaddle, Michael (1993): "Visible and Invisible Hands." In: Michael Twaddle (ed.), The Wages of Slavery: From Chattel Slavery to Wage Labour in Africa, the Caribbean and England, London: Frank Cass, pp. 1-12.

Wagner, Florian (2015): "Private Colonialism and Internationalism in Europe, 1870-1914". In: Volker Barth/Roland Czetowski (eds.), Encounters of Empires: Interimperial Transfers and Imperial Manifestations, 1870-1950, London: Bloomsbury, pp. 79-107.

Wareham, Evelyn (2002): Race and Realpolitik: The Politics of Colonisation in German Samoa, Frankfurt am Main: Lang.

Zolberg, Aristide R. (1997): "Global Movements, Global Walls: Responses to Migration, 1885-1925." In: Gungwu Wang (ed.) Global History and Migrations, Boulder: Westview Press, pp. 279-307.

Coolie Transformations – Uncovering the Changing Meaning and Labour Relations of Coolie Labour in the Dutch Empire (18th and 19th Century)

MATTHIAS VAN ROSSUM

INTRODUCTION: WHAT'S IN A NAME?

Coolie labour is often defined as indentured contract-labour migration, and its history is associated especially with the coolie trade from the 1830s and 1840s onwards. The *Encyclopædia Britannica* for example, describes the term "coolie, or cooly" as being used "in a special sense to designate those natives of India and China who leave their country under contracts of service to work as labourers abroad" (1910: 77). It provides a second, somewhat more open definition as well, mentioning that the term is "generally applied to Asiatic labourers belonging to the unskilled class as opposed to the artisan" (ibid.).

As in international historiography, Dutch studies of the history of coolie labour have focused almost exclusively on case(s) of coolie labour in the 19th century Atlantic and Asian colonial sphere fitting the first definition. These histories have been dealt with in two main historical narratives. For the Dutch West Indies, this is the history of Indian indentured contract-labour migrants (*koelies*) brought to Suriname starting in the late 19th century after the abolition of slavery. For the Dutch East Indies, this is the history of Chinese and Javanese contract labour under 'penal law' increasingly employed in the mines, on plantations, and in other industries in colonial Sumatra in the 19th century. The argument often recurs that the Dutch colonial state and entrepreneurs of the West- and East Indies based their practices of employing coolie-labour on the (earlier) British experience. The British experience, in turn, is traced back to the employment of Indian indentured contract labourers in the early 19th century (Northrup 1995).

This narrow definition of coolie labour as indentured contract migrants, and the narrative tracing the invention and employment of coolie-contracts back to the early 19th century British experience, seems to provide only a partial understanding of the origins of the coolie concept, contract labour, and mechanisms of labour exploitation. It does not include various other (longer-running) histories of work, labour relations, and exploitation in imperial-context, some of which are actually explicitly related to the notion of coolie labour in different parts of the world. The Dutch (early modern) imperial history provides an interesting case for the history of bonded labour and understanding social relations delineated with the notion of coolie.

In the 17th- and 18th-century empire of the Dutch East India Company (VOC) in Asia, the term *koelie* (coolie) was a pivotal, but ambiguous concept. The notion essentially referred to work or workers, but could include different labour relations and people of rather different social standings. The concept of coolie not only had different meaning in different regions that were part of the early modern Dutch empire, but also seems to have changed over time. In the 18th century, there seems to have been a strong regional difference between the two most important regions of the empire of the VOC, varying from temporary wage-labour (Southeast Asia) to tributary labour relations (South Asia). In the 19th century, the term coolie changed, including within the Dutch empire, and became synonym for the (formally and informally bonded) contract labour. This chapter explores the evidence for this, indicating that the historical trajectory of the concept of 'coolie labour' is not as clear-cut as it is often presented in studies on Asian contract migration. In order to do so, it explores the concept of coolie labour in different historical contexts and from different perspectives, looking at labour relations, social status, meaning, and the actual work involved. Through this explorative approach, it aims to break open dominant narratives in order to recover the different and changing meaning of the concept of coolie during especially the 18th century in Southeast Asia (particularly Batavia and surroundings) and South Asia (particularly Ceylon).

A Long History of Coolie Labour

The notion of coolie as indentured contract labour has led to lines of enquiry focusing mainly on the origins of this specific type of indentured contract migration with specifically Asian workers, and less on either the historical development of concepts of coolie labour or even that of contract labour in general. Again, the *Encyclopædia Britannica* (1910: 77) might serve as an interesting illustration of this line of enquiry:

"It is scarcely possible to say when the Indian coolie trade began. Before the end of the 18th century Tamil labourers from southern India were wont to emigrate to the Straits Settlements, and they also flocked to Tenasserim from the other side of the Bay of Bengal after the conquest had produced a demand for labour. The first regularly recorded attempt at organizing coolie emigration from India took place in 1834, when forty coolies were exported to Mauritius; but it was not until 1836 that the Indian government decided to put the trade under official regulations."

Similar perspectives have dominated in other historical studies. "The word *coolie*" has, for example, been seen as "a product of European expansion into Asia and the Americas" (Jung 2005: 679). The coolie as indentured contract worker is traced back to the "experimental contingents of indentured Indian laborers [who] were introduced to Mauritius in 1830 and 1834" (Meagher 2008: 30). The abolition of slavery, of course, had a major impact on the expansion of indentured migrant contract labour. Between 1834 and 1839, the sugar planters of Mauritius 'imported' over 25,000 Indian workers, contracted for five-year periods. This has often been seen as the beginning of indentured contract migrant labour. As some historians claimed: "Sugar planters around the world, stimulated by the success of the experiment in Mauritius, sought to adopt similar systems of indentured labor" (Meagher 2008: 30). And indeed, it is pointed out, Asian migrant contract workers appeared in the French colonies (already in the 1830s onwards), in British Malaysia, the Pacific Islands, Australia, etc.

For the Dutch West Indies, especially the plantation colony Suriname, coolies are emphasized as having been a new solution for replacing slave labour in the second half of the 19th century (ibid.: 260). In the Dutch West Indies, slavery was abolished in 1863, but 'freed' slaves were obligated to continue to work until 1873. It is emphasized that British examples were followed and British recruitment networks used to employ contract workers from British India. From the 1890s onwards, Javanese and Chinese contract workers were recruited from the Indonesian archipelago. Studies on the Dutch East Indies focus mainly on 19th century Sumatra and other parts of the 'outer districts' of the Dutch colony in the Indonesian archipelago (Houben and Lindblad 1999). Indentured contract labour was perceived by colonial authorities as a necessary solution to mobilize and recruit labour in economically unfavourable circumstances and to attract labour to – and control labour in – expanding plantation industries in undeveloped and less populated areas such as Sumatra. Special *koelie ordonnanties* – coolie ordinances or penal laws – were installed for these purposes (Breman 1992). Towards the end of the 19th century, the Dutch imperial system leaned heavily on the work of coolies, who toiled as indentured contract migrants on plantations, in mines, on roads, in harbours, and in factories in Suriname, Sumatra, Banjoewangi and other places.

It is possible, however, to provide a longer perspective on the history of coolie (and contract) labour relations. Such longer historical investigations into the early modern period, seem necessary, as recent historical findings and critiques urge us to move away from the classic historical narrative in which Europeans were the instigators of new, modernizing economic and political developments in an Asian world which was not familiar with market economies and characterized by 'despotist' modes of production prior to European colonialism (cf. Stanziani 2014; Banaji 2011). Instead, recent research indicates the presence of developed economic institutions, the widespread character of labour markets, and high levels of monetization in specific parts of South, East and Southeast Asia.[1]

It has been emphasized that markets and coercion are not exclusive, but can easily function together (cf. Banaji 2011). This is important in relation to the role of different types of unfree and free labour relations in (labour-intensive) routes to economic development. In debates on global economic development, labour-intensive paths are increasingly attributed a key role in the global diffusion of industrialization and economic development, and emphasized as the dominant trajectory "in most of Eurasia" (Stanziani 2014: 9; cf. Austin/Sugihara 2013). It has been argued that labour-intensive routes to economic development placed increasing pressures and constraints on labour and labour relations throughout the 18th and 19th century. Even more so, it has been argued that such labour-intensive production systems could be based on slavery and other forms of coerced labour, which was perceived as efficient and modern by contemporaries (cf. Mann 2012; Winn 2010).

At the same time, however, the labour-intensive ways of production in early modern Asia, especially under the VOC, could easily lean on either casual wage labour, slave labour, corvée labour, or contract labour. Often, workers in different labour relations worked side by side in the same working environments at the same time. These new perspectives indicate the importance of studying longer historical lines of labour relations and coercion, including that of coolie

---

1 On monetization and (maritime and military) labour markets see Lucassen (2014, 2012), Gommans (2002), Van Rossum (2014).

labour. The development of coolie labour relations in the long run within the Dutch empire provides an important case in testing new approaches of global labour history as well as developing new perspectives and explanations of what actually happened during this period of early globalization, increasing colonial domination, and diverging European and Asian routes of economic development.

COOLIES, PORT WORK, AND FREE LABOUR?

Let's start our exploration of coolie labour relations in the centre of the Dutch East Indian empire. In Batavia, the term *coolie* generally indicated wage labour. There was a long tradition of referring to the wage labourers working in the port as coolies. When the Batavian harbor head was lengthened in 1692, extending it further into the sea, it was reported that the costs "would soon be compensated for by the resulting reduction of the coolie wages" (Coolhaas et al. 1960-2007, vol. 5: 442) for loading and unloading the ships. From 1765, it was decided to recruit Chinese hirelings, referred to as coolies, to load and unload the ships before Batavia (Van Rossum 2014: 197-198).

In a study on 'free labour' in Java, Peter Boomgaard points out that "the term coolie" is "a convenient symbol for the appearance of free wage-labour. Its etymology, containing elements of unskilled labour, dacoitry and wages, neatly sums up the developments with which we seem to be confronted, namely, the creation of social underclass, neither slaves nor clients of Javanese patrons, cut loose from their village mooring, and living by their wits" (Boomgaard 1990: 44). He traces the emergence of the term coolie on Java to "around 1670", pointing out that "it is either related to the Western Indian caste or tribe of the Koli, associated with unskilled, menial labour and dacoitry, or to the Tamil term *kuli*, associated with wages" (ibid.).

The term *coolie* was not limited to Batavia. In other VOC-ports as well, the workers loading and unloading vessels were referred to as *coolies*. In a court case concerning the presumed smuggling of opium by the VOC-merchant Jan de Roth in 1744, declarations by port workers indicate the loading of vessels before Malacca by inland sailors and hired *koelij jongens*. Interrogated by Company officials, the hired coolie workers Cadir, Pittiromal, and Alludien, from Malacca, refer to themselves as "Coolies and free moors" – "Coelies en vrije mooren". They had been "called" near "the boom" – the toll of the water entrance of Malacca – by the "gentief" (Jew) Steven Mirandje in order to transport some chests from a vessel to a house. Their co-workers Oedeman, Polee and Asseen were also categorized as "Coolies and free Moors", referring themselves also to the "other Coolies". They received their wage at piece rate, two shillings for the transport of a chest (Boomgaard 1990: 167-167).

The term *coolie* was even employed by the Dutch for port workers in places such as Japan. The German scholar in the service of the VOC, Engelbert Kaempfer, described how in Deshima in the 1690s "some Kuli's march before carrying the gowns in boxes, one carries the board or table, on which the gowns are to be laid". Again, *coolies* seemed to be used especially to refer to hired port workers, working as casual wage labourers. Kaempfer narrates how they hired workers in the – very restricted – port area of Deshima or Nagasaki: "We were busy with packing up our baggage, hiring a sufficient number of Kuli's, or Porters, and fifteen horses for our journey." After an earthquake in October 1691, Kaempfer recalls that "[…] a Kuli, or porter, was apprehended at the gate, as he was coming away from our Island [Deshima], and some Camphire was found upon him, upon which Mr. Reinss, of whome the prisoner confess'd he bought it, was immediately carried before the mayor of the town. The Kuli himself, the merchant for whom the Camphire was bought, and his landlord were by order from the Governor secured by their Ottona's, and laid in irons". The next day, all VOC-ships "were searched, one after another." Some days later, three smugglers were caught. Although they had bought "some goods of the Chinese", Kaempfer (1727: 179) recalls "our Kuli, and some more of our servants were ordered forthwith to quit their work, and to run after the fugitives".

Company sources for Japan refer to coolie workers mainly in relation to theft while loading and unloading ships. In 1673, it was reported from Japan that "in the unloading of the ships, we had been granted great liberty, but the mischief of the coolies or labourers, who were given a free hand in their operations by the translators, has led to unbearable theft".[2] In 1729 it was mentioned, for example, that the cargoes departed from Japan were in order, with the exception of the "powder [or icing] sugar as a result of the theft by the coolies".[3] In 1692, it was decided that tin would now be melted and transported in pieces of 50 pounds apiece as a measure to counter the theft of tin by coolies loading and unloading the tin at Malacca.[4]

Not only theft and discipline, but especially also the cost of coolie labour was a continuous concern. After Company servants failed to "employ hirelings" in 1683, who were considered too expensive as they had to be paid on top of the rent of the vessels, it was decided to send 50 slaves "as coolies" to Jambi to

---

2 Generale Missiven, vol. 3, 848.
3 Generale Missiven, vol. 9, 34.
4 Generale Missiven, vol. 6, 27.

support the ten Company servants working there.[5] In 1708, reports complained about the "narrow and fast running river" of Jambi, making it impossible to sail upstream, leading to "incredible high costs" with regard to "ropes and coolie wages".[6] Two years later, after the ship *Andromeda* had run aground in the river of Jambi, it had to be unloaded by coolies, who were paid 1/8 rijksdaalder and a ration of rice per day.[7] Similar considerations, and especially comparisons between different labour relations, continually recurred. In 1702, "the requested 30 slaves" could not be sent to Malacca with the ship *Susanna*, as a consequence of which "they had to work with hired coolies".[8] In 1687, it was reported that 100 slaves had been transported from the Coromandel coast to Malacca, because the "scarce" coolies were too expensive, costing 8 stuivers per day.[9]

"COELIE SOEKEN" IN BATAVIA

Although many references involve the loading and unloading of ships, coolie labour was not restricted to port work. In 1730, it was reported from Jambi, for example, that "20 coolies had worked 44 days on raising the fundaments of the south-side of the [Company] lodgings".[10] In 1757, it was reported that it was allowed, in order to speed up the progress of works on the fortifications, to send ships carpenters and other artisans to Ambon, as well as to "recruit coolies amongst the inhabitants".[11] Two years later, reports on the financial accounts of Banda mention the "high costs" of coolies and other posts, such as building materials.[12] From the Coromandel coast it was reported in 1738 that the peeling of the nely was more expensive with a peeling mill than treading it, because the costs of the pots, copper boilers, and firewood excluded the costs of the mills, the wages of European servants and the coolie wages.[13] Other references mention coolie work or coolie wages involved in construction, ship repair (or deconstruction), logging wood, cutting stone, etc.

---

5   Generale Missiven, vol. 3, 998.
6   Generale Missiven, vol. 6, 579.
7   Generale Missiven, vol. 6, 643.
8   Generale Missiven, vol. 6, 200.
9   Generale Missiven, vol. 5, 133.
10 Generale Missiven, vol. 9, 153.
11 Generale Missiven, vol. 13, 123.
12 Generale Missiven, vol. 13, 365.
13 Generale Missiven, vol. 10, 156.

In the rural areas of Batavia, the so-called *ommelanden*, coolies performed various kinds of work. The VOC employed coolies via casual wage-labour relations. In 1743, Company coolies were mentioned to be working on the transport of drinking water in Batavia.[14] In 1750, it was decided, in order to reduce the high expenditure on coolie labour, to make sure district heads supervised the work better, to check "whether the recruited workers did indeed do their service and make the workers sign the weekly administrations".[15]

In the city of Batavia, a lively urban coolie labour market existed. The "ordinance for the coolies" ordered by Van Imhoff (1743) attempted to regulate this market by instructing the recruitment of labour should be organized through the city district heads ("wijkmeesters"). The main characteristics seemed have remained unchanged. The workers involved could be both free ("vrije mooren") or unfree workers ("slaves" being hired out or hiring out themselves). The workers in this urban coolie-labour market were used for labour that was performed in general services (carrying, loading/unloading, unskilled work) and could be hired per hour, per half day, or per day.[16]

At least before the regulations of 1743, the hiring of coolies seems to have been rather similar to the practices we encountered in the case of Malacca. Ship surgeon Johannes Knol from Colombo, for example, declared that he had taken along "a certain slave who he had called to him as [a] coolie" (Van Rossum 2015: 40-58). September of Bengal, slave of the wife of Johannes Geldzak, declared that "he had been called by a surgeon with only one eye when he was on the Middelpuntbrug [bridge in the center of Batavia] in order to carry some goods he had bought at the passer [market]". Knol would have promised him a ducaton after he had finished the job.[17]

In this lively urban coolie labour market, free workers, slaves, runaways and others could find work. Slaves were actively sent out by their masters to earn money, which they had to return (in part) to their owners. This was referred to as "bringing" "coolie money" ["coelij geld" or "coelij brengen"] (van Rossum 2015: 58).[18] An Indian sailor who had deserted his employment as contract worker in the service of the VOC survived in Batavia and its environment for some years, making a living by "coelie soeken" – "seeking coolie labour" (van Rossum 2012: 53) or day-to-day employment.

---

14 Generale Missiven, vol. 11, 107.
15 Van der Chijs, Nederlandsch-Indisch Plakaatboek, vol. 5, 648.
16 Van der Chijs, Nederlandsch-Indisch Plakaatboek, vol. 5, 379.
17 Nationaal Archief (NA), Archief van de VOC (VOC), 9375, case 18.
18 NA, VOC, 9424, case 63.

Corvée and 'Voluntary' Coolies in Ceylon

Concepts of coolie labour were not only employed in Southeast Asia. As it is often referred to as originating from South Asia, it is interesting to take a closer look at evidence of coolie labour here. In Ceylon, just as in Batavia, a broad range of work could be labelled "coolie labour". Reports on the construction works of fortifications near Trinconomale late 1780s provide an indication of the wide range of work. In July 1788, "10 heads coolies" were sent with two vessels carrying wood for the construction works.[19] In August 1788, in total 1,060 coolies were employed in the works of two forts at Trinconomale. The coolies were mentioned to be "872 large and 182 small boys".[20] Similar numbers were reported in the following months. They were employed in the loading and unloading of ships, in the warehouses, for masonry, in the gunpowder mill, for carpentry, in wood logging, in the constructing of palisades, and in the weaponry room. Another 48 coolies were employed in the public works of Trinconomale.

In this case, the concept of coolie not only referred to precarious labour relations, wage labour, or specific types of work, but also indicated social or group status. The local population of Ceylon was obligated to render specific taxes and corvée labour duties, corresponding to their status as landowners, labourers and membership of castes or communities. As a labour relation or social status, *coolie* could refer specifically to a type of corvée labour, a specific type of labour service demanded by the VOC from local populations. Alicia Schrikker explains that, for example, "the lower echelons, called *naindes*, usually formed the largest group and performed manual labour. They had to undertake specialized or coolie-labour for their headmen and the king depending on their caste. This labour was used for a variety of projects including road repair, irrigation and general building activities for the benefit of the community, but it was also used for private activities of the headman" (Schrikker 2006: 17). These *oeliam*-services – the obligatory corvée labour – required from local populations could take "the form of the Company's heavy coolie-work like dragging timber" (ibid.: 90), the loading and unloading of ships, work on fortifications as, mentioned in the case of Trinconomale, and other tasks.

As part of their system of labour extraction, the VOC administrated information on the labour services and on communities involved in land administrations, demographic registers and administrations of corvée services. The administration of corvée services of 1755, for example, contains "the name role

---

19 Sri Lanka National Archives (SLNA) 1/3164.
20 SLNA 1/3164.

of the hereafter mentioned Coolies, who were to be leaving on this morning [July 8, 1755] under supervision of the Lascorin Pintollewaddoegenainde with the second merchant and controller of Colombo the Honourable Michiel Hemme". The role listed a total of "25 heads" coming from rural districts in the hinterland of Galle, being "16 heads [coming] from the [district] Talpe Pattoe" and 9 from the district Gangebaddepattoe. One day earlier, a group of "60 heads in total" had been sent from various other districts. The "name roll" mentioned that these "Coolies had been send this morning under supervision of the lascorin named Hittigoddegamme Hewanainde in the direction of Galle in order to be send further to Colombo".[21]

Demographic registers indicate the different groups and services. In 1684, VOC accounts mentioned in total 11,280 coolies, which counted roughly for four per cent of the population and seven per cent of the total working population in maritime provinces under Dutch control (De Zwart 2014). A "translated Singalese register ola" of September 1751 listed all the male "Naindes, Wahadjas and Coolies residing under the [district] Talpepattoe" with their names, positions, and ages. In the district, there were "431 Naindes", "72 Wahadjas" and "260 Coolies". Of the 206 coolies, it was noted that 158 were "in service", 26 were schoolboys, 5 were "old and not in service anymore", 3 were ill, 41 were "out of this country, amongst which 1 old", and 32 were "active in various other services".[22] In the district Gangebaddepattoe there were "176 Naindes", "19 Wahadjas" and "79 Coolies".[23] In the district Wellebaddepattoe there were 144 Nainedes, 21 Wahadjas, and 60 Coolies, and in the district Wallallawille Corle 342 Nainedes, 96 Wahadjas, and 73 Coolies.[24]

As coolie-labour in the context of obligatory corvée labour related to both the social status of people and to the specific work involved, the use of the concept of coolie was sometimes ambiguous (cf. Tappe, this volume). As early as 1660, under the rule of Van Goens, it is mentioned that the work on the fortifications of Galle was temporarily stopped in order to let the coolies work on their land.[25] After a ship from Surat ran ashore in 1717, and the crew abandoned the vessel out of fear of the Sinhalese, the cargo of the ship was transported inland "with 300 coolies and 372 beasts of burden". In 1742, it was reported that some 3,800 bales of cinnamon were undelivered due to the "random and

---

21 SLNA 1/443.
22 SLNA 1/2758, 28.
23 SLNA 1/2758, 29.
24 SLNA 1/2758, 30-31.
25 Generale Missiven, vol. 3, 329.

disobedient behavior of the servants of the King". It was ordered that the bales should be transported by "the coolies of the mahabadde".[26] In other instances, the reference to coolie as a category of work is more explicit. In 1706, for example, it was reported that "30 chalias were left at the dessave as coolies"[27]. These workers were members of the chalias community, which was obligated to perform corvée labour for the VOC, consisting mainly of peeling and transporting cinnamon.

Court records administrating the incarceration and release of convicts also show this broad application of the concept of coolie in the context of corvée labour obligations, indicating both work and status. On January 20, 1751, five local workers were sentenced in Galle to three months' convict labour. Four cinnamon peelers were convicted over "not delivering their obligated cinnamon tax", while the "Chalias Coolie" Nabradoewe Jantjea was convicted "over being absent from his obligated service".[28] In April 1751, the cinnamon peeler Dikwellege, also named Hoenadenige Philippoe, and Philippe, "alias Poerandera Coelij", from the Mahabadde were condemned to 15 years' convict labour at the Company's public works. In October 1750, it was ordered to release from their chains the "Singalese Coolies with the names Kiembieje Wampra Goddea and d'Koeretia, because they had served their sentence of six months [of convict labour]".[29]

Coolie labour could also be employed outside the sphere of obligated labour services performed for the VOC. In 1730, it was decided that the small vessel Cochin would be taken apart, "but only if this would not lead to excessive costs in coolie wages".[30] The report on the Trinconomale construction works of September 1788 makes a clear distinction between "obligated" and "non-obligated" coolie labourers, referring to "the voluntary heads [who] have worked at the main canal". In the November report, it is noted that in total "this month daily 1108 big and 186 small and 50 voluntary" coolies were employed. The 50 voluntary coolies "finished the canal at the entrance up in the fort". The employment of large numbers of coolies, including small numbers of "voluntary" coolies, continued into the year 1789.[31] "Voluntary" in this context, however, mainly indicated non-corvée labour, and did not necessarily imply "free" or

---

26 Generale Missiven, vol. 7, 309.
27 Generale Missiven, vol. 6, 447.
28 SLNA 1/2758, 23. Original: 'Chialiasse Coelij'.
29 SLNA 1/2758, 23.
30 Generale Missiven, vol. 9, 177.
31 SLNA 1/3164.

casual labour relations. VOC administrator Jacob Burnand, for example, pointed out in the late 18th century that constraints in mobilizing corvée labourers would force the Company "to rely [more] on slave labour for coolie work" (Schrikker 2006: 112).

COOLIE WORK AND COOLIE LABOUR RELATIONS

So how do we make sense of the world of early modern coolie labour? For this, it is important to take into account labour relations, social status, meaning, and the actual work involved. One of the most striking features, perhaps, is the large variation in the labour relations themselves. A taxonomy of labour relations might help to illustrate this point. In recent studies of labour, it has been argued that labour relations were not marked by clear-cut, free versus forced, and market versus non-market dichotomies, but instead were positioned on a gradual scale between free and unfree, and between non-market-oriented and commodified. Exploring the new perspectives on the history of work opened by these insights, Jan Lucassen has argued that "market economies did not emerge only once, but several times in history in different parts of the world, and in many cases also disappeared again" (2013: 21). In accordance with this, "wage labour on a large scale, slave labour and selfemployed labour emerged several times in history, and also often declined again" (ibid.).

In the Global Collaboratory on the History of Labour Relations, these have been subdivided into reciprocal, tributary, independent, slave-, and wage-labour relations.[32] Coolie labour has been associated especially with "free" wage labour, either in the form of casual wage labour (as referred to by Boomgaard) or in the form of contract labour (although indentured, as in the 19th century). A closer look at coolie labour relations in the early modern Southeast and South Asia, however, seems to indicate that coolies were found in various different labour relations. Free persons referred to as coolies were performing (casual) wage labour side by side with slaves performing wage labour for the market referred to as coolie labour. At the same time, coolie work could also be obligated corvée (or tributary) labour. Coolies, therefore, could be more-or-less free workers (free coolies in Batavia, voluntary coolies in Ceylon) as well as coerced workers (corvée coolies in Ceylon, slaves working as coolies in Batavia or in Ceylon). This positioned workers, who were referred to as coolies, very differently in

---

32 Available online via https://collab.iisg.nl/web/labourrelations.

terms of degrees of freedom and coercion – and in terms of whether their situation was forged through mainly economic or political relations.

Types of labour relations referred to as coolie

Economic relation	Casual wage labour	Contract "indentured" labour
		Slave (hired) wage labour
Political relation		Obligated labour services
	"Free"	"Bonded"

The VOC itself used the term *coolie* in its administration and reports to indicate different labour relations (casual wage labour; corvée labour) in Southeast Asia. In South Asia, in this case in Ceylon, the VOC also used the term to indicate specific social groups. Here, the term *coolie* could refer to groups categorized as coolies who were obligated to perform *oeliam*-services, but also refer to the coolie work performed by ('voluntary') wage-labourers and slaves. The workers involved could also identify themselves as coolies, for example, in court cases. In the case of Ceylon, it is not clear whether such references primarily referred to community memberships, corvée obligations, or occupations. In the case of Malacca, the reference to their status of 'coolies' by workers who identified themselves as 'free Moors' seems to have referred to their occupation. This is more in line with the evidence for Batavia, where free inhabitants, slaves, and deserters referred to their activities as doing 'coolie' work, 'seeking coolie [work]' or bringing 'coolie money [to their masters]'.

The meaning of the term coolie was not entirely open, but was ambiguous in some aspects, such as the meaning attached to the term, and the social groups and labour relations involved (free workers, slaves, corvée workers). And although the term did not exclusively refer to work – but in many instances did indeed refer to social status or (obligations ingrained in specific) labour relations – the common element seems to have been, time and again, the work involved. In accordance with the ambiguous character of the term, the (second) very open definition of coolie work was that of unskilled and physical labour, performed in port work, transport, agriculture, construction, etc.

Transformations

So how did these early modern coolie labour relations transform into the 19th century imperial world evolving around the labour of indentured 'coolie' contract migrants? In the remainder of this chapter, two developments will be taken up that may have impacted the development of coolie labour within the Dutch imperial sphere before the well-known developments around the coolie trade within the British imperial sphere: first, the development of regulation of 'coolie work' in the early 19th century; and second, developments related to the work of migrant (contract) labourers on Java.

Despite the character of coolie labour as casual wage labour in and around Batavia, the 18th century had already witnessed some developments towards an increasing regulation of coolie labour markets (1743), and – perhaps more importantly – also towards an increasing control over workers through mediated recruitment. Some of the Chinese port workers hired by the VOC in the second half of the 18th century, for example, seem to have been recruited in a more mediated way. After the VOC decided to hire Chinese workers for the loading and unloading of the ships in Batavia in 1765, it was mentioned that "some fifty heads had already offered themselves", the rest were to be recruited via "the captain of this nation, Lim Tjipko". He was also charged with the monthly payment of the wages.[33]

In other cases, it is not even clear whether coolies were performing wage labour or whether other arrangements were involved. In 1716, for example, it was mentioned that the princes of Cheribon and other rulers "send 410 coolies in order to dredge the river of Batavia". It is difficult to say anything about the labour relations between the coolies and the local rulers (they may have been performing slave, wage or local corvee duties). For the VOC, however, the work of coolies seems to have been a gift from the local rulers to the Company. In that sense, the labour of these coolies was a sort of tribute and the reference coolie indicated especially the type of (unskilled) work involved.[34]

Early 19th century, regulations were implemented to arrange "the payment of coolies and horses employed by private travellers" on the land roads of Java.[35] In 1810, under the rule of governor-general Daendels, regulations were implemented for the provisioning of rice "to coolies working on the main road

---

33 Van der Chijs, J. A. *Nederlandsch-Indisch Plakaatboek*, Batavia Landsdrukkerij (Batavia 1891), vol. 8, 53.
34 Generale Missiven, vol. 7, 257.
35 Van der Chijs, Nederlandsch-Indisch Plakaatboek (1896), vol. 15, 824.

over the Megamendoeng". It was "decided to provide the three hundred heads, who were employed on the construction of the road over the Mechamedong, as well as the two hundred heads, who work on the roads in other districts under authority of that landdrost, with forty pounds rice per person each month".[36] In Batavia, Chinese and inland coolies were mentioned to be working in the various warehouses, the artillery warehouse, the equipage wharf, and on the ships anchored in the harbour. They were paid in monthly wages. In 1809 and 1810, their wages were raised to the rather high amount of 15 and 16 rijksdaalders respectively.[37]

This may have meant that these coolies worked not on a daily basis, but for longer periods. The Chinese coolies working in the warehouse for medicines, on the other hand, seem to have received daily bonuses of 12 stuivers.[38] On the "private" lands in the environment of Batavia, workers referred to as "coolies" often still received "daily wages" in the early 19th century.[39] The coolies recruited from Bantam and employed on the fortifications in the Meeuwenbaai earned three stuivers "to be paid for every day's work". They seem to have been recruited, however, for two weeks' work. "In order to prevent damage to the production in the rice fields or any other agricultural sector, every 14 days 200 workers would be replaced with 200 other workers from Bantam".[40]

At the same time, the pressure of colonial competition and the possibility of war may have started to impact labour relations. In 1810, for example, authorities considered the possibility of a military invasion at Batavia by European colonial competitors, developed a plan for blocking the river and arranging the (obligated) delivery of "for this work required 3,000 heads out of the inhabitants of the private lands". For every district it was decided how many of these "coolies" should be delivered by the private landowners to the authorities. They were to be supervised "by a mandadoor on every fifty men" and would "receive the ordinary daily wages of coolies".[41]

Measures were also taken to ensure the "provisioning of coolies, needed for the works at the Merakbaai" in order to continue the construction works during "the present monsoon with the best possible power". It was decided that the numbers of workers should be brought to 1,500, "excluding the government-

---

36 Van der Chijs, Nederlandsch-Indisch Plakaatboek (1897), vol. 16, 419-420.
37 Van der Chijs, Nederlandsch-Indisch Plakaatboek, vol. 15, 884; vol. 16, 45.
38 Van der Chijs, Nederlandsch-Indisch Plakaatboek, vol. 16, 77.
39 Van der Chijs, Nederlandsch-Indisch Plakaatboek, vol. 16, 484-485.
40 Van der Chijs, Nederlandsch-Indisch Plakaatboek, vol. 15, 369.
41 Van der Chijs, *Nederlandsch-Indisch Plakaatboek*, vol. 16, 484-485.

slaves, convicts and sailors", for which the district heads "of Bantam, Cheribon and Samarang were demanded to each furnish 500 men". This time the period of work was longer. The men were "to be delivered within fourteen days and would be returned three months after their arrival in the Merakbaai in order to be replaced".[42]

These practices seem to have continued into the 19th century. In 1830, for example, it was reported that "a concession was granted to a Chinese captain in order to set up a tin mine at Biliton". The contract (effective from July 1, 1827) with the Chinese captain stated that he was responsible to recruit his own labourers. It was explicitly stated, however, that the Chinese captain did not obtain any "right or authority over the native population of Biliton" (who were obligated to perform corvée labour by this time), although the captain "nevertheless had the freedom to obtain the voluntary services of the inhabitants for the burning of coal, coolie work, etc, for a reasonable payment".[43] In this period, coolie work seems still to have referred to unskilled labour payed per day or at piece rate. The Chinese operator of the tin mines, however, was not primarily dependent on the local labour force. He recruited some 300 (later up to 500) Chinese workers. Although they were not explicitly referred to as coolies, they were probably migrant contract workers.

The work of these hirelings seems to have come close to that of another interesting category of workers which should be considered in this context, namely that of the Javanese *bujang*. In the late 18th and early 19th century, these *bujang* performed work very similar to that of coolies, but were concentrated mainly in the sugar industry. As De Zwart points out, *bujang* "were temporary or seasonal workers, which represents the main difference from the coolies" (De Zwart 2015: 201). Boomgaard describes the *bujang* "as a temporary migrant", "contracted for a period of half a year or one year" to work as "free wage-labourer[s] on the sugar estates of the environs of Batavia" (Boomgaard 1990: 45). Such labour contracts were not new for Asian workers; thousands of Indian, Malayan, Javanese, Chinese and other sailors and soldiers had worked for the VOC on contracts with durations of one to three years during the 17th and 18th century (cf. van Rossum 2016). Around 1800, some 4,000 bujang were employed in the sugar mills of Batavia. On the rise from 1750 onwards, this represented, according to Boomgaard "a new phase in the development of labour relations. Whereas the coolie had cut his ties with the village society perma-

---

42 Van der Chijs, *Nederlandsch-Indisch Plakaatboek*, vol. 16, 178-179.
43 NA, Koloniaal Archief, 2.10.01, 3077.

nently, the *bujang* seems to have done so only temporarily. He probably intended to go back to his village and get married" (ibid.).

These *bujang* have often been emphasized as 'free' wage labourers (cf. Boomgaard 1990; De Zwart 2015; Van Zanden 2007). As migrant workers, however, the question of recruitment and control of *bujang* must have been of immediate interest. References in administrative sources seem to indicate that this was indeed the case. In June 1788, for example, it was stated that, "in order to counter the abuses, which have increased, it is necessary to make sure the Javanese *bujang* needed for the sugar mills, as before, are from now on recruited in the mountains by the Javanese mandoors of the mentioned sugar mills". There had been complaints that the old practice, in which *bujang* workers were recruited, brought to the mills, and escorted back by the servants of the sugar mills, had fallen in disuse in the period of the governance of Van Riemsdyk [in the period 1775-1777]. Javanese *bujang* were now being escorted by the servants of Javanese rulers, leading to a situation in which "recruiters and *bujang* were dependent on the servants of the Javanese rulers for their return". Furthermore,

"these servants [of the rulers] had also claimed them at the moment of their arrival in the mountains, which had been sufficient cause for the owners of the sugar mills to address the mentioned servants in order to be able to recruit Javanese workers, and from this a form of selling of *bujang* to the owners of the sugar mills had been born."[44]

Towards the end of the 18th century, the VOC gained such a position as to be able to demand corvée labour from local rural communities in Java. As the pressure to supply sufficient labour increased after 1800, it has been pointed out by Boomgaard that "it became more and more usual to ask Javanese and Dutch officials in Priangan, Krawang, and Cirebon to send labourers to the sugar-mills. Of course, this form of labour recruitment can no longer be regarded as hiring free labour. Although in a disguised form, we are confronted here with corvée labour" (Boomgaard 1990: 46). This seems very similar to the practice by local rulers of delivering coolies to the VOC, as we encountered earlier. Here we see important crossovers between systems of wage labour, contracted work, corvée and other forms of coercion in relation to coolie types of work.

---

44 Van der Chijs, *Nederlandsch-Indisch Plakaatboek* (1893), vol. 11, 21-22.

Conclusion

What does this say about the standard narrative? It does not aim to falsify or contradict the standard British imperial narrative, but the evidence laid out in this chapter does seem to problematize its implicit linearity. The term *coolie* was not a static concept – it was used differently between regions, and – more importantly – it changed over time. The concept of coolie labour clearly has multiple sources, stemming from the complex relations forged by early modern global interactions. The changing coolie labour relations were inherently linked to extending and changing colonial and capitalist projects of exploitation. The longer histories of coolie labour, however, seem to provide reason to question what we might call the '1830s founding myth' of (British-Indian) indentured contract labour and the coolie-trade (cf. Lindner, this volume). It indicates the importance of looking for developments connecting the dynamics of the employment of European and Asian (indentured) contract labour in the 18th century with its development and expansion in the 19th century.

One of the crucial points here – more than simply taking the innovation of the indentured contract coolie migration as the reason for its 'success' and 'spread' – is that different alternatives for mobilizing and controlling labour, such as slave-, contract-, and corvée labour, had already been available to imperial authorities and employers for some centuries. They had been employed by the VOC side by side during the 18th century. The gradual, slow abolition of slavery in the 19th century stimulated the employment of corvée and contract labour. These were alternatives that had also been available and in use previously. In the Dutch case, it seems that the importance of slave labour was already slowly diminishing towards the end of the 18th century, leading to the growth of corvée, contract- and casual wage labour (cf. Breman 2010; Boomgaard 1990). At the beginning of the 19th century, the Dutch colonial authorities would increasingly focus their attempts at mobilizing labour on expanding the corvée labour system. With the implementation of the Cultivation System in 1830, (indentured) contract work – and wage labour in general – seems to have become less important in the first half of the 19th century. The employment of contract labour in the Dutch East Indian colonial sphere, in this period, moved in the opposite direction to that elsewhere. This turned out to be only temporary, as the introduction of coolie ordinances would lead to an expansion of the system of (indentured) migrant contract workers in the second half of the 19th century.

REFERENCES

Austin, Gareth/Sugihara, Kaoru (2013): Labour-Intensive Industrialization in Global History, Abingdon: Routledge.
Banaji, Jairus (2011): Theory as history. Essays on modes of production and exploitation, Chicago: Haymarket Books.
Boomgaard, Peter (1990): "Why work for wages? Free labour in Java, 1600-1900." In: Economic and social history in the Netherlands, Vol. 2, Amsterdam: NEHA, pp. 37-56.
Breman, Jan (2010): Koloniaal profijt van onvrij arbeid. Het Preanger stelsel van gedwongen koffieteelt op Java, Amsterdam: Amsterdam University Press.
—— (1992): Koelies, planters en koloniale politiek: het arbeidsregime op de grootlandbouwondernemingen aan Sumatra's Oostkust in het begin van de twintigste eeuw, Leiden: KITLV Press.
Coolhaas, Willem Philippus/Goor, Jurrien van/Schooneveld-Oosterling, Judith Ellen/s'Jacob, Hugo (1960-2007): Generale Missiven van Gouverneurs-Generaal en Raden aan Heren XVII der Verenigde Oostindische Compagnie, Den Haag: Martinus Nijhoff.
de Zwart, Pim (2015): Globalization and the Colonial Origins of the Great Divergence: intercontinental trade and living standards in the Dutch East India Company's commercial empire, c. 1600-1800, PhD-thesis, Utrecht University.
—— (2014): "Labour Relations in Ceylon in the Late Seventeenth Century", Global Collaboratory on the History of Labour Relations 1500-2000, https://collab.iisg.nl/.
Encyclopædia Britannica, vol. 7 (Eleventh edition: New York 1910).
Gommans, Jos (2002): Mughal Warfare. Indian frontiers and high roads to empire, 1500-1700, New York: Routledge.
Houben, Vincent J.H./Lindblad, J. Thomas (1999): Coolie Labour in Colonial Indonesia. A Study of Labour Relations in the Outer Islands, c. 1900-1940, Wiesbaden: Harrassowitz Verlag.
Jung, Moon-Ho (2005): "Outlawing 'Coolies': Race, Nation, and Empire in the Age of Emancipation." In: American Quarterly 57/3, pp. 677-701.
Kaempfer, Engelbert (1727): The History of Japan: Together with a Description of the Kingdom of Siam, London: Scheuchzer.
Lucassen, Jan (2014): "Deep monetization, commercialization, and proletarization: possible links, India 1200-1900." In: Sabyasachi, Bhattacharya (ed.), Towards a New History of Work, New Delhi: Tulika Books.
—— (2013): Outlines of a History of Labour, Amsterdam: IISH.

—— (2012): "Een geschiedenis van de arbeid in grote lijnen", departure lecture Vrije Universiteit Amsterdam, 6 July 2012.

Mann, Michael (2012): Sahibs, Sklaven und Soldaten. Geschichte des Menschenhandels rund um den Indischen Ozean, Mainz: von Zabern.

Meagher, Arnold J. (2008): The Coolie Trade: The Traffic in Chinese Laborers to Latin America 1847-1874, Philadelphia: Xlibris.

Northrup, David (1995): Indentured Labor in the Age of Imperialism, 1834-1922, New York: Cambridge University Press.

Schrikker, Alicia (2006): Dutch and British colonial intervention in Sri Lanka, c. 1780-1815: Expansion and Reform, PhD-thesis, Leiden University.

Stanziani, Alessandro (2014): Bondage, Labor and Rights in Eurasia from the Sixteenth to the Early Twentieth Centuries, New York: Berghahn.

van der Chijs, Jacobus Anne (1897): Nederlandsch-Indisch Plakaatboek, Batavia: Landsdrukkerij, vol. 16.

—— (1896): Nederlandsch-Indisch Plakaatboek, Batavia: Landsdrukkerij, vol. 15.

—— (1893): Nederlandsch-Indisch Plakaatboek, Batavia: Landsdrukkerij, vol. 11.

—— (1891): Nederlandsch-Indisch Plakaatboek, Batavia: Landsdrukkerij vol. 5.

—— (1891): Nederlandsch-Indisch Plakaatboek, Batavia: Landsdrukkerij vol. 8.

van Rossum, Matthias (2016): "'Working for the Devil': Desertion in the Eurasian empire of the VOC." In: Matthias van Rossum/Jeannette Kamp (eds.), Desertion in the Early Modern World: A Comparative History, London: Bloomsbury, pp. 127-158.

—— (2015): Kleurrijke tragiek. De geschiedenis van slavernij in Azië onder de VOC, Hilversum: Verloren.

—— (2014): Werkers van de wereld. Globalisering, arbeid en interculturele ontmoetingen tussen Aziatische en Europese zeelieden in dienst van de VOC, 1600-1800, Hilversum: Verloren.

—— (2012): "A 'Moorish world' within the Company. The VOC, maritime logistics and subaltern networks of Asian sailors." In: Itinerario 36/3, pp. 39-60.

Winn, Phillip (2010): "Slavery and cultural creativity in the Banda Islands." In: Journal of Southeast Asian Studies 41, pp. 365-389.

Zanden, Jan Luiten van (2007): "Linking Two Debates: Money Supply, Wage Labour, and Economic Development in Java in the Nineteenth Century." In: Jan Lucassen (ed.), Wages and Currency: Global Comparisons from Antiquity to the Twentieth Century, Bern: Peter Lang, pp. 169-192.

Variants of Bonded Labour in Precolonial and Colonial Southeast Asia

OLIVER TAPPE

INTRODUCTION

In 1888, the French explorer Pierre-Paul Cupet (2000 [1900]: 38) rescued a young upland Tai[1] girl from Chinese slave-traders. Indignant about the 'uncivilized' practice of slavery in the uplands of Laos, Cupet decided to return the girl to her village. However, on arriving at her mother's village, he did not receive the gratitude he had expected. Cupet's interpreter explained to him: "She has no money to give you [...] to buy back her daughter and she believes that you will take her along tomorrow morning" (ibid.: 49). Cupet deplored the 'barbaric' legacy of slavery in Southeast Asia. His position reflected the moral undertone of the French colonial *mission civilisatrice*, even if certain forms of servitude and coerced labour continued to exist under French rule.

Indeed, the French administrative attitude towards labour relations in Indochina was characterized by contradictions and hypocrisy. The colonial administration faced the challenge of providing an indigenous workforce – without resorting to slavery – for labour-intensive enterprises such as plantations and mines, as well as for large-scale infrastructure projects in sparsely populated regions. As in many other colonial environments in late 19th-century Asia and Africa (see Lindner's chapter in this volume), the solution was a combination of forced requisition and voluntary recruitment of cheap labour: in the case of

---

1 The many different upland Tai groups (not to confuse with the lowland Thai in Thailand) in the Lao-Vietnamese borderlands belong to the Tai-Kadai language family – like the Lao, Thai, Shan, Lü, Zhuang, etc.

Indochina, from empoverished, landless Vietnamese or, more rarely, from semi-nomadic uplanders. Both groups of labourers were called 'coolies'.

The cultural misunderstanding described above stemmed from fundamentally different views of slavery: on the one hand, as a socioeconomic phenomenon involving exchange and obligations; on the other hand, as a morally problematic form of exploitative labour (even if tolerated by colonial authorities; cf. M. Klein 1998; Testart 2001).[2] In this chapter, I will explore aspects of coercion and bondage in precolonial and colonial labour relations, with a particular focus on continuities and transformations during the colonial encounter. The role of debt within Southeast Asian labour relations – from bonded servitude in 19th-century Siam to the colonial coolie system – will deserve particular scrutiny as key element of bonded labour.

The chapter will focus mainly on the regions that came to be known as Indochina under French colonial rule, in particular Laos and Vietnam and their vast mountainous, ethnically heterogeneous borderlands. For the discussion of precolonial variants of slavery and servitude, Thailand/Siam will be another case in point. After a general overview of variants of bonded labour in precolonial mainland Southeast Asia, I will discuss the Tai-Lao concept of *kha* (slave/serf), which not only refers to a socioeconomic category but also includes connotations of ethnic difference and racial discrimination.

In addition, the chapter addresses the impact of French colonialism on local labour relations and patterns of servitude such as traditional *corvée* obligations (for example, requisition of peasant labour by ruling elites for the purpose of agriculture, public works, and military service). It also investigates the colonial coolie system (indentured or contract labour in the plantation and mining economy), followed by a discussion of debt and indebtedness as a key factor of labour relations in past and present (cf. Reid 1983; Bush 2000; Derks 2010). In precolonial and colonial times, bonded labour was linked with debt as an economic, social, and cultural phenomenon.[3]

---

2   For a general discussion on the historical variants of unfree labour, see the introduction to this volume, and Brass/van der Linden 1997.

3   This paper was presented during the workshop *Forms of bonded labour: Conceptual approaches towards a new comparative research framework* (University of Cologne, 23-24 June 2014). I would like to thank the participants of the workshop for their helpful comments and inspiring discussions. Special thanks are reserved for my colleagues of the research group 'From Slave to Coolie' at the Global South Studies Center in Cologne (Ulrike Lindner, Sabine Damir-Geilsdorf, Gesine Müller, Michael

PATTERNS OF SLAVERY AND SERVITUDE IN MAINLAND SOUTHEAST ASIA

Precolonial Southeast Asian sociopolitical organization was characterized by a huge variety of forms of slavery and servitude (Condominas 1998). Besides the widespread pattern of debt-bondage in agrarian societies, the enslavement and integration of other people was an important factor for early state-building (cf. Reid 1983; Day 2002; see Mabbett 1983 for the case of Angkor). According to Anthony Reid's pioneering work on slavery in Southeast Asia,

"[...] the movement of captive peoples and slaves was the primary source of labour mobility in Southeast Asia. Typically it took the form of transferring people from weak, politically fragmented societies to stronger and wealthier ones." (Reid 1983: 27; Michaud 2006: 219-220)

Both slavery and servitude implied notions of patron-client relations and control of people.

In contrast to, for example, American slavery, the distinction between 'slavery' and 'freedom' was fluid in many respects. Allegedly 'free' commoners were obliged to supply unremunerated labour and to pay in-kind taxes. Often this burden resulted in a paradoxical phenomenon unknown in other slave systems: commoners selling themselves into slavery or bonded servitude to escape tax and *corvée* requisitions (cf. Campbell 2003; Bush 2000; Reid 1983; Turton 1980). Consequently, it is difficult to clearly classify the different forms of bonded labour in precolonial Southeast Asia as either slavery or servitude. An overview of different regional examples will illustrate these analytical challenges.

In 13th- and 14th-century Vietnam, the class of slaves was mainly constituted by "peasants who sold themselves into slavery to improve their lives, or prisoners of war, or people from other lands brought by merchants. They served many functions from manual laborers to skilled craftspeople" (Taylor 2013: 122). Here, as we will also see in the case of precolonial Tai states, the boundary between so-called slaves and free peasants or craftspeople was fluid. During that period, large estates emerged that were farmed by slaves or by peasants in a slave-like situation. The Vietnamese aristocracy could accumulate slaves and serfs particularly after natural disasters when peasants lost land and harvests, and ended up in debt servitude – while others tried their luck at banditry.

Zeuske, Michael Hoffmann, and our valiant assistants Bebero Lehmann and Fabian Heerbaart).

With the beginning of the Lê dynasty in the 15th century, a new legislation on land ownership and village government encouraged villages that were organized on the basis of free peasants with enough land to support their families and pay taxes (ibid.: 190). Yet bonded servitude remained a basic condition for the Vietnamese peasantry, and debt bondage again resurfaced under French land legislations (see below). In addition, Vietnamese and Chinese pirates specialized in capturing women and children to sell as slaves in China. This practice was only abandoned after French influence and military intervention.

In general, precolonial Vietnamese society was characterized by a huge gap between a landlord class – the mandarins – and the peasants. Sociopolitical organization built upon systems of *corvée* and peasant mobilization in the case of warfare. Peasants were obliged to work in the ricefields of the mandarins, including doing hard work such as digging irrigation canals and dykes. Furthermore, the peasants were exploited for prestigious projects such as the well-known citadels (see Dutton 2006: 137-140). New land legislations under the Nguyên dynasty in the 19th century resulted in an even more explicit asymmetry in the agricultural labour relations (cf. Cleary 2003; Brocheux and Hémery 2009).

Systems of slavery and servitude were arguably more complex in the Tai states such as the early Thai kingdoms of Sukhothai and Ayutthaya (later Bangkok/Siam), the Lao kingdom of Lan Sang, and the Northern Tai kingdom of Lan Na (Chiang Mai). As Terwiel (1983) demonstrates for the Siamese case, the general binary between commoners (*phrai*) and slaves (*kha, that;* Skr. *dāsa*) was further subdivided into a detailed hierarchy, with different levels of bondage and labour requirements. No form of labour was exclusive to slaves, and – as mentioned above – the boundary between *kha* and *phrai* was fluid (cf. Turton 1980; Rabibhadana 1969). For peasants in times of, for example, misery due to famine it appeared to be more advantageous to enter a relation of bondage since patrons were expected to provide for the subsistence and security of their dependent peasant families.

In the Tai-speaking world, slavery and servitude that resulted from forcibly resettled war captives was also significant, and constituted an important demographic factor (cf. Grabowsky 1999; 2004; Bowie 1996). In his demographic history of Lan Na (Northern Thailand), Volker Grabowsky (2004) shows that a considerable part of the population (one quarter to one third) were categorized as 'slaves'. Instead of being an outcast part of the population, they were integrated to a certain degree into the social hierarchy of the respective kingdom, although the lowest stratum was consigned to all kinds of hard labour. In Siam, captured agricultural populations were resettled in villages and urban quarters of people who shared a common ethno-linguistic background (cf. Turton 1980; van Roy 2009).[4]

Even if Thai nationalist historiography used to describe Siamese slavery as benign and characterized by a relation of royal patronage, the raids and deportations were violent and entailed a considerable blood toll (cf. Bowie 1996). When in the 19th century the whole of Laos, including parts of the upland frontier bordering Vietnam, became the target of large-scale military campaigns and slave raids, many of the deported died on the way to Siam or suffered the harsh conditions of plantation work (cf. Bowie 1996; Grabowsky/Turton 2003).

For James Scott (2009), the lowland state in Southeast Asia was a manpower-generating machine, accumulating people, and thus driving others into the hills if they wished to avoid submission to exploitative feudal states. Scott refers to Karl Marx in stating that "[...] there was no state without concentrated manpower; there was no concentration of manpower without slavery [...]" (2009: 85). He declares precolonial Burmese and Tai states as "slaving states" (ibid.: 89) that either conducted regular slave raids in the surrounding uplands themselves or at least stimulated the emergence of a market for slaves (with some upland ethnic groups preying upon one another).

The historian Victor Lieberman criticized Scott's hypothesis, and specified that at times it was rather over-population that was a problem for lowland states, and that slave raids gained momentum mainly with the transforming global economy of the 19th century (Lieberman 2010: 339). The global trade and demand for Southeast Asian commodities indeed triggered labour demand and different forms of labour requisition, especially in booming port cities such as Bangkok (cf. Reid 1999; Beemer 2009), but according to Lieberman (2010: 341) there is little historical evidence for Scott's hypothesis that the populating of the Southeast Asian uplands was a result of settlement by escapees from lowland slaving states.

What both authors agree upon is the fact that warfare in Southeast Asia was more concerned with manpower than with territory. It should be noted here that it was not only feudal states that engaged in different practices of enslavement. The Red Karen of the Burmese-Siamese upland frontier were notorious for their slave-raiding among neighbouring groups such as the Sgaw and Pwo Karen, and even in the Buddhist Shan principalities (Grabowsky/Turton 2003: 238; Turton

---

4   The British envoy Bowring (1969 [1857]: 190) estimated that during the reign of Rama III (1824-1851), 46,000 war slaves inhabited the kingdom of Bangkok, including 20,000 Lao, 10,000 (South) Vietnamese, and several thousand Burmese and Malay (cf. Bowie 1996).

2004). They sold the slaves mainly to the court of Chiang Mai. So lucrative seemed the slave trade in the 19th century that in Burma abolition took place quite late:

"[the British] came to an agreement with the Kachin and Shan chiefs that the freedom of the slaves would be purchased by Government, with the provision that all slaves would be freed by 1 January 1928. This was accepted 'with reluctance' by the Kachin and Shan headmen." (Leach 1954: 294)

Southeast Asian slavery can also be considered as a nexus of cultural transfer, since different groups of slaves were integrated to different degrees into the social fabric of their captor societies (cf. Beemer 2009). For example, when the Burmese invaded the central Thai kingdom of Ayutthaya in 1767, they deported an estimated 30-100,000 Thai to the Burmese realm (ibid.; James 2000). In the Burmese royal chronicles, the slaves are listed and categorized according to twenty skills (van Roy 2009: 492).[5] Thai artisans enjoyed a privileged status within the slave community and were even better off than ordinary Burmese peasants; for example, they were exempted from *corvée* labour.

The Lao war captives in 19th-century Siam are a similar case in point. In fact the origins of the jewellery district in Bangkok today can be traced back to a settlement of Lao goldsmiths who were enslaved and forcibly deported after the destruction of the Lao capital Vientiane by the Siamese in 1828, when many thousands of Lao were deported (cf. van Roy 2009; Ngaosyvathn/Ngaosyvathn 1998; Tappe 2013). Some of them received the privileged status of royal slaves (*kha luang*) and farmed the king's lands along the Bangkok periphery to supply the royal granaries, while others were donated, as acts of merit, to royally sponsored temples as temple slaves (van Roy 2009: 61).

This Siamese practice came to a halt after the British (India, Burma) and French (Vietnam, Laos, Cambodia) colonial expansion in the 19th century, when Bangkok faced considerable political and economic pressure. Due to economic concessions (e.g. trade privileges for the British in Bangkok) and the Franco-British agreement to allow a Siamese 'buffer state' between British Burma and French Indochina, Siam escaped direct colonization (cf. Thongchai 2011). As part of his path toward Western-style 'modernization', King Chulalongkorn (1853-1910) responded to the European abolitionist discourse and officially abolished slavery in 1905 to underline the allegedly 'civilized' status of his kingdom.

---

5   For the history of the Thai-Burmese wars see Lieberman (2003) and Myint-U (2006).

As Edward van Roy (2009: 62) convincingly argues:

"The very existence of captive labour villages became an acute embarrassment. It was imperative that their [ethnic] identity be officially suppressed and their [origins] denied. An obvious first step was the abandonment of the 'captive labour' caste designation within the Thai legal system."

This strategy not only helped the king to avoid the 'slavery argument' as a Western pretext for colonial intervention, but also transformed the political culture within his kingdom. By abolishing slavery, Chulalongkorn deprived local nobles of their traditional source of power and prestige, thus further centralizing Bangkok's power (cf. Thongchai 1994).

Formal slavery may have ended in Southeast Asia, but other forms of dependence continued (Turton 1980). While terms such as *that* disappeared from official rhetoric in Siam, the reference *kha* remained in use as denominator for the non-Tai-speaking groups of the highlands, mainly marginalized groups belonging to the Mon-Khmer language family such as the Khmu, Rmeet, Phong, Katu, Ta-Oy, Katang, Cheng, and many more (cf. Pholsena 2006; Michaud 2006). This convergence of social and cultural classification deserves closer attention.

THE *KHA* CONCEPT

The term *kha* in Lao and Thai language refers both to the category of slaves/serfs and to non-Tai people in general. For European colonial administrators, these two meanings created some confusion between a social and an ethnic category – emblematized by the category *kha* in French colonial censuses (Pholsena 2006: 224). In precolonial Lao and Thai society, both meanings converged in traditional statecraft and sociopolitical organization. An old saying goes: "*kep phak sai sa kep kha sai müang*" ("gather vegetables and put them into baskets; gather [non-Tai] people/serfs and put them into the *müang*/polity"), which refers to the need of underpopulated Tai polities to integrate non-Tai people (cf. Grabowsky 2001; Turton 2000; Condominas 1990) – usually into the lowest strata of the traditional feudal hierarchy, and thus associated with subservient status.

Indeed Mon-Khmer-speaking people such as the Khmu often entered relations of bonded labour or *corvée* for Tai elites, and performed the "hardest and most disgusting jobs to do in the *müang*" (Condominas 1990: 64). In the Tai-Lao speaking world, the term *kha* (*sa* in other upland Tai languages) signifies relations of unfree labour – but is also used to refer to the highland people beyond the confines of lowland polities. In consequence, French observers identified the *kha/sa* 'race' as "the most miserable one we know" (Diguet 1895: 27). As the explorer Lefèvre-Pontalis added in 1892: "It is in the final analysis the eternal question of the Thai exploiting the Kha and searching to obtain their workforce at the best price […]" (2000 [1902]: 338).[6]

Figure 1: Colonial visualisation of the Tai-Kha hierarchy: Tai Deng (Red Tai) woman and a Khmu servant (1920s NE Laos).

Source: Foropon 1927.

---

6   The French also observed considerable differences in the status of the different Mon-Khmer-speaking groups that were classified as *kha*. While the Khmu in the Lao principality of Luang Prabang appeared to hold significant economic and ritual positions (cf. Holt 2009), the uplanders of the Bolaven plateau in southern Laos were targets of ruthless slave raids (Keay 2006: 105; de Carné 1872: 123).

As mentioned above, the slaves/serfs were integrated into the social hierachy of the precolonial state in Southeast Asia. In principle, the boundary between commoners and slaves was fluid. Poor peasants could enter servitude to avoid taxation or to redeem their debts. Slaves could climb the social ladder through manumission and marriage. We know, from Edmund Leach's (1954: 221-3) seminal book "Political Systems of Upper Burma", the example of a Kachin uplander marrying a Shan girl. The groom had to move to the house of his father-in-law according to the principle of uxorilocality and became a *de facto* slave, including being obliged to do hard work on the family's fields. His children, however, inherited the status of their mother and became 'free' Shan.

Unlike the term 'slave' suggests, some *kha* groups were in an economically advantageous position. In his study of the Rmeet (Lao: Lamet) of northern Laos, the Swedish anthropologist Gustav Izikowitz (2001 [1951]) noted that in precolonial times, the uplanders provided not only forest products but also rice for the lowland Lao in exchange for iron and salt (cf. Jonsson 2014). An English traveler in the 19th century even stated: "Without the Khas, their lazy, pleasure-loving, opium-smoking masters would have to work, or die of hunger." (Hallet 1988 [1890]: 22) The term *kha* here denotes the lowest strata in the Tai-Lao social hierarchy, without necessarily reflecting actual enslavement or servitude.

The situation in other regions of the Southeast Asian massif was indeed very different. Driven by the increasing labour demand of 19th-century Siamese economy, a veritable slave trade developed throughout the highlands. In the mountains bordering China, marauding bands abducted people and sold them into servitude, as the introductory vignette illustrated. Such instances provided a pretext for the French intervention and colonial *mission civilisatrice*, with some French contemporaries partly blaming the practice of slavery for the alleged 'backwardness' of parts of the Indochinese population (cf. Délaye 2002).[7] With the abolition of slavery, exploitative labour relations did not cease to exist, however.

---

7   The French position towards slavery was ambivalent, however, oscillating between condemnation and acquiescence (see Conklin 1997 and M. Klein 1998 for the French colonies in Africa; see Pétré-Grenouilleau 2004 for the abolitionist discourse as pretext for colonization; cf. Lindner, this volume). It should be noted that the explorer Cupet himself took advantage of porters provided for him by local notables from their own slaves (Délaye 2002: 309).

COLONIAL CORVÉE AND COOLIE LABOUR: TRANSFORMATIONS AND CONTINUITIES

After the abolition of slavery, variants of servitude and coerced labour still prevailed in Indochina. The French category of coolie[8] referred to three forms of bonded labour: 1) ad hoc recruitment of porters, often uplanders enrolled by force, modification of *kha* discrimination; 2) 'traditional' *corvée* requisitions (e.g. for colonial public works), directed towards lowland (Vietnamese, Lao, and Khmer) peasants and upland slash-and-burn cultivators alike; 3) indentured labour, mainly in the plantation and mining sectors of the colonial economy, with Chinese and Vietnamese labourers working under three-year contracts. The following passages describe the first two forms of coerced labour, while the third – colonial coolie labour *par excellence* – will be discussed in the next part of this chapter.

In November 1901, the colonial gazette *Bulletin Économique de l'Indochine* reported on the ad hoc recruitment of 360 indigenous – possibly Khmu – coolies to transport teak trunks, tied together to form rafts, down the Mekong river at Luang Prabang. The report points out the difficulties of longer engagements and stressed the importance of a trusting relationship with the local population, and of appropriate remuneration. Not mentioned is the fact that seasonal labour migration was common among the Khmu, who since the early 19th century had worked on Siamese Teak plantations to gain money and prestige goods (cf. McCarthy 1994 [1900]; Évrard 2006). This experience certainly made it easier for the French to recruit coolies among them.

In other cases the population resented coolie and *corvée* requisition. It was particularly Lao and Vietnamese mandarins taking advantage of their more privileged status and land appropriation that led to more assymetric power relations and increased the vulnerability of both small tenants and shifting cultivators. Sometimes Lao and Vietnamese landlords insisted on 'traditional' *corvée* obligations for themselves so that small tenants and swiddeners often faced a double burden of labour requisitions. In the case of upland Laos, many subaltern groups resented the collaboration of Lao elites who took advantage of the privilege to collect taxes and to organize *corvée* (cf. Gunn 1990; Foropon 1927).

---

8   Borrowed from the English term, itself a loanword from Hindi (see general introduction of this volume for a discussion of this concept). On the ambiguity of the term – 'coolie' as signifier for specific kinds of work and/or a social status – see van Rossum, this volume.

The category of coerced labour that the French called *corvée* – the obligation to provide labour service for the state – was not so different from previous relations of servitude between landlord and serf. While in France the institution of *corvée* was abolished after the revolution, in the colonial context it remained part and parcel of taxation schemes. The French created a perfidious tax system that included considerable *corvée* obligations. While in precolonial times, *corvée* labour was fitted into the schedule of agricultural practice (e.g. in the dry season after harvest), the constant demand by the French for public works did not allow for this. With the new system, both peasants and skilled labourers were forced into *corvée*, which they could only avoid by paying additional taxes – that is, a choice between neglecting field and artisanal work, or risking indebtedness (Adams 1978: 293-4).

The combination of tax and *corvée* with arbitrary labour requisition included the use of force, justified by the alleged reticence of local labour. Public works such as roads and bridges depended on aggressive labour recruitment and subsequent exploitation. As Eric Jennings drastically illustrates with the example of the hill station of Dalat in the highlands of Central Vietnam, such colonial infrastructure "[…] was literally built on the backs of Vietnamese and indigenous minority laborers and peasants" (2011: 4). His account provides disturbing impressions of the abuse of allegedly 'traditional' labour regimes and their colonial modifications. Jennings introduces the colonial functionary Victor Adrien Debay, who was notorious for his violence:

"[Debay] deliberately picked on village chiefs and elders, he strategically terrorized villagers into paying a variety of arbitrary levies, he willfully used the language of requisitions, corvées, and forced labor, and he intentionally turned victims on each other, ordering coolies to beat other coolies. He subsequently pointed to the inadequacy of rules governing labor recruitment to justify his use of force." (Jennings 2011: 32)

This all occurred under the Code de l'Indigénat that denied the 'indigènes' many basic human rights (cf. M. Klein 1998; Benton 1999). Violent assaults on Vietnamese coolies were usually only mildly punished or fined, whereas resistance to labour requisition was severely punished – and again taken as pretext for the necessity of force to get people to work. Beatings or imprisonment could in some cases be replaced by the payment of penalties that, however, added to the already existing financial burdens and increased the risk of indebtedness.

At the turn of the 20th century, Vietnamese and Chinese coolies had already replaced the scarce locally available workforce in the uplands. On the construction sites for mountain roads and railroads, they suffered from a high mortality rate, from malaria, accidents, and exhaustion. The construction of the Hanoi-Yunnan railroad after 1897, in particular, witnessed an immense death toll in spite of French claims of improved medical support and work security. 12,000 of a total of 60,000 Vietnamese and Chinese workers died along its tracks (cf. Del Testa 2001; Brocheux and Hémery 2009). In addition, brutal and racist overseers maltreated the indigenous workers as inferior races that had to be beaten to learn discipline and order (ibid.). As a result, labourers often voted with their feet. As Jennings put it with regard to road construction: "After each pay, masses of emaciated, fever-ridden workers simply left" (Jennings 2011: 66).

The term 'coolie' marks the blurred boundary between precolonial and colonial labour relations, since it designates both traditional *corvée*/servitude (induced by economic and/or moral primordial debt, as explained below) and 'modern' variants of indentured labour. Bush (2000; cf. Derks 2010) distinguishes between contract work performed by state agents, and that by private actors, a distinction blurred in the case of French Indochina. Especially the plantation and mining sectors were characterized by entanglements and contestation between the colonial bureaucracy, private enterprises, and various local actors when it came to recruiting and disciplining coolie labour.

COOLIE SYSTEM IN THE PLANTATION AND MINING ECONOMY

Since the mid-19th century the French took control of the territories of present-day Vietnam, Laos, and Cambodia. Coolie labour became a crucial factor for French strategies of economic development and their – in the end, failed – attempt to create a cost-efficient colony (cf. J.-F. Klein 2012). The program of development was known as *mise en valeur* (cf. Sarraut 1923). It was part and parcel of the colonial *mission civilisatrice* that aimed at the modernization of economic practices, modes of thought, and social relations, and the disciplining of minds and bodies according to the norms and the requirements of industrial work (cf. Conklin 1997; Brocheux/Hémery 2009).

This policy had a great impact on agrarian society, starting with the intensification of a rice-exporting economy since the 1860s, followed by a period of industrial, mining, and plantation development, initiated in 1897 by the *gouverneur général* Paul Doumer. When the rubber boom in southern Indochina began in 1926 and continued until 1930, the cultivated acreage jumped from 18,000 hectares to almost 80,000 (Brocheux/Hémery 2009: 127). The rubber industry employed 70,000 coolies, mainly contractual workers from Tonkin and

Annam, usually under three-year contracts. Labour migration reached its peak in the 1920s with an annual average of more than 12,000 Vietnamese from densely populated Tonkin moving to the south, and around 2,000 moving to the Pacific islands (cf. Delamarre 1931; Boucheret 2008).

The labour migrants worked under a system of indentured labour or contract labour, known in France as *engagisme*. The history of French indentured labour dates back to the 17th century, when French migrants moved to America, mainly in Quebec, under the so-called *trente-six mois* (cf. Mauro 1986). They worked on farms for 36 months and were allowed to buy and own the land they had cultivated after they finished the contract. However, this was a scheme for prospective white settlers, widely differing for later coolie contracts.

These patterns of labour migration happened before the heyday of colonial slavery. Asian indentured/coolie labour migration to Africa and the Americas gained momentum towards the end of slavery in the mid-19th century. European and Asian systems of indentured labour differed in many respects, most notably concerning racial issues (cf. Mauro 1986). In the colonial context the legal framework of contract labour was reframed under the infamous Code de l'Indigenat, which implied considerable legal differences between French citizens and colonial subjects (cf. Conklin 1997; Boucheret 2008). The coolie system became not only a key pillar of the French colonial economy but also – similarly to the labour systems of other colonial powers – a means of control and discipline (cf. J.-F. Klein 2012; Slocomb 2007; see Houben/Lindblad 1999 for Indonesia).

Rubber plantations were established in rather thinly populated regions in many Asian colonies in the late 19th century: well-known enterprises included Goodyear in Sumatra (Dutch colony), Dunlop in Malaya (British Colony), and Michelin in South Vietnam and Cambodia (French colonies) (cf. Tully 2011; Murray 1992; Panthou/Binh 2013). In the latter case, plantations were mainly established on the high plateaus (known as 'red earth'), thinly populated by different subsistence-farming ethnic groups (cf. Aso 2012). The latter were often displaced, and usually resisted requisition as plantation workers. The French colonialists required a large workforce, and found it in the densely populated delta region of the Red River in Northern Vietnam near the large capital Hanoi (cf. Gourou 1955; Bunout 1936; Boucheret 2008).

In the French sources this displacement of labour is often depicted as a 'solution' to the alleged overpopulation of the Red River Delta (cf. Pasquier 1918; Robequain 1939). However, this demographic problem had resulted from previous transformations of property relations in the region. While in precolonial times there was already a clear picture of a feudal society with a land-holding aristocracy and a mass of small tenants, French administrative interventions aggravated the situation (cf. Cleary 2003; Hardy 2003). The French developed a land code that privileged large landowners and latifundia capitalism. Colonialism was also characterized by the appropriation and privatization of communal land. Wealthy Vietnamese landlords collaborated with the French and accumulated the farmland while a large, subordinate class of tenant farmers emerged, often working on sharecropping contracts whose detailed conditions were imported from France. The class of poor Vietnamese tenant farmers was dispossessed, often hopelessly indebted, and thus open to the idea of signing coolie contracts.

Indeed, the French were able to recruit thousands of Vietnamese coolies for plantation work without too much effort. Vietnam already had a history of population movements, most famously including the southward move, the settlement of the Vietnamese coast from the North to the Mekong Delta in the South. In contrast to the colonial stereotype of Vietnamese peasants' 'natural' attachment to their villages (cf. e.g. Bunout 1936) – cultivated by the French authorities to sustain population control – Andrew Hardy (2003) shows how especially for land-poor peasants the option of moving around looking for work, either as agricultural labourers or as soldiers, was appealing.

Such mobility was a way of earning the means to start family, to buy land and a house, and to gain higher status after returning to the village. It was not an easy decision, because having to leave the community to look for work and money elsewhere meant to admit one's own poverty, and was thus a challenge to saving face and maintaining dignity (cf. Hardy 2003; Do 2005). Sometimes the socioeconomic conditions left people with no choice anyway. They were forced to move, and the French took advantage of this situation for their own projects of economic development and population management. Thus, we have to consider different economic, sociocultural, and political factors that contributed to the colonial coolie system.

The interwar years, in particular the years just before the world economic crisis, witnessed an intensification of the French policy of economic development. Industrial plantations, most prominently of rubber and coffee, along with the mining sector constituted the pillars of the French colonial economy, which was oriented mainly towards resource exploitation. The demand for labour rapidly increased, and the colonial administration faced the claims of different economic interest groups including the Société Le Nickel in Nouvelle-

Calédonie.[9] The local administrations in Tonkin and Annam criticized uncontrolled labour recruitment, not least because some provinces had their own agendas of economic development that, for example, involved labour-intensive infrastructure projects.[10]

Figure 2: Coolie migration in French Indochina

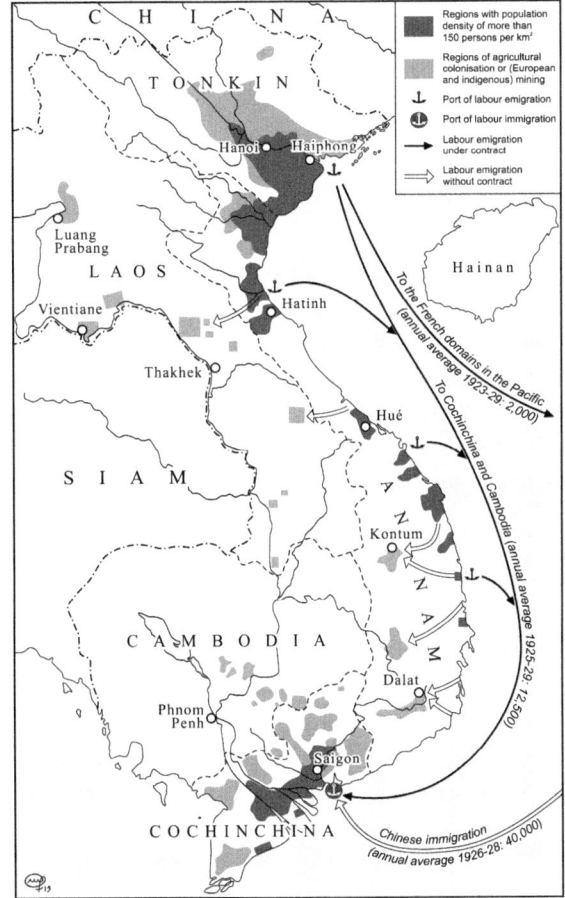

Source: Revised map based on Delamarre 1931.

---

9 Angleviel 2001; Archives nationales d'outre-mer (ANOM), Aix-en-Provence, AF/INDO 111, F81.

10 Les Cahiers Coloniaux de l'Institut Colonial de Marseille, no. 491, 25 June 1928, pp. 254-6 (ANOM, FM/AFFECO 26).

However, Tonkin remained the main source of available manpower, and the flow of labour migrants towards the Mekong delta and beyond continued. The population of Tonkin rapidly increased under French rule, while the ongoing latifundia system was reproducing a mass of poor peasants, their plight aggravated by regular inundation and poor harvests. The colonial administration agreed on certain quota for migration, though: an annual 25,000 coolies for southern Indochina and 2,500 for the Pacific Islands (ibid.). The economic lobby, represented mainly by the powerful rubber barons, continued to call for more flexibility of the labour market, as it were, for reduced bureaucracy, and free circulation of labour. Also during the rubber boom in the interwar years, critique of the exploitative coolie system emerged both in French colonial newspapers and among the emergent educated Vietnamese middle class in Hanoi and Saigon (cf. Boucheret 2001, 2008; Aso 2012; Brocheux/Hémery 2009; Del Testa 2001, 2002).

In 1927, the colonial government set up a survey of labour conditions by the Inspection Général du Travail (cf. Boucheret 2001). Its agents conducted surveys in different parts of the colony to check the working and living conditions at plantations and mines. They noted, for example, the widespread practice of corporal punishments for the smallest offence, and the scandalous sanitary and medical conditions.[11] On the rubber plantation of Phu-Rieng, inspector Delamarre visited a clinic where half of the patients had been injured by beatings, and he noted numerous dirty sheds containing coolies shackled and close to starvation (Binh 1978: 37).

On the plantation of Mimot in Cambodia, the local Khmer notables complained about the mistreatment of the Tonkinese coolies at the hands of the overseers, who acted like "conducteurs de buffles et de boefs".[12] The Belgian overseer Verhelst was particularly notorious for arbitrarily beating the coolies with canes and whips (Ngo Van 1997: 412). His blatant abuses could not be ignored by Inspector Delamarre, yet still the Mimot company protested against his dismissal, revealing the pervading racism of colonial society that considered the *indigènes* second-class citizens.[13]

---

11 Some reports are quoted in the annex of Ngo Van's (1997) account of the early years of the Vietnamese anti-colonial struggle; see also ANOM, FM/AFFECO 25; Boucheret 2008.

12 Letter 6 March 1929, Gouverneur Général d'Indochine to Minister of Colonies in Paris (ANOM, FM/AFFECO 26).

13 Ibid.; cf. Aso 2012. The plantation owners in fact argued that disciplinary measures, including occasional violence, were necessary to guarantee a stable and dutiful work-

The inspections provoked a considerable paper trail within the French administration.[14] However, as the contemporary Paul Monet (an official of the colonial *Service géographique*) deplores in his pamphlet *Les Jauniers* – 'yellow-slaves trader', derived from *négriers* – the inspection failed to change the miserable living conditions of the coolies (cf. Monet 1930). Tran Tu Binh, who in 1930 became one of the leaders of a workers' revolt on the rubber plantation of Phu-Rieng (Cambodia), even indicated that the French inspectors were corrupt and let the enterprises go on, accepting ineffectual promises to improve the working and living conditions of the coolies (Binh 1985 38).

Indeed, the planters' lobby claimed to care about medical support for and the hygiene of the workers, which in the end should improve their living conditions, arguably bringing about greater 'civilization'. This clearly echoed the colonial claim of the *mission civilisatrice*, the French ideology of improving the social, cultural, and moral standards of the colonized (cf. Conklin 1997; Aso 2012). The interests only collided when it came to the aspect of violence and to excessive exploitation of the workers because the colonial government tried to maintain the myth of a morally justified and benevolent colonization. In general, however, it was common sense among the different colonial interests that contract labour and coolie migration was indispensable, for demographic and economic reasons (cf. Boucheret 2008).

Therefore, coolie labour can be considered as a kind of hybrid between wage-labour and forced labour – politically institutionalized and legitimized. According to the law, it was possible to leave the contract when advances and other costs were paid off. However, it was almost impossible for the coolies to do so. They rather accumulated more debts, and the system of exploitation continued (cf. J.-F. Klein 2012; Maurer 2010; Angleviel 2001). Meanwhile, the planters' lobby responded to the growing critical voices with publications defending their efforts for the improvement of the economic and social conditions in the colony. Reports of violence and abuse were renounced as fables and lies of leftist groups.

In 1928, the socialist *gouverneur général* Varenne introduced new labour regulations in response to a growing number of alarming reports about the harsh labour- and living conditions in the coolie camps of the plantations and mines,

---

force. Underlying this view was a racist attitude linked to the common idea that the *indigènes* were still not sufficiently 'civilized' and, thus, had to be disciplined in order to function according to the requirements of the colonial *mise en valeur*; that is, economic development (see Jennings 2011).

14 See the ANOM files FM/AFFECO 25 and 26.

and also in response to the International Labour Organization's campaign against forced labour.[15] The French authorities claimed to protect the indigenous workers, but did not even think about abandoning the coolie system as such. The new regulations fixed some of the workers' rights, such as working hours of nine hours per day, a specific number of days off, and the obligation of the companies to explain the contract in all details to the workers, who often could not read them. In general, the labour reforms only secured the existence of the coolie system and consolidated the legal divide between coolies and free workers (cf. Boucheret 2001, 2008).

One example of this was the introduction of the so-called *carte speciale d'ouvrier contractuel*, a specific passport for coolies that replaced the ordinary ID card. This passport was modelled after that created for the *Légion Étrangère*. The place of origin did not matter. Rather, the name and place of the employer, for example a plantation company, was written on the passport.[16] This means that the worker was actually bound to the plantation or mine in that he was not allowed to change either employer or place of residence. In fact, any leave was treated as desertion and severly punished. Only after the contract had finished could the coolies exchange the *carte speciale* for a regular passport. Being a coolie indeed appears to have implied a different identity, a different legal and social status – in fact, a very precarious one.

COOLIE PRECARITY AND THE DEBT FACTOR

Debt provides a key to the understanding of the precariousness of the lives of labourers under conditions of both bonded servitude and indentured labour (cf. Derks 2010). Relations of debt bondage, albeit prone to exploitation, appeared in precolonial times as option in precarious circumstances because it implied mutual obligations. However, such relationships often entailed a vicious circle of further indebtedness and quasi-slavery. The coolie system implied similar ambivalences with regard to the interplay of precarity and allegedly legal security, and the significance of debt.

Jean Michaud's observation for the Southeast Asian uplands can be extended for labour relations in Southeast Asia in general: "In many cases, especially after slavery was made illegal, enslavement became more a matter of usury and

---

15 Decree 25 Oct 1927, in: Journal Officiel de l'Indochine (9 Nov 1927).
16 Letter 24 Septembre 1928, Gouverneur Général d'Indochine to Ministry of Colonies in Paris (ANOM, FM/AFFECO 26).

economic exploitation, using the leverage of debt to enslave defaulters. When a debtor could not repay what he had borrowed, the creditor used him as free labor for varying periods of time, sometimes years, even for the rest of his life." (2006: 220) Even the French coolie system can be included in such a definition, since indebtedness was a crucial factor in both entry into and eventual inability to exit the contract (cf. J.-F. Klein 2012; Derks 2010; Testart 2001; Northrup 1995).

Since debt is a crucial factor of present-day contract/indentured labour as well (see Derks 2010; Killias 2010; Huong 2010; Damir-Geilsdorf, this volume), it seems a promising vantage point for the study of labour relations from a *longue durée* perspective. For the duration of the contract, the workers – both in colonial times and the present – faced a temporary suspension of basic rights, and thus experienced vulnerability and di-stress. Precolonial conditions of debt bondage, arguably a temporary state of exception, can also be discussed within this framework.

The historian Baas Terwiel (1983) estimates that in the 18th-19th century a quarter to half of the Siamese population was in a position of debt bondage to someone. As Katherine Bowie argues, precolonial "state power and state policy was integrally involved in the maintenance of human servitude" (1996: 137), and slavery and/or bonded servitude must be considered as the physical imposition of the state, rather than as a mere fiscal option for poor peasants. Instead of a voluntary choice, debt bondage was often a combined result of structural coercion and natural calamities, but was certainly also a consequence of gambling and money lending.

The colonial mechanisms of *corvée* and coolie labour also served the economic and administrative interests of the state (cf. Northrup 1995; Laviña/ Zeuske 2014). After the abolition of slavery, other means of capitalist exploitation had to satisfy the needs of colonial economic interests. Coolies became another form of disposable labour, caught in a precarious interplay of contract security and exploitation, debt and economic opportunity. As a kind of "voluntary slavery" (Angleviel 2001), coolie labour was simultaneously both voluntary and coerced (notably by generally precarious socioeconomic conditions), perhaps including aspects of the conditions of both precolonial servitude and postcolonial wage labour.

The precarity of the contract workers under colonialism is reflected in literary works by Vietnamese ex-coolies and descendants of coolies. The book "The Red Earth" by Tran Tu Binh (1985) describes the hardships of coolie life on the rubber plantations in southern Indochina (cf. Monet 1930; Tully 2011). Tran Tu Binh was a communist activist who went to the plantations to mobilize the workers in the south to follow "the road to proletarianized revolutionary struggle" (Binh 1985: 12). His detailed observations of coolie life are written with Marxist jargon, as is often the case with Vietnamese anticolonial literature (cf. Truong 2000). Such accounts offer much material with which it is possible to assess the impact of colonial labour regimes on individual biographies.

Binh provides drastic descriptions of the various corporal punishments the coolies had to endure from the hands of the overseers, "the terrible, cruel demons of this hell on earth" (Binh 1985: 24). The coolies were forced to work from six to six with only a short break. Many of them suffered from exhaustion, injuries (induced by accidents or the overseers' relentless beatings), malaria, and dysentery, and thus many coolies died and "became fertilizer for the capitalists' rubber trees" (ibid.: 27). They received only rice rations of bad quality, for which they had to pay ridiculous prices at the shops owned by the plantations. Though in theory they were allowed to quit the contract after 18 months – given that they had paid back advances and recruitment costs (cf. Boucheret 2001) – the coolies were often already heavily indebted. According to Monet (1930: 26), the suicide rate among the coolies was high, with up to ten suicides per months on certain plantations.

In contrast to Tran Tu Binh, the author of another illustrative book, Jean Vanmai, was not an eyewitness but the son of a coolie in the nickel mines of Nouvelle-Calédonie, born in 1960. The title of his book, "Chân đăng" (1980), refers to the self-designation of the Vietnamese coolies, with *chân đăng* literally meaning 'feet under contract', i.e. contract labourers. This book is based on interviews with Vietnamese coolies, but written in a fictional style. The reason for this was that the Vietnamese community wished to leave this part of its history behind and feared the reaction of the dominant French population of the island. Indeed, the publication of this book caused some heated debate about the dark heritage of Nouvelle-Calédonie, the legacy of the island as a penal colony and labour camp (cf. Do 2005; Angleviel 2001; de Deckker 1994).

Jean Vanmai describes the *chân đăng*'s feeling of exile, vulnerability and estrangement. Like Binh, he sketches the everyday violence in the workplace, from a casual slap in the face to attempts at rape (Vanmai 1980: 100).[17] Generally, the contracts listed punishments for "insubordination", which could mean anything, even fainting from exhaustion. Brutal overseers – some of them veterans of the French army, or even having worked in the Belgian Congo previously – considered the beating of coolies as a legitimate means of enforcing

---

17 Female coolies were particularly vulnerable, often subjected to sexual harrassment or given as sex slaves to loyal foremen (Binh 1985: 24). The female-male ratio in 1929 was about 1:5 in Cambodia and Nouvelle Calédonie (Delamarre 1931: 36; 44).

discipline (cf. Angleviel 2001; Jennings 2011). Since it was impossible to quit the contract without becoming hopelessly indebted, as already mentioned, and with running away punished in the same way as desertion from the army, the coolies had to endure the mistreatment at the hands of their overseers. As one protagonist in Vanmai's book laments:

"Que pouvons-nous faire d'autre ici, sur cette petite île? Impossible de fuir. Et nous sommes bien loin de notre pays. Il ne nous reste donc qu'une seule solution: travailler et obéir pour éviter les fouets des contremaîtres et les violences des gendarmes." (Vanmai 1980: 137-8)

Writing about Javanese and Vietnamese coolies in Nouvelle-Calédonie, Maurer (2010) and Angleviel (2001) emphasize the significance of indebtedness for the precarity of the labourers in the colonial plantation and mining economy. Usually food and clothes allowances were guaranteed by the contract. However, often the rice and dried fish were of such poor quality that the workers were forced to buy additional food in the local shops, which were usually run by the companies (see above; Binh 1985: 27). These shops also sold other items like needles for sewing clothes, and sometimes turned into gambling halls in the days following payday. Many coolies bought credit, and the gradual accumulation of debt forced them to sign consecutive contracts – attaching them "as semi-slaves to their employer" (Maurer 2010: 877).

The combination of advances and retainers was another factor contributing to the risk of indebtedness: advances that lured coolies into signing work contracts were deducted from their salaries over the first year, while the company withheld a portion of the salary as so-called 'pécule', an amount of money only paid on the ending of the contract. According to Angleviel (2001: 76), in 1926 the French mining company *Société Le Nickel* withheld 30% of its workers' salaries. Not surprisingly, the reduced salary and the precarious life on the working sites resulted in indebtedness. It thus appears to be only a very small step from contract labour to bonded labour or even forced labour.

Accounts of the everyday lives of the Vietnamese coolies also provide information about the motivation of the peasants from Tonkin to sign such contracts. On the one hand, Binh and Vanmai mention the plight of the Vietnamese peasantry in colonial Indochina, in particular their chronic indebtedness. On the other hand they refer to a kind of moral debt that especially young men feel towards their parents and ancestors. In Vietnam, filial piety is considered a keystone of morality, and thus one can understand why the sons of poor peasant families took their chances working abroad to save money for a small plot of land (cf. Vanmai 1980; Angleviel 2001; Hardy 2003).

Tran Tu Binh notes how the recruiters exploited the situation in the Red River Delta, where recruitment stalls mushroomed at intersections and marketplaces:

"When they were unable to recruit enough labor, the French colonialists threw in Vietnamese contractors to coax and con farmers in the Red River delta who had lost their land and were down on their luck with no opportunity to escape their lot. There was an abundance of recruiting activity everywhere. The contracting gangs tried to outdo each other in spinning fantastic images of the out-of-this-world way of life on the rubber plantations, because they received two piasters [four times the daily wage for coolies; OT] for each person they handed over to the French." (Binh 1985: 12)

Examples of both Vietnamese and Javanese coolies in Nouvelle-Calédonie show the chain reactions triggered by the first recruitment, the first contract signed under precarious circumstances – sometimes due to indebtedness, sometimes because of the generally poor socioeconomic conditions. While in the case of the Vietnamese the process of colonial land appropriation aggravated landlessness and poverty, in Java rapid population growth and scarcity of agricultural land led to the acceptance of emigration and coolie labour. Arguably, the legacy of precolonial debt bondage in Southeast Asia enabled the emergence of a disposable workforce for colonial capitalism.

Conclusion

The economic anthropologist David Graeber shows in his influential book, *Debt: The First 5,000 Years*, that since antiquity "the struggle between rich and poor has largely taken the form of conflicts between creditors and debtors – of arguments about the rights and wrongs of interest payments, debt peonage, amnesty, repossession, restitution, the sequestering of sheep, the seizing of vineyards, and the selling of debtors' children into slavery" (Graeber 2011: 8). Graeber considers debt as a means of enacting violence, and a lever of exploitation. This is evident in the context of the colonial and precolonial state in Southeast Asia.

When comparing the coolie system with precolonial forms of bonded labour, we have to distinguish between debt resulting from coerced labour relations, and debt preceding these precarious arrangements. Asian peasants in precolonial and colonial times always ran the risk of becoming trapped in a vicious circle of indebtednes and exploitation. Even if we consider certain mechanisms of security (mutual obligations within traditional patron-client relations and legal frameworks of colonial labour), the general precarity of the labourers in the grey zone between slavery and wage labour remains a crucial issue.

Without question, variants of coerced labour shaped socioeconomic relations in precolonial and colonial mainland Southeast Asia to a large extent. In precolonial Vietnam and Laos, as well as in Siam, different forms of slavery and servitude reflected the strong hierarchization of society. Feudal aristocratic and/or landlord classes took advantage of *corvée* obligations and other forms of coerced labour extracted from subaltern peasants, small tenants, or upland swiddeners – the latter classified as *kha* (slaves/serfs) in Laos and northern Thailand.

The French, following the British in Burma, officially abolished slavery in their Indochinese possessions as a keystone of their alleged *mission civilisatrice*. However, some practices such as *corvée* labour persisted as a form of taxation, and the infamous coolie system was established to guarantee labour influx for the booming plantation and mining economy. Both variants can be considered bonded or coerced labour, since they imply different degrees of force, coercion, and violence. Examples of victims of such conditions are the *kha* who were exploited by the French and their Lao allies for *corvée* labour, and the Vietnamese coolies enduring structural violence on the colonial rubber plantations: "Like life imprisonment without jail" (Binh 1985: 28).

The factor of debt exemplifies the historical continuities of precolonial and colonial variants of bonded labour, thus allowing for a *longue durée* perspective on labour relations in mainland Southeast Asia in general. Precolonial debt bondage in many respects resembles the conditions that forced poor Vietnamese peasants in the Red River Delta into signing the coolie contract, sometimes followed by additional indebtedness, and thus *de facto* bondage to their employers.

As Annuska Derks and others have pointed out for the present, such forms of bonded labour have also prevailed in the postcolonial era. Transnational labour migration sometimes follows schemes envisaged by the colonial powers, in particular the new forms of contract/indentured labour (cf. Derks 2010). Vietnamese, Lao, and Thai migrants also form part of this global system of labour relations and mobility. The interplay between poverty and indebtedness on the one hand, and bound contracts and exploitation on the other, remains a critical issue for research into current economic tendencies in the Global South.

REFERENCES

Adams, Nina S. (1978): The Meaning of Pacification – Thanh Hóa under French Rule 1885-1908. PhD diss., Yale University.

Angleviel, Frédéric (2001): "De l'engagement comme, esclavage volontaire. Le cas des Océaniens, Kanaks et Asiatiques en Nouvelle-Calédonie (1853-1963)." In: Journal de la Société des océanistes 110, pp. 65-81.

Aso, Michitake (2012): "Profits or People? Rubber plantations and everyday technology in rural Indochina." In: Modern Asian Studies 46/1, pp. 19-45.

Beemer, Bryce (2009): "Southeast Asian Slavery and Slave-Gathering Warfare as a Vector for Cultural Transmission: The Case of Burma and Thailand." In: The Historian 71/3, pp. 481-506.

Benton, Lauren (1999): "Colonial Law and Cultural Difference: Jurisdictional Politics and the Formation of the Colonial State." In: Comparative Studies in Society and History 41/3: 563-588.

Binh, Tran Tu (1985): The Red Earth: A Vietnamese Memoir of Life on a Colonial Rubber Plantation, Athens: Ohio University, Center for International Studies.

Boucheret, Marianne (2008): Les plantations d'hévéas en Indochine (1897-1954). PhD diss., Université Paris I.

—— (2001): "Le pouvoir colonial et la question de la main-d'œuvre en Indochine dans les années vingt." In: Cahiers d'histoire 85, pp. 29–55.

Bowie, Katherine A. (1996): "Slavery in nineteenth century northern Thailand: archival anecdotes and village voices." In: Edward Paul Durrenberger (ed.), State power and culture in Thailand, New Haven: Yale University Press, pp. 100–138.

Bowring, John (1969[1857]): The Kingdom and People of Siam, Kuala Lumpur: Oxford University Press.

Brass, Tom/van der Linden, Marcel (eds.) (1997): Free and Unfree Labor: The Debate Continues, Bern: Peter Lang.

Brocheux, Pierre/Hémery, Daniel (2009): Indochina: An Ambiguous Colonization, 1858- 1954, Berkeley: University of California Press.

Bunout, René (1936): La main-d'œuvre et la législation du travail en Indochine, Bordeaux: Imprimerie-Librairie Delmas.

Bush, Michael L. (2000): Servitude in Modern Times, Cambridge: Polity Press.

Campbell, Gwyn (2003): "Introduction: Slavery and other forms of Unfree Labour in the Indian Ocean World." In: Slavery & Abolition 24/2, pp. 4-32.

Cleary, Mark (2003): "Land codes and the state in French Cochinchina, c. 1900-1940". In: Journal of Historical Geography 29/3, pp. 356-375.

Condominas, Georges (ed.) (1998): Formes Extrêmes de Dépendance. Contributions à l'Étude de l'Esclavage en Asie du Sud-Est, Paris: École des Hautes Études en Sciences Sociales.

—— (1990): From Lawa to Mon, from Saa' to Thai: Historical and anthropological aspects of Southeast Asian political spaces, Canberra: Australian National University.

Conklin, Alice L. (1997): A Mission to Civilize: The Republican Idea of Empire in France and West Africa, 1895-1930, Stanford: Stanford University Press.

Cupet, Pierre-Paul (2000 [1900]): Travels in Laos and Among the Tribes of Southeast Indochina. The Pavie Mission Indochina Papers, Vol. 6, Bangkok: White Lotus.

Day, Tony (2002). Fluid Iron: State Formation in Southeast Asia, Honolulu: University of Hawaii Press.

de Carné, Louis (1872): Voyage en Indo-Chine et dans l'empire Chinois, Paris: E. Dentu.

de Deckker, Paul (ed.) (1994): Le peuplement du Pacifique et de la Nouvelle-Calédonie au XIXe siècle: Condamnés, Colons, Convicts, Coolies, Chân Dang, Paris: L'Harmattan.

Délaye, Karine (2002): "Esclavage et représentations coloniales en Indochine de la seconde moitié du XIXe au début du Xxe siècle." In: Outre-mers 89/336-7: 283-319.

Del Testa, David W. (2002): "Workers, Culture, and the Railroads in French Colonial Indochina, 1905–1936." In: French Colonial History 2/1, pp. 181–98.

—— (2001): Paint the Trains Red: Labor, Nationalism, and the Railroads in French Colonial Indochina, 1898–1945. PhD diss., University of California.

Delamarre, Paul Emile (1931): L'émigration et l'immigration ouvrière en Indochine, Hanoï: Imprimerie d'Extrême-Orient.

Derks, Annuska (2010): "Bonded Labour in Southeast Asia: Introduction." In: Asian Journal of Social Science 38, pp. 839-852.

Diguet, Edouard (1895): Etude de la langue Tai, Hanoi: F.H.Schneider.

Do, Tess (2005): "Exile, Rupture and Continuity in Jean Vanmai's Chan Dang and Fils de Chan Dang." In: Portal: Journal of Multidisciplinary International Studies 2/2, pp. 1-20.

Dutton, George (2006): The Tây Sơn Uprising: Society and Rebellion in Eighteenth-Century Vietnam, Chiang Mai: Silkworm Books.

Évrard, Olivier (2006): Chroniques des cendres: Anthropologie des sociétés khmou et dynamiques interethniques du Nord-Laos, Paris: IRD.

Foropon, Jean (1927): "La province des Hua-Phan (Laos)." In: Extrême-Asie 14, pp. 93-106.

Goscha, Christopher E. (2012): Going Indochinese: Contesting Concepts of Space and Place in French Indochina, Copenhagen: NIAS Press.

Gourou, Pierre (1955): The peasants of the Tonkin Delta: A study of human geography, New Haven: Human Relations Area Files.

Grabowsky, Volker (2004): Bevölkerung und Staat in Lan Na: Ein Beitrag zur Bevölkerungsgeschichte Südostasiens, Wiesbaden: Harrassowitz.

—— /Turton, Andrew (2003): The Gold and Silver Road of Trade and Friendship. The McLeod and Richardson Diplomatic Missions to Tai States in 1837, Chiang Mai: Silkworm Books.

—— (2001): "Note on Kep Phak Sai Sa Kep Kha Sai Müang." In: Aséanie 8, pp. 67-71.

—— (1999): "Forced Resettlement Campaigns in Northern Thailand During the Early Bangkok Period." In: Journal of the Siam Society 87/1-2, pp. 45-86.

Graeber, David (2011): Debt: The First 5000 Years, New York: Melville House.

Gunn, Geoffrey (1990): Rebellion in Laos. Peasant and politics in a colonial backwater, Boulder, Colorado: Westview Press.

Hallet, Holt (1988 [1890]): A Thousand Miles on an Elephant in the Shan States, Bangkok: White Lotus.

Hardy, Andrew (2003): Red Hills: Migrants and the State in the Highlands of Vietnam, Honolulu: University of Hawai'i Press.

Holt, John C. (2009): Spirits of the place: Buddhism and Lao religious culture, Honolulu: University of Hawai'i Press.

Houben, Vincent/Lindblad, Jan Thomas (eds.) (1999): Coolie Labour in Colonial Indonesia. A Study of Labour Relations in the Outer Islands, c. 1900-1940, Wiesbaden: Harrassowitz.

Huong, Lê Thu (2010): "A New Portrait of Indentured Labour: Vietnamese Labour Migration to Malaysia." In: Asian Journal of Social Science 38, pp. 880-896.

Izikowitz, Karl G. (2001 [1951]): Lamet: Hill Peasants of French Indochina, Bangkok: White Lotus.

James, Helen (2000): "The Fall of Ayutthaya: A Reassessment." In: Journal of Burma Studies 5: 75–108.

Jennings, Eric T. (2011): Imperial Heights: Dalat and the Making and Undoing of French Indochina, Berkeley: University of California Press.

Jonsson, Hjorleifur (2014): Slow Anthropology: Negotiating Difference with the Iu Mien, Ithaca: Cornell University Press.

Keay, John (2006): Mad About the Mekong. Exploration and Empire in South East Asia, New York: Harper Perennial.
Killias, Olivia (2010): "'Illegal' Migration as Resistance: Legality, Morality and Coercion in Indonesian Domestic Worker Migration to Malaysia." In: Asian Journal of Social Science 38, pp. 897-914.
Klein, Jean-François (2012): "Esclavages, engagismes et coolies, histoire des sociétés coloniales au travail (1850-1950)." In: Jean-François Klein/Claire Laux (eds.) Sociétés impériales en situations coloniales. Afrique, Asie, Antilles (années 1850- années 1950), Paris: Ellipses, pp. 163-182.
Klein, Martin A. (1998): Slavery and Colonial Rule in French West Africa. Cambridge: Cambridge University Press.
Laviña, Javier/Zeuske, Michael (eds.) (2014): The Second Slavery: Mass Slaveries and Modernity in the Americas and in the Atlantic Basin, Münster: Lit.
Leach, Edmund (1954): Political Systems of Highland Burma, London: Athlone.
Lefèvre-Pontalis, Pierre (2000[1902]): Travels in Upper Laos and on the Borders of Yunnan and Burma, Bangkok: White Lotus.
Lieberman, Victor (2010): "A zone of refuge in Southeast Asia? Reconceptualizing interior spaces." In: Journal of Global History 5, pp. 333-346.
—— (2003): Strange Parallels: Southeast Asia in Global Context, c. 800–1830, Cambridge/New York: Cambridge University Press.
Mabbett, Ian (1983): "Some remarks on the present state of knowledge about slavery in Angkor." In: Anthony Reid (ed.), Slavery, bondage, and dependency in Southeast Asia, New York: St Martin's Press.
Maurer, Jean-Luc (2010): "The Thin Red Line between Indentured and Bonded Labour: Javanese Workers in New Caledonia in the Early 20th Century." In: Asian Journal of Social Science 38, pp. 866-879.
Mauro, Frédéric (1986): "French indentured servants for America, 1500-1800." In: Piet C. Emmer (ed.), Colonialism and Migration: Indentured Labour Before and After Slavery, Dordrecht: Martinus Nijhoff, pp. 83-104.
McCarthy, James (1994 [1900]): Surveying and exploring in Siam, Bangkok: White Lotus.
Michaud, Jean (2006): Historical Dictionary of the Peoples of the Southeast Asian Massif, Lanham: Scarecrow Press.
Monet, Paul (1930): Les Jauniers, Paris: Gallimard.
Murray, Martin J. (1992): "White Gold or White Blood?: The Rubber Plantations of Colonial Indochina, 1910–40." In: E. Valentine Daniel/Henry Bernstein/Tom Brass (eds.), Plantations, Proletarians, and Peasants in Colonial Asia, London: Frank Cass, pp. 41-67.

Myint-U, Thant (2006): The River of Lost Footsteps; Histories of Burma, New York: Farrar, Straus and Giroux.

Ngaosyvathn, Mayoury/Ngaosyvathn, Pheuiphanh (1998): Paths to conflagration: fifty years of diplomacy and warfare in Laos, Thailand and Vietnam, 1778–1828, Ithaca: Cornell University Southeast Asia Program.

Ngo Van (1998): Viêt-nam 1920-1945: révolution et contre-révolution sous la domination coloniale, Paris: L'Insomniaque.

Northrup, David (1995): Indentured Labor in the Age of Imperialism, 1834-1922, New York: Cambridge University Press.

Panthou, Eric/Tran Tu Binh (2013): Les plantations Michelin au Viêt-Nam, Clermont-Ferrand: La Galipote.

Pasquier, Pierre (1918): La colonisation des terres incultes et le problème de la main-d'œuvre en Indochine, Saigon: Ardin.

Pétré-Grenouilleau, Olivier (ed.) (2004): From Slave Trade to Empire: Europe and the colonisation of Black Africa, 1780s–1880s. Abingdon/New York: Routledge.

Pholsena, Vatthana (2006): Post-war Laos – The Politics of Culture, History, and Identity. Ithaca: Cornell University Press.

Rabibhadana, Akin (1969): The Organisation of Thai Society in the Early Bangkok Period 1782–1873, Ithaca: South East Asia Program, Department of Asian Studies, Cornell University.

Reid, Anthony (1999): Charting the Shape of Early Modern Southeast Asia, Chiang Mai: Silkworm Books.

—— (1983): "Introduction: Slavery and Bondage in Southeast Asian History." In: Anthony Reid (ed.), Slavery, Bondage and Dependency in Southeast Asia, New York: St. Martin's Press, pp.1–43.

Robequain, Charles (1939): L'évolution économique de l'Indochine française, Paris: Paul Hartmann.

Sarraut, Albert (1923): La mise en valeur des colonies françaises, Paris: Payot.

Scott, James C. (2009): The Art of Not Being Governed: An Anarchist History of Upland Southeast Asia, New Haven: Yale University Press.

Slocomb, Margaret (2007): Colons and Coolies: The Development of Cambodia's Rubber Plantations, Bangkok: White Lotus Press.

Tappe, Oliver (2013): "Thailand und Laos – Eine historische Hassliebe." In: Orapim Bernart/Holger Warnk (eds.), Thailand: Facetten einer südostasiatischen Kultur, München: Edition Global, pp. 35-68.

Taylor, Keith W. (2013): A History of the Vietnamese, Cambridge: Cambridge University Press.

Terwiel, Baas (1983): "Bondage and Slavery in Early Nienteenth Century Siam." In: Anthony Reid (ed.), Slavery, Bondage and Dependency in Southeast Asia, New York: St. Martin's Press, pp. 118-137.

Testart, Alain (2001): L'Esclave, la Dette et le Pouvoir, Paris: Editions Errance.

Thongchai Winichakul (2011): "Siam's colonial conditions and the birth of Thai history." In: Volker Grabowsky (ed.), Southeast Asian historiography: unravelling the myths, Bangkok: River Books, pp. 20–41.

—— (1994): Siam Mapped: A History of the Geo-Body of a Nation, Honolulu: University of Hawai'i Press.

Truong, Buu Lam (2000): Colonialism Experienced: Vietnamese writings on Colonialism, 1900-1931, Ann Arbor: University of Michigan Press.

Tully, John (2011): The Devil's Milk: A social history of rubber, New York: New York University Press.

Turton, Andrew (1980): "Thai Institutions of Slavery." In: James L. Watson (ed.), Asian and African Systems of Slavery, Oxford: Basil Blackwell, pp. 251-292.

—— (ed.) (2000): Civility and Savagery: Social Identity in Tai States, Richmond: Curzon.

—— (2004): "Violent Capture of People for Exchange on Karen-Tai Borders in the 1830s." In: Gwyn Campbell (ed.), The Structure of Slavery in Indian Ocean Africa and Asia, London: Frank Cass, pp. 69-82.

van Roy, Edward (2009): "Under duress: Lao war captives at Bangkok in the nineteenth century." In: Journal of the Siam Society 97, pp. 43–65.

Vanmai, Jean (1980): Chân đăng, Nouméa: Publications de la société d'études historiques de la Nouvelle-Calédonie.

"His Original Name Is . . ." – REMAPping the Slave Experience in Saudi Arabia[1]

ALAINE S. HUTSON

For years, European and American scholars have stressed the differences between slavery in the Middle East and the Atlantic World, and they have been very cautious about comparing slavery in the two regions or using scholarship on the Atlantic to interpret data from the Middle East.[2] Since at least the 19th century European travelers and scholars and Middle Eastern elites have portrayed slavery in the Middle East as more benign than its oppressive Atlantic brother. Scholars attributed the 'benign' quality of the slave experience partially to the 'non-productive' work in which Middle Eastern slaves were engaged and partly to the Islamic norms and laws governing the holding of slaves. Some authors have started breeching this academic divide, revealing the inadequacies of the scholarship on slavery in the Middle East, bypassing the cautions against comparison and unearthing the malignant side of the institution (cf. Zilfi 1997; Erdem 2010; Frank 2012; Zdanowski 2013). Bernard Lewis (1990: 99-102) has written that the capture, transport, and sale of slaves in the Atlantic World and Middle East were probably equally horrific. Matthew Hopper (2006) has written

---

1 The author would like to thank Amde Mitiku of www.Ethiotrans.com for help with the identification and social context of Ethiopian names. A Missouri State University Summer Faculty Fellowship funded the original archival research for this article. A Sam Taylor Fellowship grant from the United Methodist Church purchased the JMP software used for the statistical analysis and a Faculty Residency Fellowship from UNCF/Mellon enabled the building and online publishing of the REMAP Database.

2 Gordon (1989: 48-49), Lewis (1990), and Philips (1993: 161) emphasize the difference in the use of slave labor and treatment in the Middle East.

on slaves put to "productive use" in the palm date and pearl industries of the Arabian Peninsula. Ehud Toledano (2009: 14) has called for scholars to "reexamine the argument that Islamic slavery was so much milder than its counterparts that it perhaps cannot be discussed in the same analytic framework."

However, Lewis believed that differences in the two systems would most likely show up in research on the labor conditions for slaves in the Middle East. In other words, the use of slaves, laws governing them and their owners, and owners' treatment of slaves would reveal the differences in the two systems. Lewis further surmised that thoase differences would stem from the economic systems into which slaves were forced to labor: large-scale plantation slavery in the Americas versus the usually small-scale domestic slavery of the Middle East. Certainly differences abound between slavery in the two regions, due to many factors. Laws in the two regions varied dramatically over the subject of inheriting slave status. The systems in the regions did not share age preferences for slaves, and, as David Barry Gaspar (1985: 93) has pointed out, slave's lives were largely shaped "by the work they were made to do, which implied exposure to diverse patterns of subordination" even within a region, system, or time period.

The aim of this chapter is to offer up sharper pictures of the lives of Africans enslaved in 20th-century Saudi Arabia.[3] These pictures suggest that the reverse of Gaspar's statement is also true. When made to do similar work (rural agricultural or urban domestic) slaves in Saudi Arabia experienced patterns of subordination similar to the enslaved in the Americas. This research also amends Gaspar's thesis by suggesting that slaves' work, along with their owners' expectations about Africans' cultures and their owners' notions of power, governed these patterns. The article's findings indicate the need for more comparative research and analysis so that scholars can move beyond the paradigm of "benign Islamic slavery" created by Ottoman "amplification" and the need for scholars to engage in reconstructing the lived experiences of the enslaved.[4]

---

3   This is part of larger research on runaways' narratives from around the Arabia Peninsula in the early 20th century. Here I do not use the "voice" in a conscious effort not to engage in what Gayatri Spivak (2010: 27) terms "the ventriloquism of the speaking subaltern."

4   Toledano (1993: 477-506) discusses what he calls the "amplification" of certain slaves' roles by the Ottoman Empire in its defense of slavery to the British and other European powers. In their dealings with European abolitionist sentiments Ottoman officials emphasized slaves put to work in the military, administration, and the harem.

Eve Troutt Powell (2006: 254) states that "a detailed understanding of the lives of African slaves does not emerge in the archives of the Public Record Office". I argue that when read and analyzed using qualitative and quantitative methods, these records "obviously both linguistically and culturally filtered [...] as limited as they are, can form the basis of a viable and credible social reconstruction" (Toledano 2009: 10). The basis of this article's reconstruction of the lives of enslaved Africans is the records of the British Legation in Jeddah, Saudi Arabia from 1926 to 1938. During this time, the British were freeing and repatriating runaways slaves as stipulated in Article 7 of the 1927 Treaty of Jeddah.[5] All together the Foreign Office files give information on 263 people.[6] For 60 fugitives there are brief but detailed handwritten narratives or typed questionnaires. I have compiled and coded the data from these documents, as well as high-resolution images of the archival documents and full citation of the archival sources, into a free, online searchable database for researchers – Runaways Enslaved and Manumitted on the Arabian Peninsula (REMAP; www.REMAPdatabase.org). When citing information from individual runaways I will be using their REMAP database ID number.

Readers may question whether the data and findings of this research are peculiar to Saudi Arabia or indicative of general trends in 20th-century Middle Eastern slavery. Further questions about the data's reliability are raised because

---

5 Britain relinquished this right in 1936, the same year King Ibn Saud decreed the Saudi Arabian slave regulations. See Miers (1989: 102-28) for more on the provisions of the slave regulations and their relationship to the renunciation. Two years later, fugitive slaves continued to seek manumission from the British. These slaves were turned away, but the British did record the incidents and they were included in the data set and statistical tests.

6 There are both summarized reports and individual documents for the former slaves. F.O. 905/11, Embassy and Legation, Saudi Arabia: General Correspondence. Slaves: General Question. 1934 contains one of the reports (206 are listed in the report, 7 of whom have individual documents: 6 in F.O. 967/1 Legation, Hejaz: Various Papers. Slave traffic. 1926 and 1 in F.O. 905/62 Embassy and Legation, Saudi Arabia: General Correspondence. Slaves, Slavery and slave trade: Gabor Ahmed. 1938.); F.O. 905/28, Embassy and Legation, Saudi Arabia: General Correspondence. Slaves: Manumission: Individual cases. 1935 contains updated reports of manumissions from 1930-1935 (53 listed in the updates, 51 of whom have individual documents); F.O. 905/61, Embassy and Legation, Saudi Arabia: General Correspondence. Slaves, Slavery and Slave Trade: General. 1938 contains the narratives from the two 1938 runaways.

the British or their consulate employees recorded the narratives and held an official anti-slavery position. This question can only be answered by further comparative research, but there are indications that runaway slaves from Saudi Arabia were like runaways in other parts of the Peninsula.[7] As for British influence in the narratives, the British ambivalence about their role in manumission and the diversity of information found in the documents, indicate that the British did not attempt to skew the narratives to shine a strictly negative or positive light on Saudi slavery.[8] The British relinquished their rights to manumission after ten years, noting that the number of slaves who sought refuge was miniscule compared to their numbers in the kingdom which indicated, to the British, that slaves were content in their enslaved status and therefore their manumission efforts were not needed. British relinquishing of this right so quickly and their rationalization for it provides an example of ambivalence toward manumission.

Data from the British Saudi records provide information that Saudi slaveholders had patterns of subordination and control of slaves that were also used by American slaveholders in several areas including: 1) owners' naming practices, 2) owners' assignments of labor based on a slave's country of origin, and 3) Saudi Arabia's drafting of fugitive slave laws and treaties in response to slaves' seeking British manumission and help in repatriation. These narratives speak not only to slaves' lived experiences but also to owners' cultural, labor, and political practices. These parallels not only tell historians about the conditions of Middle Eastern and Atlantic slavery, they reveal insights about the nature of power in owner-slave social and labor relationships and in slave states experiencing resistance to slavery outside from international powers and inside from slaves themselves (cf. Simawe 1999).

Owners, across from both coasts of Africa, attempted to project their hopes for slaves' temperaments and natures through renaming them. Arabs, Americans, and Europeans created fictions about slaves' identities by fashioning stereotypes for slaves from different parts of Africa. Finally, owners tried to stave off escapes by unleashing the judicial weight, and sometimes violence, of the state against runaways.

This work contributes to the trend of newer scholarship that is abandoning the 'benign Islamic slavery' paradigm for a more nuanced and detailed picture of Middle Eastern slavery and its lived rules from the perspective of the enslaved. It

---

7 Hutson (2002: 51, 53, 56-8) discusses data from British offices in Bahrain.
8 For a further description of the data see Hutson (2002: 51-53).

argues that those rules in Saudi Arabia were often aimed at compartmentalizing slaves' names, jobs, and actions in order to better control them.

NAMING PRACTICES

In the narratives several runaways report that their names were changed after being enslaved. For those slaves from Ethiopia like Abdul Kheyr, Salim, Said, and Feyruz whose original Amharic names were Dagfeyh, Nagashi Lejawannis, Araro, and Aggafari that is not surprising.[9] However this renaming also appears to have been a common practice even for people who were Muslim prior to being enslaved. One Nigerian had a perfectly good Muslim name of Arabic origin when he was captured as a teenager: his parents named him Adam. Despite that his new owner renamed him Mabruk, which means "Blessed."[10] Other narratives reveal some patterns to this renaming with certain names being used especially for male slaves. Bakr a teenage boy from Borno (another Nigerian) reported being renamed Bakhit (Lucky) upon his enslavement at the hands of Bedouins at the age of three while on hajj with his parents; Su'da, a seventeen year old originally from the Sudan was renamed Na'im (Comfort); and Bilal, a Sudanese slave in his mid-thirties had been renamed Faraj (Relief).[11]

In all, 13 of the 60 narratives (over 20%) refer to original names and aliases, nicknames, or alternate names used in slavery. Nigerians, Ethiopians, and Sudanese are equally represented among the thirteen, but Su'da is the only woman. The British designed the questionnaires used in this study to collect information pertinent to their particular slavery policy goals in Saudi Arabia, so there was no specific question or attempt to find out if slaves had been renamed.[12] One-fifth is likely a slight under representation of men slaves' renaming, perhaps women slaves renaming is underrepresented too. In

---

9   REMAP #241, REMAP #248, REMAP #250, and REMAP #251, respectively. Araro, may be a mistransliteration of "Areru" a typical Amharic slave name. "Araru" was also a slave name meaning dark like the color of an over roasted coffee bean. Amde Mitiku, email message to author.

10 REMAP #3.

11 REMAP #7, REMAP #256, and REMAP #245, respectively.

12 Among the British interests were determining: slaves' origins so the Legation could repatriate them, bill the appropriate government for the transportation costs and try to stop the trade at the source; the route and method used to import slaves; who brokered and bought slaves in Arabia; and how and where owners were using slave labor.

scrutinizing all 133 names of runaways in the data this under representation for men is evident. While names for women slaves were varied, men's names showed definite trends. Of the 40 names for women the only names repeated more than twice were fairly common Arabic names – Salima (Peaceful or Safe), Jamila (Beautiful), and Sa'ida (Fortunate). However, in a general population of Muslim men one might expect to find many named Muhammad, Ali, Ahmed, Hassan, or Usman: there was only one Muhammad, one Ali, and one Hassan and two each for Ahmed and Usman. But names like Faraj, Johar (Jewel), Mabruk, Jaber (Comforter), Sa'ad (Good luck) and Surur (Joy) were used for nearly a quarter of the escaped men. In fact the one man originally named Ali appears to have been given the slave name of Murjan (Coral).[13] Though women's names were varied, they also included names like Mabruka, Bakhita, and Bushra (Good omen), as well as very unusual names like Ghuzlan and Kelyba.[14]

This naming data adds to the increasing evidence that Arab and other Middle Eastern and Muslim owners had patterns of naming specifically for slaves. Bakhita was also a name commonly given to Sudanese women slaves in Egypt. Jonathan Miran points out that in Ethiopia slave names were often "names of flowers, gems, precious substances and aesthetic features" (Miran 2013: 147-148).

Special "slave names" was also a phenomenon observed in Atlantic slavery. Commonly owners in the Americas gave slaves classical Greek and Roman names, Christian names, and "generic African names" (Hine/Hine/Harrold 2000: 41).[15] Gaspar interprets this renaming of slaves to be an act of social control on the part of slave owners because it "allowed owners to define and fully claim [Africans] as their property while attempting to strip them of an identity associated with their original names" (Gaspar 1985: 131). The Saudi data seems to indicate owner's felt the need to control men more strongly than women.

To establish what Arab slave owners' patterns might have been requires more research and more knowledge of the meaning and etymology of Arabic names, however some patterns do emerge from the Saudi data. King Abd al-Aziz Ibn Saud told Munshi Ihsanullah, a British Legation officer that West Africans

---

13 REMAP #218 says "also called Murjan."
14 I could not find meanings for these last two names and some others. They are not Arabic.
15 Cf. Dunn (1972: 252) for more on owners' common practices when naming African slaves. Mullin (1992: 86) indicates that at times planters named new slaves in conjunction with trusted slaves or left naming up to them entirely. There is no indication of this so-called seasoning practice in Saudi Arabia.

"lived like beasts, that they were much better off as slaves, and that if he had his way he would take all (West African) pilgrims as his slaves, raising them thus out of their depraved state and turning them into happy, prosperous and civilised beings."[16] The names Blessed (Mabruk/a), Lucky (Bakhit/a), Comfort (Na'im), Relief (Faraj), and Good Luck (Sa'ad) indicate that other Saudi slave owners fully expected their slaves to be happy in their situations and probably considered African captives lucky to be enslaved on the Arabian Peninsula. Owners projected those expectations onto slaves through names.

These expectations and the positive names that went with them were consistent with 19th-century American theories of the "positive good" of plantation slavery and gives further support to Larry Tise's work on proslavery thought. Tise argues that "the notion that slavery could be a positive good for slaves and slave society appears in proslavery literature of all nations and in nearly all eras" (Tise 1987: 97).[17] Tise's analysis of proslavery literature from a variety of regions and over a century indicates "that the proslavery argument or rather arguments were virtually the same wherever one found slaveholding on the defensive" (ibid.: 10). The concept of slavery, anywhere in the world, was being questioned and attacked in Europe during the 19th and 20th centuries. Middle Eastern slavery was certainly scrutinized in orientalist literature and threatened by the British who manumitted slaves throughout the Arabian Peninsula.

Thise includes a discussion of the religious arguments for seeing slavery as a positive good. A century before Ibn Saud made his feelings known to Ihsanullah, Reverend Richard Furman made a parallel argument that Africans enslaved in South Carolina "have their situation bettered by being brought here & held as Slaves, when used as the Scriptures direct" (Furman, quoted in Tise 1987: 40). Half a world apart an American Christian minister and Saudi Muslim king expressed the same thoughts that African slaves' conversions to monotheistic world religions made slavery a happy, uplifting experience.

European orientalist literature, both pro- and antislavery, coupled with the portrait of slavery painted by Ottoman officials gave birth to the enduring image of benign slavery in the Middle East and the notion that it was incomparable

---

16 F.O. 403/460 Confidential Print Africa. Africa and Slave Trade. Correspondence Part I. Mr. Bond to A. Henderson (enclosure, 14), 6 March 1930. The Indian Vice Consul Ihsanullah, a Muslim who spoke to the King on the evils of slavery, reported this.

17 Cf. Finkelman (2003: 1-44) for more on the various defenses of slavery employed by southerners in the US.

with Atlantic slavery.[18] Both literatures used arguments of positive good that are also found in the pre-emancipation Americas. The Dutchman C. Snouck Hurgronje makes the following observations about Africans enslaved in Mecca.

"The thousands of negroes and Abysinnians who have been carried off into Moslim [sic] lands and there remember their earlier life consider themselves as made into men by slavery: all are contented, and not one wishes to return to his native land." (1970 [1888-9]: 19)

Charles Doughty, a late 19th-century traveler and writer, expressed anti-slavery opinions, but also wrote that "[slaves] can say 'It was his grace' since they be thereby entered into the saving religion [...] for such do they give God thanks that their bodies were sometimes sold into slavery!" (1936: 605). Doughty argued that slaves' contentment was one of the worst aspects of Middle Eastern slavery. Even an enemy of slavery held notions about Africans that coincided with the proslavery image of the happy slave who felt lucky to be enslaved by followers of the god of Abraham.

The contented slave on the Arabian Peninsula was no doubt a composite of European authors' own observations, mixed with what Ehud Toledano has termed the "amplification" of *kul*/harem slavery by 19th century Ottoman officials, and the opinions of Middle Eastern slave owners with whom Europeans interacted. The Ottoman *Tanzimat* period produced this amplification as a defense of slavery in a Turkish Muslim empire that was trying to prove itself a modern society capable of reform. As members of the elite, *Tanzimat* officials were slaveholders themselves and portrayed slavery in the empire as mostly an elite affair that involved: pampered women in the harem; clever perfumed eunuchs creating court intrigue; or strong, well-fed lazy *janissary* soldiers who did not want to fight but still reaped the spoils of war and military life.

This notion of the fortunate *kul*/harem slave is ubiquitous in various academic circles. Balkan parents begging for their children to be taken as slaves in order to have a better life is given as the proof that slavery in the Ottoman controlled world of the Middle East was a benevolent institution. However, as Toledano (1993) points out, the bulk of work performed by slaves and most slaves themselves were domestic and agricultural slaves whose patterns of subordination were quite different from *kul*/harem slaves. Toledano argues that

---

18 Cf. Toledano (1993) for more on Ottoman "amplification" of benign *kul* (slaves in the empire's military and administration) and harem slavery and "deletion" of domestic and agricultural slavery as a reaction to European abolitionism.

British abolitionists made a strategic mistake by lumping all slaves together in their quest to abolish Ottoman slavery. This article argues that academics make the same mistake when analyzing slavery in the Middle East. This research focuses on the lives and work of slaves engaged in lowly, domestic and manual labor in close proximity to their owners and their owners' demands, control, and punishment not the sexual services of the vast harem, the administrative plotting of eunuchs or the rewards of successful military service.

The difference in the physical spaces in which slave work occurred in the Peninsula and the Americas probably further differentiated for Europeans slavery in the two regions. In the Americas the work of slavery could be more readily seen or read about in abolitionist literature. Slaves toiled in fields under the crack of a driver's whip, whip marks could be seen on the exposed bodies of working slaves, and illustrations of bizarrely forged iron implements for punishing slaves were referred to in owners' diaries as well as anti-slavery tracts. But the work (and punishment) of slaves in the Middle East was within households, not visible to most visiting Europeans. Slaves were certainly on the streets and in fields but most of their interaction with owners and other authority figures most likely took place in the home, not out in public.

Though authors on Middle Eastern slavery differ in their nationalities, eras, and support of slavery, the one thing all these observers had in common was the power and privilege of being free, educated, elite, mostly male, and in some cases slave holders. This similarity seems to indicate that many of these opinions about the nature of African enslavement in these various contexts tell historians little about the actual conditions, circumstances, and workings of slavery and much more about the nature of power and propaganda in slave societies.

There are also indications that slave owners' expectations and stereotypes about Africans from different regions may have affected naming practices. Bushra was the name for two slave women, one from French Equatorial Africa (the Ouaddaï region of eastern Chad).[19] Good omen may denote that owners, like others on the early 20th century Arabian Peninsula, believed that women of African descent had healing powers associated with spirit possession cults such as *zar* and *bori, zar* coming from East Africa and *bori* from West Africa. While both regions provided ritual experts in these cults, West African *bori* adepts still travel to Mecca and Medina during hajj season and report being sought after as healers for Saudi women suffering from mysterious illnesses that biomedical

---

19 REMAP #139, REMAP #191. The second Bushra could not be associated with a specific woman's narrative; she may have been from Ouaddaï, Ethiopia, or the Sudan.

doctors have failed to cure.[20] More research is warranted but the two West African Bushras may indicate a preference for West African *bori* practices among the women of Saudi Arabia.

Johar was the name given to three slave men, all were most likely from Ethiopia and all were definitely commercial workers including a "shop boy" and a sailor.[21] Only three out of ten Ethiopians reported being commercial workers, so it seems significant that all Johars had similar slave work experiences and may have shared a country of origin. All three being named Jewel may suggest that they had the classic Ethiopian light skin color and slim features which many Arabs considered beautiful.[22] The name could also indicate that many slaves were to be used in the jewelry trade – either in jewelry shops or on pearl diving boats. Pearl diving was a trade rife with slaves.

The fact that slave women had more common Arabic names may indicate that slave women were performing similar roles as free women in families; beauty is expected of concubines and hoped for in wives; wives, sisters, mothers, and slaves are given the tasks of keeping a peaceful home, raising happy children, and pleasing husbands. Unlike the Americas there were no laws restricting Arab men from marrying their slaves and status was inherited from the father so lives of slave women had the potential to more closely parallel those of free Arab women. However, it appears that like the Americas most slave women did work and inhabited spaces not attempted by free Arab women. Slave women went out in public to carry water and washing to urban households and performed agricultural work in rural areas. The narratives are not explicit on exactly what jobs women had in agriculture or how they were expected to dress and act when out in the city. During this time Arab women became veiled and more secluded as Ibn Sa'ud and his Wahhabi supporters gained more control of

---

20 Cf. Toledano (2007: 204-254) for more on the creolization of the two spirit possession traditions; Doumato (2000: 170-184) for the practice of spirit possession healing in Arabia, Bahrain and Kuwait associated with Sudanese and Ethiopian women; O'Brien (1999: 29) for more on the role of Nigerian women in 20th-century Saudi Arabia.

21 One Johar was among four men who reported to the Legation together, whose information was clumped together, and who were repatriated together. Their individual information cannot be matched with certainty to their names, but all reported being commercial workers of some type and one was Ethiopian.

22 Fair (2001: 94-95) gives an example of 'Arab' standards of beauty by quoting an elite man from the Arab-dominated Swahili coast who described long thin noses and straight hair as marks of beauty and Miran (2013: 138) comments on concubines from Ethiopia as being sought after in Arabia.

what became the 1932 Saudi state. It is clear from narratives of runaway women that they saw being a slave and being a wife as markedly different, but from naming practices and documentary evidence it appears that males - Arab owners and British officials, may have perceived a smaller difference.[23]

Regardless of the meanings of the names it is clear that the act of renaming itself, both on the Arabian Peninsula and in the Americas, was an attempt by slave owners to strip Africans of their former identity, especially African men who had formerly known freedom. The men named Murjan help build the case that owners had used certain slave names for at least two generations. One man was renamed Murjan but two men who had been born to enslaved parents had the moniker ibn Murjan (son of Murjan).

In the Americas some slaves remembered their original African names as a form of protest and resistance: the most famous but fictionalized example being Kunta Kinte's resistance of his slave name Toby (Haley 1976: 180-181, 183, 216).[24] Saudi slaves' use of their original names in their manumission narratives (their official record of running away and becoming free) mirrors the Atlantic form of slave protest.

LABOR ASSIGNMENTS

The experiences of the fugitive slaves in Saudi Arabia confirms Gaspar's notion that slaves' work heavily influenced the terms of their subordination. Statistical tests found that slaves' jobs affected and interacted with many aspects of their lives: their work helped determine how many years they were enslaved, patterned the number of owners they had, and were factors in their reasons for running away.[25] Gender and country of origin also influenced what occupation slaves plied.[26] Fugitive slaves reported 19 different occupations.[27] In order to

---

23 Swidler (2003: 343-356) makes similar observations about the perception gap in late 19th-century Balochistan.
24 Cf. Gaspar (1985: 132) for analysis of this form of slave protest.
25 The chi-square test results were as follows: labor assignment and number of years enslaved (n = 117, $X2 = 11.89$, df = 2, $p < .01$); labor assignment and number of owners (n = 122, $X2 = 9.44$, df = 4, $p < .06$); and labor assignment and reasons for running away (n = 65, $X2 = 22.78$, df = 6, $p < .001$).
26 Gender and labor assignment (n = 221, $X2 = 41.82$, df = 2, $p < .001$) and country of origin and labor assignment (n = 217, $X2 = 14.88$, df = 8, $p < .07$).

conduct statistical tests these 19 trades were categorized as domestic, agricultural, or commercial labor.[28] Occupations are recorded for 221 fugitives, 101 were domestic laborers (46%), 71 were commercial labor (32%), and 49 were agricultural workers (22%).

Table 1: Labor Assignment and Country of Origin[29]

Type of labor	Agricultural		Commercial		Domestic		Total	
	n =	%	n =	%	n =	%	n =	%
Ethiopia	9	19	25	35	39	39.5	73	34
French Equatorial Africa	4	9	6	9	6	6	16	7
Nigeria	3	6	10	14	5	5	18	8
Sudan	29	62	29	41	43	43.5	101	47
Yemen	2	4	1	1	6	6	9	4
Total	47	100	71	100	99	100	217	100

Table 1 shows that Ethiopians were utilized as domestic slaves, Nigerian slaves worked in commerce, and Sudanese people made up the bulk of agricultural slaves. Perhaps stereotypes or prior experience operated to channel slaves from certain countries into certain jobs, which was the case for slaves laboring in the New World.[30]

---

27 The categories were domestic, agricultural labourer or labourer, camel driver, chauffeur, concubine, milkboy, miller, pearl diver, porter, sailor, shepherd, shop boy, soldier, stone cutter, water carrier, bodyguard, washer woman, and motor driver.
28 Domestic, chauffeur, and concubine were categorized as domestic labor. Agricultural labourer or labourer, milkboy, and shepherd were deemed agricultural labor. Camel driver, miller, pearl diver, porter, sailor, shop boy, soldier, stonecutter, water carrier, washerwoman, bodyguard, and motor driver were considered commercial labor.
29 This table originally appeared in Hutson (2002: 64), but has been modified here by putting washerwoman in commercial instead of agricultural labor. All subsequent references to tables from this article reflect this modification.
30 Even though Ethiopians were 34% of the table, they were only 19% of agricultural workers. Ethiopians were, in fact, twice as likely to work as domestic laborers as agricultural workers. Nigerians were only a small percentage of the sample (8%) but they were over-represented (15%) in the commercial labor sector. Conversely, Sudanese people were 62% of agricultural workers but only 47% of the sample.

There is evidence of planters in the New World employing slaves in different jobs based on ethnicity. David Geggus observed that sugar and coffee plantation owners had preferences for slaves from different "nations" in Africa depending on stereotypes about their average height, agricultural traditions, experience with livestock, perceived common health problems, etc. (Geggus 1993: 79-84 and 86-88). Planters in the Americas also looked at slaves' diets in their homelands (including whether they were supposed cannibals), purported temperament, and the attractiveness of a nation's women.[31] In Brazil, the Yoruba who built large cities in West Africa were put to work in urban areas like Salvador (Schwartz 1985: 475). The Fulbe were often employed to take care of livestock (Geggus 1993: 88). Africans who grew rice in their African homeland were sought by owners in South Carolina in order to make New World rice cultivation successful (Littlefield 1981: 135).

Again more research must be done to conclusively establish the reason for the job patterns of slaves in Arabia, however there are some clues. As West Africans, Nigerians are part of a long history of commercial interactions with Arabs in North Africa and across the Red Sea. Trans-Saharan trade routes from Northern Nigeria, Ghana and Mali to Mediterranean ports and cities have been documented since the tenth century (Bovill 1995: 61). And West Africans have used those routes and one through the Sudan to make the pilgrimage to Mecca and Medina. West Africans are still known today for amassing wealth and prestige by conducting commerce while on hajj (cf. Rosander 1997; O'Brien (1999: 12, 31). In the 19th and early 20th centuries West Africans had reputations for even selling their children. However, looking at a few Nigerian fugitive slaves reinforces their penchant for commerce and negates the idea they sold their own children.

After the death of his father in Nigeria, Adam bin Mohammed went on *hajj* with his Quranic teacher at the age of fourteen. In Jeddah his teacher sold him into slavery. Adam became part of the commercial system in Saudi Arabia when he was sold to a Bedouin camel man and began working in the Bedouin's business.[32] As a commercial worker Adam lived in Bahra, a town on the road from Jeddah to the commercial center of Saudi Arabia, Mecca.

As with others enslaved as preteens and teenagers, Adam could remember something of his home and family. Though renamed Mabruk, Adam gave the British Legation officers his real name and the names of his cousins, mother, and

---

31 For more on how ethnic stereotypes effected planters buying and employing preferences see Littlefield (1981: 13-17) and Debien (1974: 41-52).
32 REMAP #3.

his town. One can imagine that these were pieces of information that Adam and other captives would try to engrave in their memories, hoping to hang onto something of their homeland and to use them in order to have any chance to find their way home.

Adam had two sets of owners, though one set appears to have been slave dealers who owned him only in transit.[33] Like the transatlantic slave trade in West Africa it appears that slaves in Saudi Arabia could be traded several times before reaching the place where they would live and work. Once firmly entrenched in the house of an owner, slaves were not necessarily there for life. The data shows that an average slave had three owners during twenty-two years of captivity. Seven to ten years is often given as the common length of enslavement in the Ottoman Empire and throughout the Arab Muslim world. It is not attached to *Sharia* or Sunna, but rather "Ottoman social practice" (Toledano 2009: 14).

Khadija bint Gummiog had the average number of owners but under different circumstances. She was not sold but inherited and was a slave before she came to Saudi Arabia. She was presumably on her way from Nigeria to Mecca with her Nigerian owner, when he died in the Kordofan in Sudan.[34] She was subsequently inherited by another member of his family and brought to Jeddah, where her second owner died. Another family member then inherited her. Like Adam, she too was a commercial worker. Khadija was like a few other West African women engaged in commercial labor who were "sent out to work, [...] as water-sellers who parade the street balancing a petrol-tinfull [sic] of water on their heads."[35] Saudi slave owners also hired out slave women's labor in other trades that required mobility such as washerwomen.[36]

West Africans reportedly sold their children while on hajj, but data from Saudi runaways indicate that parents and relatives did not sell their children on hajj. Instead the children who got sold were vulnerable children, like Adam who no longer had the protection of fathers or poor children like Khadija who were already servants or slaves in wealthier households. Only one man from French West Africa, Jaber ibn Muhammad, reported being sold as a child by a relative,

---

33 For Adam, and all slaves the first slave dealer they were sold to, was not counted as an owner unless the dealer kept and worked the slave for more than a few months.

34 REMAP #262, Khadija's story is also discussed in Hutson, "Enslavement and Manumission," 58-59. Khadija is actually described as a "Takruni Fellata" which was the way the British in Saudi Arabia usually described someone from Nigeria.

35 F.O. 905/11, Memorandum on Slavery in Saudi Arabia 1934.

36 The two washerwomen in this study were both from Ethiopia.

his uncle. Certainly children might not have been aware of all the circumstances which preceded their journeys to Saudi Arabia, or their parents' dealings while on hajj and the fugitives who reported being captured while on hajj with their parents may have been the victims of their parents' financial circumstances. However, the narratives cannot be used to support the prevalence of this practice. Instead, there are at least three poignant stories of parents who hoped to find their children and looked for years, over a decade, supporting fugitive narratives of being stolen. These mothers and fathers employed the British colonial governments where they lived, friends and relatives traveling and living in Saudi, Saudi *shariah* courts and returned to Saudi Arabia several times themselves to track down and finally reunite with their then adult children.[37] The narratives from Adam, Khadija, and Jaber also make it clear that West Africans resident in Saudi Arabia were very much involved in the enslaving and trading of Africans in Saudi Arabia, just not their own children.

Sudan is part of the agricultural tradition of the Nile Valley. It was during the early 20th century that many Sudanese agricultural workers were employed on the Gezira cotton scheme between the Blue and White branches of the Nile. Raising crops near the desert, the Sudanese would have been accustomed to a similarly hot arid desert climate. These characteristics may have made the Sudanese valued agricultural workers. One such agricultural slave was Rizgullah, a Sudanese man in his early thirties. Kidnapped as a child from the Nuba Mountains by a West African he served for two years under his first owner in Jeddah. Rizgullah was then sold to a Bedouin in a rural area where he spent the majority of his captivity as an agricultural worker, probably for over 20 years.[38] His owner treated him badly, so he ran away one day. It took him two days to make his way to Jeddah. His owner was called to the Legation and he

---

37 REMAP #244 tells the story of Rogaya and her father and REMAP #246 Bakur and his mother. F.O. 902/28 3 February 1934 and F.O. 905/61 7 July 1938 appear to chronicle the attempts of one father Abdul Qader to trace his son Muhammad. The first file lists the surname of the father as Housani and places his son's kidnapping sometime between 1914 and 1917. The second file, which tells of the father's final success in locating his son, gives the father's name as Abdul Qader Mohamed Hausawi and the date as 1344 AH (1925). This first attempt was reported to the Legation by Abdul Qader's sister and may account for the difference in dates. This case was only counted once in the data as REMAP #261.

38 REMAP #226 Rizgullah did not report an approximate age for his enslavement, but most were enslaved at a median age of 7 and therefore at 32 with only one owner beforehand, Rizgullah spent approximately twenty-three years with his second owner.

said he liked Rizgullah and apparently valued him enough to offer Rizgullah freedom certified in *shariah* court and work as a free man.[39] Rizgullah refused to return under any circumstances, presumably because of the past ill treatment and probably because living as a manumitted slave in Saudi Arabia was very close to living in slavery. He was repatriated to the Sudan.

WOMEN, COUNTRY AND LABOR

Most enslaved women were engaged in domestic labor in Saudi Arabia,[40] however, table 2 shows that country of origin was even more keenly significant among women. European slave owners in the Americas considered women from Cape Verde, Sierra Leone, and Guinea to be "comely of body", Sudanese women were "pleasing concubines" (Freyre 1966: 302-303) and all were employed in domestic occupations; the data indicates that Saudi Arabians may have had the same perceptions of Ethiopian women, considering them beautiful in part because of their straight features. These stereotypes may have been a major cause for Ethiopian women predominately having domestic jobs – including concubinage.[41]

Only two women, both Ethiopian, were described in the data set specifically as concubines. However, several other women's narratives make it clear they were concubines or domestics to whom their owners had sexual access. The narratives are unclear on how concubinage worked; if it was primarily for the sexual pleasure of owners, the production of children for his lineage or both; and whether it was interconnected with other domestic duties.[42] British officials also note that some domestic slaves were "often of a special character and used for

---

39 In his study of South Carolina, Littlefield (1981: 126) found that Gambians were "more highly represented among runaways than among imports, [...] which strongly suggests that their agricultural skills were sufficiently desirable to counterbalance their tendency to run." It seems Rizugullah's owner was willing to make the same trade off to keep a valuable agricultural worker.

40 F.O. 905/11, Memorandum on Slavery in Saudi Arabia 1934.

41 This was also true for the two Yemeni women in the test. Yemeni women from the other side of the Bab el Mandeb from Ethiopia would be even lighter-skinned. They were both domestics.

42 F.O. 403/460, 12 British officials believed it was the latter, stating that women slaves were wives and servants to poor Arabs without the means to marry a "regular wife."

immoral purposes," which made settling their cases "by no means simple."[43] The amplification of benign slavery often indicates that being a slave wife or child of a slave mother held no shame or disadvantage in a family. However domestic slave women's narratives include stories of forced abortion, refusal to acknowledge children and beatings from women in the owner's household. Apparently some Arab men or their kinswomen did not wish to have children born of slave women.[44]

Table 2: Women's Labor Assignments and Country of Origin[45]

Type of labor	Agricultural		Commercial		Domestic		Total	
	n =	%	n =	%	n =	%	n =	%
Ethiopia	0	0	2	40	14	35	16	33
French Equatorial Africa	1	25	1	20	2	5	4	8
Nigeria	0	0	2	40	2	5	4	8
Sudan	3	75	0	0	20	50	23	47
Yemen	0	0	0	0	2	5	2	4
Total	4	100	5	100	40	100	49	100

LABOR AND PATTERNS OF SUBORDINATION

The narratives in combination with statistical tests also give us insight into how the jobs African slaves worked in Saudi Arabia led to diverse patterns of subordination: agricultural slaves were enslaved longer than other slaves and ill treated, but they were more likely to have one owner; commercial workers appeared to have more skills than other slaves and therefore to be more viable as free people. As Toledano noted of slaves in 19th century Ottoman territories, not all slaves were similarly situated, some like these runaway commercial workers in Saudi Arabia had the language and labor skills to navigate the social terrain and earn enough to provide shelter, food and clothing for themselves (Toledano 2009: 17). In 1920s and 30s Saudi Arabia commercial slaves were most

---

43 F.O. 967/1, 13 February 1926.
44 Cf. Altorki (1986: 144) on how women of elite Saudi Arabian families do not see children of slave mothers as desirable or equal in families' marriage strategies.
45 (n=49, $X2 =15.37$, df=8, p<.05)

threatened by sale to another owner. Women were more likely to be domestics and had less viability as free autonomous persons. They opted for local manumission instead of repatriation. These findings are reflected in the reasons commercial and agricultural slaves gave for running away. Table 3 shows that Rizgullah's story of ill treatment was typical for agricultural workers. In fact, 93 percent of runaway slaves in agricultural work cited ill treatment as the reason they had fled. Despite the fact that they appeared to be property whom owners valued highly and kept for longer periods than others, agricultural slaves' value did not improve the treatment they received.[46]

Table 3: Labor Assignment and Reason for Running Away[47]

Type of labor	Agricultural		Commercial		Domestic		Total	
	n =	%	n =	%	n =	%	n =	%
Family reasons	0	0	4	16	2	8	6	9
Free status threatened	1	7	4	16	4	16	9	14
Ill-treatment	14	93	7	28	13	52	34	52
Sale	0	0	10	40	6	24	16	25
Total	15	100	25	100	25	100	65	100

Statistical tests also showed that slaves of Sudanese origin like Abdul Kheyr Said were more likely to be born to slave parents in Saudi Arabia than slaves of other countries. Of course being born slaves they were enslaved on average longer than others – a median of 30 years. Abdul Kheyr Said was a 35-year-old man whose slave parents, both from Sudan, had both died. Abdul Kheyr Said had recently married and lost his father. He ran away because his owner was poorly feeding him and his wife. Abdul Kheyr Said only reported having the one owner, probably that of his parents.[48] His story illustrates the finding that those born a slave in Saudi Arabia were more likely to have one owner than those captured for the Saudi market.

---

46 See Hutson (2002: 65) for more on the value of agricultural slaves in Saudi Arabia.
47 ($n = 65$, $X2 = 21.40$, $df = 6$, $p < .002$). This table originally appeared in Hutson (2002: 66).
48 REMAP #232.

Table 4: Status and Country of Origin[49]

Status	Born a slave in Saudi Arabia		Enslaved elsewhere		Captured for Saudi market		Total	
	n =	%	n =	%	n =	%	n =	%
Ethiopia	2	8.5	1	11	78	37.5	81	33.5
French Equatorial Africa	0	0	2	22.25	15	7	17	7
Nigeria	1	4	2	22.25	15	7	18	7.5
Sudan	20	83.5	2	22.25	95	45.5	117	48
Yemen	1	4	2	22.25	6	3	9	4
Total	24	100	9	100	209	100	242	100

On a comparative basis, agricultural laborers were 3.7x more likely than commercially utilized slaves to give ill treatment as a reason for running away. Commercial workers were more likely than domestic or agricultural workers to leave their owners because of an impending sale. Abdul Kheyr, a 25-year-old camel driver, ran away from his owner, Meccan slave dealer Abdulla Gari, in 1935.[50] Abdul Kheyr had tried to run away three years before, but he had been apprehended by the Jeddah police and sent back to Mecca.[51] His reason for running the first time is not recorded. However, on his second attempt, Abdul Kheyr cited his imminent sale to Amir Abdullah, the brother of King Ibn Saud and a man with a reputation for cruelty to his slaves. Abdul Kheyr's story shows that sale was a gamble for commercial slaves; their circumstances and treatment would change with their new owners, perhaps for the worst like Abdul Kheyr's

---

49 (n=242, X2 =27.83, df=8, p <.001). Note for the category "Enslaved elsewhere": These people served as slaves in other countries before traveling to Saudi Arabia in the caravans of pilgrims and travelers. European travelers described these people as slaves sold as "traveller's checks" to help pay for their owner's stay in Saudi Arabia or return home.

50 REMAP #241. Abdul Kheyr's story is also discussed in Hutson (2002: 66).

51 Petrushevsky (1985 [1966]: 157) notes that *shariah* provides a sort of fugitive slave law. Fugitive slaves had to be arrested and returned to their owner. Saudi Arabia had a specific fugitive slave law based on this *shariah* concept. Al-Nawawi (1975: 296) includes a *hadith* chronicled by Muslim and related by Jabir that prohibits a slave from running away from his owner.

case. His commercial skills may have emboldened him, and his actions may denote that commercial slaves knew they had skills that made their freedom viable.

Women's viability in freedom in Saudi Arabia or Africa was more in doubt. Living in a patriarchal, family-oriented society as a single woman with no patron or family and only domestic experience was not ideal for Saudi Arabia and not realistic for repatriation to Africa. Furthermore/Besides, most of these women only had a knowledge of Arabic and their owner's families. These doubts and societal conditions may have limited the number of women who sought refuge at the legation and led many runaway women without husbands (or without their husbands) or adult children to request local manumission.[52]

Children, the natural results of slave marriage or concubinage, also limited and shaped women's choices. Table 5 shows that although women were only 37 percent of the table,[53] they represented 75 percent of those locally manumitted. Hasina bint Hamad, an Ethiopian woman enslaved in Jeddah, ran away with her son, Bashir, and requested local manumission "for the sake of her son."[54] For concubines or slave women who had children with free Arab men in their owner's households, children were significant obstacles to repatriation. Unlike the Americas, Islamic codes of law based children's status on their paternity, so one could have a slave mother and free Muslim father and still be born free. However, slave women were only allowed to keep their freeborn children with them until the age of seven, at the latest (Petrushevsky 1985 [1966]: 156-157). The Saudi government acted several times throughout this period to stop the British from removing children of free Saudi fathers from the country/Saudi Arabia. So slave women with freeborn children also chose local manumission for the sake of their children.

---

52 Most scholarship on slavery indicates that more African women than men were sold into the trans-Saharan and other slave trades bound for the Arab Muslim world (Cf. Austen 1979: 44; Robertson/Klein 1983: 4). Yet, in the Saudi Arabian statistics, men outnumbered women 2.64 to 1. Women accounted for 27.5 percent of those who sought refuge at the British Legation (n = 72), whereas men were 72.5 percent (n = 190). While women appear to be underrepresented, the number of women who ran away is a significant one and gives a female perspective on slavery.

53 The table has statistics for the 103 runaways for whom there is documentation of the outcome of their bid for freedom.

54 REMAP #213.

Table 5: Gender and result of bid for freedom[55]

	Women			Men			Total	
	n =	% of women	% of result	n =	% of men	% of result	n =	%
Free person with safety issues	1	3	33	2	3	67	3	3
Left without manumission	2	5	25	6	9.25	75	8	8
Local manumission	18	47	75	6	9.25	25	24	23
Manumitted and repatriated	17	45	25	51	78.5	75	68	66
Total	38	100	37	65	100	63	103	100

In fact, table 5 shows that gender significantly affected how slaves acted once they reached the legation. Women were 5.13x more likely to be locally manumitted than men, and men were 1.75x more likely to leave the legation without manumission or to be manumitted and repatriated than women.

REPATRIATION AND FUGITIVE SLAVE LAWS

These statistics seem to indicate that both women and men slaves in Saudi Arabia engaged in what Gabriel Debien (1966: 3-44) described as *petit marronage* that is, they used running away as a strategy to negotiate better treatment. Debien also details permanent forms of running away such as *grand marronage* or the construction of independent African maroon communities. In another article I have argued that local manumission was a form of *petit marronage*, a negotiation tactic for slaves in Saudi Arabia. Although there were no maroon communities described in the Saudi data, here I analyze repatriation, the permanent way out of slavery open to those slaves. Edward Alpers (2003: 59) has described this kind of running away as "an important intermediary point

---

55 (n=103, X2 =19.34, df=3, p<.001). Free person with safety issues indicates ex-slaves whose lives or freedom were threatened by their owners or others. This table will also appear in Hutson (forthcoming).

along the continuum from *petit marronage* to *grand marronage*." John Thornton (1998: 273) has described African background (if slaves had lived in Africa) or culture (in part determined by their ethnicity and country of origin) as important in determining if slaves in the Americas would attempt to permanently run away. On the whole, the pattern for the Saudi data is for the locally manumitted who were threatened with resale, Sudanese runaways (primarily men working in agriculture outside the cities), and unaccompanied young children to engage in repatriation. Again table 5 and table 6 below are instructive for establishing these patterns.

Rizgullah's story illustrates the plight of Sudanese agricultural runaways and Saudi Arabia's establishment of fugitive slave laws and measures. Once Rizgullah ran away and arrived in the city, he experienced the measures the Saudi Government took to apprehend runaway slaves. Four policemen chased him into the Italian Legation by accident, where one policeman hit him with a stone before the legation staff expelled the police. Other runaways who were caught by the Saudi police were given short prison sentences and then returned to their owners. Under a Saudi fugitive slave law any one could apprehend a runaway slave in order to return him or her to enslavement.[56] The Italian Legation helped Rizgullah find his way to the British and eventually freedom, because the British were the only Europeans who drafted rights of manumission into their treaties with the Saudi government.

Rizgullah and Abdul Kheyr's stories make clear that Ibn Saud and the Saudi Arabian Government had implemented a fugitive slave law. British Legation officials also noted that along a major road from Mecca to Jeddah there were Saudi police patrols which frequently stopped public transportation to search for escaping slaves. British officials and travelers found that the Saudi public and local officials were also part of efforts to counter the threat of grand marronage posed by British manumission and repatriation of slaves: along the Mecca-Jeddah road village officials had been ordered to "watch all cars […] and to keep a strict eye on all pedestrians" for escaped slaves and Saudis were to notify local officials upon discovering a runaway.[57] Local Saudi officials were charged with arresting and returning slaves to their owners (Thomas 1931).

---

56 Petrushevsky (1985 [1966]: 157) notes that this Saudi law was in step with the *shari'a* which provides for fugitive slaves to be arrested and returned to their owner.
57 F.O. 905/28, 2 July 1935.

Table 6: Country of origin and result of bid for freedom[58]

	Free persons with safety issues		Left without manumission		Local manumission		Manumitted and repatriated		Total	
	n	%	n	%	n	%	n	%	n	%
Ethiopia	0	0	4	50	13	62	20	29.5	37	37.5
French Equatorial Africa	0	0	0	0	0	0	1	1.5	1	1
Nigeria	1	50	2	25	0	0	8	12	11	11
Sudan	0	0	2	25	5	24	39	57	46	46.5
Yemen	1	50	0	0	3	14	0	0	4	4
Total	2	100	8	100	21	100	68	100	99	100

Not only were newly runaway slaves in Saudi Arabia threatened with the fugitive slave law and re-enslavement, several freed Africans who were repatriated made the mistake of setting foot back on the Arabian Peninsula and had to run to freedom again. Three men reported their misfortune in encountering ex-owners unexpectedly. An Ethiopian seaman had the rotten luck to come face-to-face with his former owner in 1926 in the port of Rabegh. As a result, his owner reclaimed him and immediately sold him.[59] Aman Ibn Hassan was equally cursed in a port outside of Saudi Arabia.[60] As a slave, the fifty-year-old Ethiopian man was an agriculturalist. After running to freedom and repatriation in 1929 Aman took up work as a seaman on a dhow. In early 1935 his ex-owner just happened to be buying grain at the same Yemeni port where Aman's ship had docked. His owner recognized him and had Yemeni soldiers seize him. Jaber Ahmed, a Sudanese domestic, had been enslaved while on hajj in 1908 at the age of twenty-six.[61] He escaped, was freed and repatriated to Sudan in 1927. Jaber attempted once more to perform the hajj as a freeman in 1937. Though he was an employee of the British government in Sudan and on a

---

58 (n=99, $X2 = 33.65$, df=12, p <.001). This table will also appear in Hutson (forthcoming).
59 REMAP #12.
60 REMAP #246.
61 REMAP #69, also referred to as Gaber Ahmed.

legitimate Sudanese passport he was identified by his old owner and seized by the Saudi police. Their refusal to accept the terms of the Treaty and British manumission rights probably stemmed from financial self-interest but was Islamically upheld as well by a *hadith* (saying of the Prophet) that prohibits a slave from running away from his owner.[62]

Just as officials in American slave owning societies had to negotiate treaties in order to stop other European and Native American communities from taking in runaways, a stronger Saudi Government negotiated a new treaty with the United Kingdom in 1936. Because Ibn Saud had solidified his control of the peninsula he insisted on rescinding Section 7 of the old treaty.[63] Britain acquiesced on the condition that the king would promulgate and enforce a thorough set of regulations that was to slowly choke off the institution of slavery by stopping the importation of slaves and assuring the welfare of those already enslaved while they waited to be manumitted on their owners' initiatives or die.[64]

After the end of manumission in 1936, it is clear that Africans know the Saudis and British have closed the path to manumission and repatriation. Only two African cases were documented at the Jeddah Legation after 1936. It is clear from their stories and subsequent British inquires that the Saudi slave regulations are not widely known or followed. Jaber Ahmed's aforementioned case of re-enslavement provides an example that even the Saudi police did not follow the 1936 regulations. Jaber experienced the full gamut of British-Saudi relations regarding slavery. Immediately before the Treaty of Jeddah was signed he escaped to the Legation where the British had been manumitting slaves for years. He was manumitted and repatriated. He returned to perform his interrupted hajj on a passport issued by the British to shield its subjects from harm, but the Saudi police confiscated his passport and when Jaber refused to return to his supposed owner they imprisoned him for four months. Despite the facts of the case and the laws of the land, when Jaber's wife asked for him to be released through the British Legation the Saudi Government's first response was that slaves and slavery were no longer a British concern. The British did press the case by pointing out the Saudi Government's new regulations and the understanding that

---

62 Muslim: Kitab al-Iman, Bab Tasmiyyat al abd al-abiq kafiran. Cited from Nawawi no. 347.

63 Oil was not actually found in Saudi Arabia until 1938, but oil had been found in the region and oil concessions had been negotiated by 1936.

64 F.O. 905/27 Embassy and Legation, Saudi Arabia: General Correspondence. Slaves: manumission: general question: Draft Saudi Regulation on Slavery, 19 July 1935.

had given birth to them, and nearly two years after his capture Jaber was set free by order of King Ibn Saud himself. Unfortunately his wife had passed away in the interim.[65]

Interestingly, children under the age of fifteen who ran away and did not accompany an adult family member were also repatriated.[66] All the children but one reported being enslaved in Jeddah.[67] No doubt an unaccompanied trip from a village a walk of a day or two away would be a hard task for a preteen or teenage to attempt and would be noticed by authorities and passersby. Most were domestic slaves, two of the Sudanese boys were water carriers.[68]

Again, it is unclear if and how the British made manumission decisions for children. One would think that as unaccompanied children repatriation would put them in a vulnerable position unless the British felt sure their parents could be found. The British did attempt to record the names of children's hometowns and as many relatives as possible on questionnaires before sending them on the boat across the Red Sea. Ex-slaves' typed questionnaires were their boat ticket and therefore arrived with them in Sudan or Ethiopia. British officials on the African side apparently took over ex-slaves cases. This shepherding of cases was most likely how Jaber Ahmed found gainful employment with the Condominium government in Kassala. British officials note the formation of Ethiopian ex-slave communities in Sudan and Ethiopian coffee-producing areas.[69] The British contributed to these communities by sending them escaped Ethiopian slaves. Slaves registered at Gedaraf, Sudan went to the Sudanese communities where work was found "without difficulty for the men and husbands for the unmarried women."[70] The documents directly state that repatriated slaves from Saudi

---

65 F.O. 905/62, 1 November 1938.
66 There were ten children under the age of 15 who came to the Legation without an adult and applied for manumission: four Ethiopians, four Sudanese, one Nigerian, and Faraj from Yemen. All were boys except one Ethiopian girl. Yemen was not considered a place for repatriation so Faraj was the only one locally manumitted.
67 One 12-year-old Sudanese boy who had worked as an agricultural laborer was from outside Jeddah - Wadi Fatma.
68 REMAP #34, #43, #46, #54, #67, #68, #178 and #227. REMAP #56 and #57 were the water carriers.
69 D.O. 35/169/4 Dominions Office and Commonwealth Relations Office: Original Correspondence, Slavery. 21 January 1928. There is no indication of how or by whom these communities were formed.
70 D.O. 35/169/4.

Arabia went to the coffee production areas in Ethiopia where work was plentiful. Perhaps the communities' efforts stretched to finding parents for minor children. There is no mention in the documents of ex-slave communities being started for Sudanese and West African refugees, but British officials whose jurisdiction included the villages and towns from which these children reported being stolen may have made further efforts for these children.

Conclusion

This research has shown that some Saudi owners seemed not to recognize repatriation as a permanent form of freedom or legitimate no matter the year it occurred. Their slaveholding practices such as naming, using stereotypes for work assignments, and one could argue having children with slave women were attempts to create and keep contented slaves and their labor. These slaveholding practices produced patterns of subordination similar to the enslaved in the Americas. This research also amends Gaspar's thesis by suggesting that owners' expectations and practices also help govern these patterns, not just the type of slave work. It shows that gender, nationality, and age profoundly affected how individual slaves experienced slavery and mapped out their choices about freedom.

References

Al-Nawawi, Muhyiddin (1975): Gardens of the Righteous, translated by Muhammad Zafrulla Khan, London: Curzon Press.
Alpers, Edward A. (2003): "Flight to Freedom: Escape from Slavery among Bonded Africans in the Indian Ocean world, c.1750–1962." In: Slavery & Abolition 24/2, pp. 51-68.
Altorki, Soraya (1986): Women in Saudi Arabia, New York: Columbia University Press.
Austen, Ralph (1979): "The Trans-Saharan Slave Trade: A Tentative Census." In: Henry A. Gemery/Jan S. Hogendorn (ed.), The Uncommon Market: Essays in the Economic History of the Atlantic Slave Trade, New York: Academic Press.
Bovill, Edward (1995): The Golden Trade of the Moors, Princeton: Marcus Weiner Publishers.

Debien, Gabriel (1974): Les esclaves aux Antilles francaises, Basse Terre: Société d'Histoire de la Guadeloupe.
—— (1966): "Le marronage aux Antilles française au XVIIIe siècle." In: Caribbean Studies 6, pp. 3-44.
Doughty, Charles (1936): Travels in Arabia Deserta. 2 Volumes, New York: Random House.
Doumato, Eleanor (2000): Getting God's Ear, New York: Columbia University Press.
Dunn, Richard S. (1972): Sugar and Slaves: The Rise of the Planter Class in the English West Indies, 1624-1713, Chapel Hill: University of North Carolina Press.
Erdem, Y. Hakan (2010): "Magic, Theft and Arson: The Life and Death of an Enslaved African Woman in Ottoman Izmit." In: Kenneth M. Cuno/Terence Walz (eds.), Race and Slavery in the Middle East: Histories of Trans-Saharan Africans in 19th Century: Egypt, Sudan, and the Ottoman Mediterranean, Cairo: American University in Cairo Press, pp. 125-46.
Fair, Laura (2001): Pastimes and Politics: Culture, Community, and Identity in Post-abolition Urban Zanzibar, 1890-1945, Athens: Ohio University Press.
Finkelman, Paul (2003): Defending Slavery: Proslavery Thought in the Old South, Boston: Bedford/St. Martin's.
Freyre, Gilberto (1966): The Masters and Slaves: A Study in the Development of Brazilian Civilization, New York: Alfred Knopf.
Frank, Alison (2012): "Children of the Desert and the Laws of the Sea: Austria, Great Britain, the Ottoman Empire, and the Mediterranean Slave Trade in the Nineteenth Century." In: The American Historical Review 117, pp. 410-444.
Gaspar, David Barry (1985): Bondmen and Rebels: A Study of Master-Slave Relations in Antigua, Baltimore: The Johns Hopkins University Press.
Geggus, David (1993): "Sugar and Coffee Cultivation in Saint Domingue and the Shaping of the Slave Labor Force." In: Ira Berlin/Philip D. Morgan (eds.), Cultivation and Culture: Labor and the Shaping of Slave Life in the Americas, Charlottesville: University Press of Virginia.
Gordon, Murray (1989): Slavery in the Arab World, New York: New Amsterdam Books.
Haley, Alex (1976): Roots, Garden City: Doubleday.
Hine, Darlene Clark/Hine, William C./Harrold, Stanley (2000): The African American Odyssey, Upper Saddle River: Prentice Hall.
Hopper, Matthew (2006): The African Presence in Arabia: Slavery, the World Economy, and the African Diaspora in Eastern Arabia, 1840-1940, PhD diss., University of California (UCLA).

Hurgronje, C. Snouck (1970 [1888-9]): Mekka in the Latter Part of the 19th Century, Leiden: E.J. Brill.

Hutson, Alaine S. (forthcoming): "REMAPping the African Diaspora: Place, Gender, and Negotiation in Arabian Slavery." In: Olajumoke Yacob-Haliso/Toyin Falola (eds.), Gendering Knowledge in Africa and the African Diaspora, Amherst: Cambria Press.

—— (2002): "Enslavement and Manumission in Saudi Arabia." In: Critique 11, pp. 49-70.

Lewis, Bernard (1990): Race and Slavery in the Middle East, New York: Oxford University Press.

Littlefield, Daniel (1981): Rice and Slaves: Ethnicity and the Slave Trade in Colonial South Carolina, Baton Rouge: Louisiana State University Press.

Miers, Suzanne (1989): "Diplomacy versus Humanitarianism: Britain and Consular Manumission in Hijaz, 1921–1936." In: Slavery & Abolition 10, pp. 102-28.

Miran, Jonathan (2013): "From Bondage to Freedom on the Red Sea Coast: Manumitted Slaves in Egyptian Massawa, 1873–1885." In: Slavery & Abolition 34/1, pp. 135-157.

Mullin, Michael (1992): Africa in America: Slave Acculturation and Resistance in the American South and British Caribbean, 1736-1831, Urbana: University of Illinois Press.

O'Brien, Susan (1999): "Pilgrimage, Power and Identity: The Role of the *Hajj* in the Lives of Nigerian Hausa *Bori* Adepts." In: Africa Today 46/1-2, pp.11-40.

Petrushevsky, I.P. (1985 [1966]): Islam in Iran, transl. by Hubert Evans, London: Athlone Press.

Philips, John Edward (1993): "Some recent thinking on slavery in Islamic Africa and the Middle East." In: Middle East Studies Association Bulletin 27, pp. 157-162.

Powell, Eve Troutt (2006): "Will the Subaltern Ever Speak? Finding African Slaves in the Historiography of the Middle East." In: Israel Gershoni/Amy Singer/Y. Hakan Erdem (eds.), Middle East Historiographies: Narrating the Twentieth Century, Seattle: University of Washington Press, pp. 242-261.

Robertson, Claire/Klein, Martin (1983): Women and Slavery in Africa, Madison: University of Wisconsin Press.

Rosander, Eva Evers (ed.) (1997): Transforming Female Identities: Women's Organizational Forms in West Africa, Uppsala: Nordiska Afrikainstitutet.

Schwartz, Stuart (1985): Sugar Plantations and the Formation of Brazilian Society, Cambridge: Cambridge University Press.

Simawe, Saadi (1999): "Color and Race in the Poetry of Black Poets in Arabic: A Comparative Study of Images of Blackness and Africanness in Arabic and African American Literature." Paper presented at "Slavery and the African Diaspora in the Lands of Islam." Northwestern University April 30-May 2, 1999.

Spivak, Gayatri (2010): "Can the subaltern speak?" In: Rosalind C. Morris (ed.), Can the subaltern speak?: Reflections of the History of an Idea, New York: Columbia University Press, pp. 21-80.

Swidler, Nina (2003): "On the Difficulty of Telling a Slave from a Wife." In: Carina Jahani/Agnes Korn (eds.), The Baloch and Their Neighbours: Ethnic and Linguistic Contact in Balochistan in Historical and Modern Times, Wiesbaden: Reichert, pp. 343-356.

Thomas, Bertram (1931): Alarms and Excursions in Arabia, Indianapolis: Bobbs-Merrill.

Thornton, John (1998): Africa and Africans in the Making of the Atlantic World, 1400-1800, Cambrigde: Cambridge University Press.

Tise, Larry (1987): Proslavery: A History of the Defense of Slavery in America, 1701-1840, Athens: The University of Georgia Press.

Toledano, Ehud (2009): "Bringing the Slaves Back." In: Benhaz Mirzai/Ibrahim Musah Montana/Paul Lovejoy (eds.), Slavery, Islam and Diaspora, Trenton: Africa World Press, pp. 7-20.

—— (2007): As If Silent and Absent: Bonds of Enslavement in the Islamic Middle East, New Haven: Yale University Press.

—— (1993): "Late Ottoman Concepts of Slavery (1830s-1880s)." In: Poetics Today 14, pp. 477-506.

Zdanowski, Jerzy (2013): Slavery and Manumission: British Policy in the Red Sea and the Persian Gulf in the First Half of the 20th Century, Ithaca: Ithaca Press.

Zilfi, Madeline C. (1997): Women in the Ottoman Empire: Middle Eastern women in the early Modern Era, Leiden: Brill.

Contract Labour and Debt Bondage in the Arab Gulf States. Policies and Practices within the *Kafala* System

SABINE DAMIR-GEILSDORF

Since the discovery of oil on the Arabian shore of the Gulf in the 1930s, the first oil-induced economic boom, and the compensation of the lack of human resources by imported labour, the Arab Gulf States have experienced a continual rise in the number of foreign workers. In particular, from the 1960s onwards, the influx of foreign workers – initially primarily from neighboring Arab countries, but, due to political reasons, in recent decades mostly from South and Southeast Asia – has increased.[1] According to a United Nations database of 2015, the six member states of the Gulf Cooperation Council (GCC), namely Bahrain, Kuwait, Oman, Saudi-Arabia, Qatar, and the United Arab Emirates, have one of the largest migrant stocks worldwide with around 25 million migrant workers, who together constitute about 60 per cent of the area's total population.[2] Numbers vary from country to country; in the United Arab Emirates (UAE) and Qatar for instance, nationals comprise a mere 12 per cent of the total population (United

---

1 Cf. Seccombe/Lawless (1986) and Errichiello (2012) for details on labour migration patterns to the Arab Gulf before the oil boom in the 1970s, and for the problem of lacking reliable data for that time.
2 Calculation by the author on the basis of source data provided by the United Nations 2016. However, these numbers are only estimates, and vary in the relevant literature. Since data on population from statistical centers of the Gulf States often do not provide a breakdown by nationalities, information on the share of foreign workers mostly rely on estimates of the sending countries. Furthermore, these figures do not consider the presumably high number of irregular migrants, which might be 15 per cent of the total workforce (cf. Shah 2014).

Nations 2016; Snoj 2013). However, in all GCC states, the clear majority of the labour force are migrant workers, composing approximately 70 per cent of the regional labour market (Babar 2013: 122). In some countries such as Qatar and the emirate of Dubai their share is as high as 96 per cent of the total workforce (De Bel-Air 2015: 10). India, the Philippines, Nepal, Bangladesh, and Pakistan are the main sending countries.

Figure 1: International migrant stocks in the UAE 1990-2015

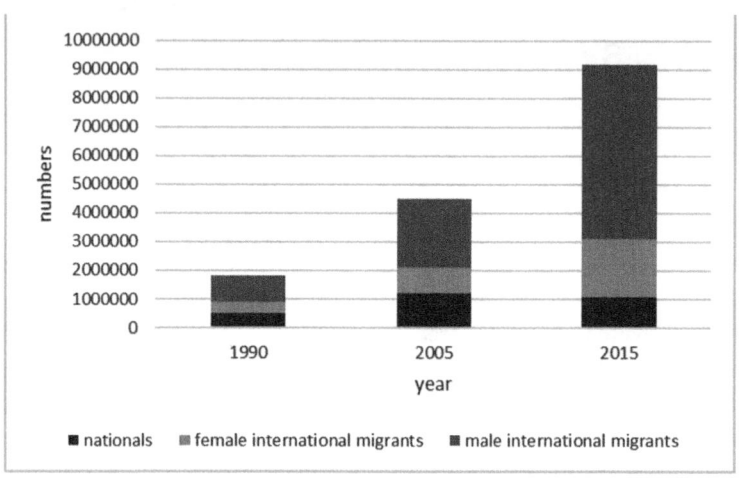

Source: Chart by the author, based on data of United Nations, Department of Economic and Social Affairs, Population Division (2015).

Since the GCC states do not conceive of themselves as immigration countries, governmental rhetorics do not refer to the imported labour workforce as migrants but as "temporary contract workers", "foreign workers", or "expatriates". Both the migrant workers' residency and their employment are regulated by a specific sponsorship system (*kafala*), a kind of "extensive and institutionalized inter-Asian guest worker scheme" (Lori 2012: 15), moving millions of people and generating billions of dollars for sending and receiving countries. Long-term stay, permanent settlement, and naturalization are not possible under the *kafala* system. Therefore, migrant workers usually arrive in the Arab Gulf States with contracts valid for a period of two years, or sometimes up to four years. They are supposed to leave the country immediately after the expiration of their contracts if not renewed or extended. Regulations in the framework of the *kafala* system tie temporary contract labourers closely to their local employers, who are legally and economically responsible for them during their stay, and often control their mobility and ability to leave the country or change employers.

This chapter examines the main aspects and legal frameworks of the *kafala* system, and the recruitment policies and practices for labour migration to the Arab Gulf until the year 2016. Focussing on the UAE and Qatar and the findings of ethnographic fieldwork conducted 2014 in Dubai and Doha,[3] it explores official recruitment practices, as well as perspectives of migrants and employers. The chapter illustrates illegal practices, which employers, recruitment agencies, labour brokers, and intermediaries have developed to circumvent certain provisions of both sending and receiving countries in order to generate additional profits out of migration processes. I will show that the *kafala* regulations cannot be assessed in general as a system of bonded labour, but that especially low-income Asian labour migrants often end up in situations of debt-bondage. This is particularly the case when they fall victim to deceptive recruitment, contract frauds or illegal visa trading.

THE *KAFALA* SYSTEM: GENERAL TRAITS AND LEGAL FRAMEWORKS

The Arabic term *kafala*, which is usually translated as sponsorship, means "guarantee" and it is in this context that a migrant worker is required to have a sponsor (*kafil*) who functions as a kind of guarantor and bears legal and economic responsibility for him[4] during the contract period until he leaves the country. The *kafil*, who is also the employer of the migrant worker, can be a national individual, or a company belonging to at least 51 per cent nationals.[5] Only for domestic workers (housemaids, nannies, gardeners, drivers, cooks, cleaners etc.) may a *kafil* be a non-national, provided that his salary matches a

---

[3] I would like to thank the Global South Studies Center (GSSC, Cologne, Germany) for financing the research visits in Dubai and Doha.

[4] The male pronoun is used in this chapter to refer to both male and female individuals, unless indicated otherwise.

[5] Exceptions are free economic zones in the UAE which have their own rules and regulations, and in which migrant workers are not sponsored by their employers but by the respective free zones (cf. Khan/Harroff-Tavel 2011: 294).

specific rate set by the respective GCC country.[6] As a guest-worker scheme, organizing the process of imported manpower, the *kafala* system was established in the 1950s, when several states of the region abolished slavery.[7] In Saudi Arabia, for instance, the residency law from 1952 required every foreigner to have a local *kafil* (Fargues/De Bel-Air 2015: 156). The roots of this specific sponsorship system are uncertain, and disputed in academic literature. Some authors hint to its origins in Bedouin traditions of hospitality which sets obligations regarding the treatment and protection of foreign guests (Khan/Harroff-Tavel 2011: 294, Zahra 2014: 11). The explanation offered by Longva (1997: 103-106) is more convincing. Longva sees striking similarities between the *kafala* system and former patterns of indentured labour in the Arab Gulf States that lasted until the 1950s. At the start of the pearling season, boat captains or boat-owner merchants used to give families of divers a loan to live on during the divers' absence. The diver was supposed to pay off the debt at the end of the season, when profits where distributed among the crew. However, at least from the 1930s onwards, most divers could not bring home any money, and so had to pledge to work for the same merchant or captain in the following season (ibid.: 104). These divers usually worked as sailors outside the pearl season, and were also tied closely to their other employers who had to give written permission to the pearl boat owners to use the service of their sailors (ibid; cf. Hopper 2013). Furthermore, certain characteristics of the current *kafala* system that tie migrant workers closely to local employers were probably also influenced by recruitment practices brought in by the British and international oil companies in the 1930s when bringing foreign workers to the Gulf (cf. Seccombo/Lawless 1986; Dusche 2011: 41). As Baldwin-Edwards suggests, the origins of the *kafala* system lie in the attempt to benefit national unskilled workers, and to provide "temporary rotating labour that could be rapidly bring into the country in economic boom and expelled during affluent periods" (ibid. 2011: 37).

What makes the current Gulf States' system for governing and regulating migrant workers unique in comparison to other contemporary migrations policies is not merely the fact that it seeks to avoid any kind of long-term stays or permanent settlement. Above all, it is the fact that the state delegates substantial portions of the responsibility for controlling foreign workers' entry, stay,

---

6   In the UAE, for instance, the minimum monthly salary necessary to be a *kafil* of a domestic worker is currently (August 2015) 6,000 AED; approximately 1,630 USD (cf. Hukumat Dubai 2013).

7   Cf. Miers (2003: 339-357) for an overview on the end of slavery in the Arab Gulf States between 1950 and 1970.

mobility, and exit after the termination of the employment relationship – in other countries a state prerogative – to citizens and their proxies (De Bel-Air 2015: 5, Gardner 2014: 4-5). Due to this dependence of the particular labour migrant on his *kafīl* (employer), the *kafala* leads to a kind of "privatization of migration governance" (Babar 2013: 123). It produces not only a high variability in the foreign workers' experiences (cf. Gardner et al. 2013: 15), but also a high vulnerability of migrant workers for abuse and exploitation.

Certain provisions of the *kafala* system vary from one GCC country to another and change frequently, but in general migrant workers arrive under fixed-term contracts. Since all GCC countries attempt to avoid long-term settlement of migrant workers, there is a salary cap for bringing in family members. As most migrant workers are below this ceiling, they and their families live under "transnationally split" conditions (Rahman 2011: 390) and workers remit back home to support family members left behind. At the same time, this policy results in probably unique worldwide demographic imbalances of some GCC countries. In Qatar, for instance, according to statistical data of June 2015, three quarters of the country's total population were male (Ministry of Development Planning and Statistics 2015: 8). Although labour migrants are employed in almost all areas of work (construction, education, hospitals, service sector, education etc.), most of them are so-called "low-skilled" workers occupying low-paid jobs in sectors such as construction and service. In Qatar, around 60 per cent had below secondary school education in 2010 (De Bel-Air 2014: 5). Since low-skilled workers usually live in labour camps which by law must be outside of cities and "family areas", according to surveys from 2010, more than half of Qatar's total resident population dwelt in such camps (ibid.: 7), usually sharing a room with five to seven other persons, with communal bathrooms and kitchens.[8] Domestic workers are usually housed in the homes of their employers.

THE ROLE OF THE SPONSOR

A worker's visa status in all GCC countries is closely tied to his *kafīl*, which provides him with wide-ranging control over the worker's mobility. In Qatar, all

---

8 New guidelines issued in 2013 ban double-decker beds in labour camps, and prescribe that not more than four workers are to be housed in one room and that each worker should have a free space of at least 4 sqm in the shared room (cf. Perumal 2014). However, the implementation of these guidelines is still pending.

foreign workers require an exit permit issued by their *kafil* if they want to leave the country, whether for a short time or permanently; in Kuwait this applies to those employed in ministries and other governmental institutions. This requirement very obviously violates the freedom of movement as articulated in the Universal Declaration of Human Rights[9] and the International Convention on the Elimination of All Forms Racial Discrimination, as also bemoaned for example by the UN's Special Rapporteur of human rights of migrants (Crépeau 2014: 8). International criticism triggered also the so-called "no objection certificate" (NOC), which guest workers in Qatar and most other GCC states require as a permit of their *kafil*, if they want to change employers before their contracts expire or during a non-limited contract. This NOC is even required after the expiry of contracts, when workers do not want to leave the country immediately but choose to stay with new employment. Reforms announced in 2014, but as yet (February 2016) not implemented, promise among other things that employers may be changed after the end of contracts without an NOC and without the previous work barrier of six months, or in case of a non-limited contract after a period of five years (State of Qatar 2014; Kovessy 2014).

In the UAE, until 2011, the regulations for NOCs and labour bans after the expiry of contracts where quite similar to those in Qatar. Workers required the *kafil*'s NOC after the termination of their work contracts to be allowed to transition to another company. Otherwise, they had to return to their home countries with a labour ban for at least six months. With ministerial resolution 1186, which was put into force in January 2011, workers now do not necessarily face a six-month ban on taking up new employment after the expiration of their contracts. They can take up a new employment, provided the following conditions are met: Firstly, that the former *kafil* of his own accord terminates or neglects to renew the work relationship; and secondly, that the employee had spent at least two years under his former contract. Exceptions to the requirement of the two-year-period and a NOC are for professional and skilled employees who have completed one full year of service and fulfill certain provisions. They must hold at least a high school diploma and must receive a certain minimum salary in their new jobs (minimum 5,000 AED [1,360 USD] for those with a high school diploma, 7,000 AED [1,906 USD] for diploma holders, and 12,000

---

9   The Universal Declaration of Human Rights states in article 13: "1. Everyone has the right to freedom of movement and residence within the borders of each State. 2. Everyone has the right to leave any country, including his own, and return to his country."

AED [3,268 USD] for bachelor degree holders) (Al-Imarat al-'arabiyya al-Muttahida 2010).

Nonetheless, according to UAE labour law (Paragraph 4, article 116)[10] workers who leave their employers before the end of the contract term have to compensate the "losses" of their employers. Only in Bahrain, since 2009, workers of all professional fields are allowed to change employers after only one year of service (Zahra 2015).

Workers who leave their *kafil* (employer) without an NOC are categorized in official rethoric as "absconders" and "runaways", and are subject to immediate detention and/or deportation. Moreover, if they continue to stay in the country without valid papers, they face additional fines for overstaying their visas. Their *kafil* will also be held responsible and fined, if he does not file an official complaint in the form of an "absconding report". If for example in the UAE a *kafil* does not report his "absconded" housemaid, and the maid is caught working illegally for another employer (which she most probably will do, since she can't leave the country without her *kafil*'s NOC), the *kafil* will be charged with a fine of up to up to 50,000 AED, approximately 13,600 USD (Al-Sadafy 2012). For persons who employ her as an undocumented housemaid, current fines are up to 70,000 AED, approximately 19,061 USD (Hukumat Dubai 2013). However, an absconding report can be quite complicated.[11] In order "to save time and effort" in 2014 the Qatari Ministry of the Interior introduced a new feature in its e-governance service, which enables employers to lodge complaints about absconding workers via their smartphones (Hukumi 2014).

Especially for low-skilled migrant workers with low income it is difficult to receive an NOC before the expiration of their contracts, since the *kafil* usually demands the reimbursement of the "investment" he paid for their recruitment, e.g the fees of an agency as the intermediary, plane ticket, medical tests, residence visa, health card, etc. For a domestic worker in the UAE for example, in 2014, depending on the home country of the worker, a sponsor would pay a recruitment agency between 10,000 and 14,000 AED (around 2,723 – 3,813 USD).[12] With a monthly minimum salary of a housemaid, as dictated by law, ranging according to the housemaid's nationality from 750 AED (204 USD) to

---

10 Compare labour laws at the homepage of the UAE's Ministry of Work: "Qanun al-'amal", http://www.mol.gov.ae/molwebsite/ar/labour-law/labour-law.aspx.
11 See for example "Abscond Reporting at Labour & Immigration – UAE", http://www.visaprocess.ae/beta/abscond-reporting-at-labour-immigration-uae/.
12 Interview with Louis, manager of a recruitment agency for domestic workers in Dubai, March 15, 2014. All names of interlocutors have been anonymized.

1,400 AED (381 USD) (Government of Dubai 2014), it is extremely difficult for a maid to reimburse her *kafil*. Ann, a Filipina maid employed by a cleaning company and taking care of three to five large houses every day, with often more than 12 hours work per day and sometimes no days off in a month, had been repeatedly threatened by her Moroccan supervisor: "If you break the contract, you will have to pay me 13,000 AED [3,540 USD]."[13] Saving this sum from her monthly income of around 1,400 AED (381 USD) was far beyond Ann's reach.

Furthermore her children, who lived in the Philippines with her sister and other family members, relied on her remittances. Ann's migration to Dubai was, like many other cases, a family-driven decision to improve living conditions at home. Besides, it was also a kind of "personal escape", since she separated from her husband, but is still married, because divorce is not legal for Catholics in the Philippines. However, her hopes for a more independent life in Dubai turned out to be false. According to Ann, far worse than being overworked was sexual harassment: "It happens all the time that they touch you [...] Here you have no dignity, you are nothing, you are not a human being", she said. For domestic workers it is difficult to report rape or sexual assault, because they risk the accusation of consensual sex under the charge of "illicit relations", which are forbidden by law (cf. Amnesty International 2014: 8). After a friend of Ann's who worked for the same company was nearly raped, the two decided to quit and return together to the Philippines with the help of their embassy. At the same time, she feared her family's reaction, since they considered her the one who "will make it for all" of them. Therefore, she was still hoping to find another sponsor in order to be able to continue working in Dubai, while waiting for the legal procedures undertaken by her embassy to enable her returning home.

In addition to the threat of having to bear the costs of reimbursing the *kafil*, workers who break a contract before its termination and want to return home also have to bear the costs of the return flight, which would otherwise have been covered by the *kafil* (cf. Tappe, this volume, for similar restrictions within coolie contracts in colonial Southeast Asia).

'MAID-TRADE' AND PERSECUTION OF 'RUNAWAY MAIDS' IN SAUDI ARABIA

Especially in Saudi Arabia, many citizens use social media to bemoan the high costs involved in recruiting housemaids. Depending on the maid's country of

---

13 Interview with Ann, Dubai, March 14, 2015.

origin, recruitment costs in 2014 ranged from 20,000 to 25,000 SAR, approximately 5,333-6,666 USD (al-Umran/al-Utaibi 2014). Official procedures for hiring domestic workers via a recruitment agency take several months, and many Saudi families complain that they face difficulties in finding domestic help at all. The latter situation also arises due to bans preventing several Asian and African countries from sending housemaids to work in Saudi Arabia. The high recruitment costs probably contribute to the perception on the part of some Saudi sponsors of their domestic workers as a kind of personal property, in which they have invested money.

Numerous profit-seeking Saudi companies and also some individuals trade sponsorships of domestic workers by advertising on internet forums offering to "take over" housemaids and to compensate their sponsors for their investment, efforts, and time. In other advertisements they offer these maids to "hand over" (*li-l-tanazul*), often openly labelling the women as "for sale" (*li-l-bayʻ*) and mentioning their "price" (*siʼr*).[14] It is strongly to be doubted that the domestic workers who are offered in such advertisements are not trafficked, but are able to participate in the decision on their future stay and employment.

The "trading of housemaids" is most frequent in Saudi Arabia, but also occurs in other GCC countries. On a Kuwaiti online advertisement portal, for instance, in February 2015 a *kafil* posted a picture of the passport of his 27-year-old Filipina maid and offered her for the "price" of 1,200 KWD (3,965 USD). Explaining that the reason for her "handover" was the return of his former housemaid, he stipulates a direct transfer without probation time, and contact via WhatsApp.[15] However, these attempts are at the margins of the law in the respective countries or, if human trafficking can be proven, are punished, as highlighted by the example of an Emirati newspaper article on a *kafil* in Dubai who was arrested for trying to sell his maid for a sum of 3,000 AED (817 USD).[16] Nevertheless, financial losses of sponsors whose maids have "absconded" are an issue which is frequently discussed in Saudi newspapers and social media.[17] In order to avoid the costs of recruiting a new one, or to force the

---

14 Cf. for example the numerous ads in the following forums: "Mauqiʼ Khadimat" [Servant Forum]: http://www.shrte.com/ and "ʻAlam al-Marʼa [World of the Woman]"; http://www.womenw.co/fl46/.
15 Cf. 1808080.com: http://www.1808080.com/viewlisting.php?view=25493.
16 Cf. "Muqabil 3000 alaf Dirham – Dubay: Tajir bashar yaʼrud khadima lil-bayʻ wa-l-shurta taqbid ʻalayhi bi-kamin," 24, May 10, 2015, http://bit.ly/1CGAOjk.
17 Cf. for example "Runaway domestics cost families SR 1 billion"; http://www.arabnews.com/saudi-arabia/news/620891; August 26, 2014; Toumi 2013.

"runaway" maid to reimburse the *kafil*'s recruitment costs, Saudi sponsors of maids do not only rely on legal persecution by the government, but have also developed several strategies to find their runaway maids by themselves. In the Saudi twitter site "khadimat haribat@maidescape", for example, sponsors post pictures of their "runaway" maids, often with copies of their passports, with the hope that others will recognize them and turn them in to the police.[18] Often this is also accompanied by accusations against the respective maid, such as that she "stole money", "didn't leave anything in the house which she didn't break" (plates, glasses, electrical appliances) or "showed very suspicious behavior with a man of her nationality who helped her and two of her relatives to flee".[19] Saudi newspapers take up such efforts as well, as for an example in an article in which a *kafil* offered a reward of 50,000 SAR (13,333 USD) for his "absconded" maid, who was accused of having poisoned the neighbour's family and then escaping with her lover (Al-Ufuq News 2015).

A rather new strategy of Saudi sponsors to protect themselves against financial losses for recruitment costs in case of "runaways" is by taking out insurance, which has emerged as a new industry. A Saudi company offers sponsors an insurance policy of 375 SAR for a housemaid, promising a compensation of up to 8,000 SAR in the case that she absconds. It also hints at the fact that the policies are more expensive when they are to cover employees of certain nationalities, such as Ethiopians and Indonesians, because they are more likely to run away (al-Muriki 2014).

At the same time, a flourishing black market has developed in Saudi Arabia for undocumented "freelance housemaids", who have entered the country in irregular ways, overstayed their visas, or "absconded" from their *kafil*s. According to data from the Statistical yearbook of the Saudi Labour Ministry, in 2013 around 65,000 domestic workers (49 per cent female, 51 per cent male) were absent from work (Wizarat al-'amal 2014; cf. Damir-Geilsdorf/Pelican 2015).

HIRING PRACTICES AND DEBT BONDAGE

In labour recruitment to the Arab Gulf, a chain of recruitment agencies, labour supply agencies, brokers, contractors, and sub-contractors and other intermediaries is involved in both sending and receiving countries. As a "profit-seeking

---

18 Cf. "Khadimat haribat@maidescape", https://twitter.com/maidsescape.
19 Ibid.

industry" (Gardner 2014: 6), all these different actors and sponsors try to benefit from the process. Furthermore, some sending countries also rely significantly on remittances from their citizens abroad. In Nepal in 2013, for example, remittances comprised around a quarter of the country's gross domestic product (Knight 2014). In Kerala (India), where around 90 per cent of migrant workers stay in the Arab Gulf, remittances were 31 per cent of the state's GDP (Jayan 2012; cf. Philip 2014).

Kafala regulations in the GCC countries require that sponsors bear the entire recruitment costs, including the employee's return flight after the termination of the contract. Nonetheless, recruitment agencies in the GCC states always cooperate with recruitment agencies and brokers in sending countries who in turn charge the migrants. Depending on their countries of origin, labour migrants on average pay around 1,000 USD for their recruitment; some up to 3,000 USD. However, as several studies have shown, recruitment costs also depend on the skills of the labour migrants, since skilled workers often pay only half of the recruitment costs that low-skilled ones have to bear (Jureidini 2014: 30).

In most sending countries private recruitment agents operate under licence from the government, according to detailed rules and regulations (Shah 2010). In an attempt to protect their citizens from unscrupulous brokers and intermediaries, some sending countries also prescribe a maximum recruitment fee by law. Bangladesh, for example, set 84,000 BDT (1,230 USD) as the maximum recruitment fee to the Gulf, but surveys showed that the Bangladeshi labour migrants leaving to Saudi Arabia nonetheless on average pay 3,000 USD for their recruitment (Rahman 2011: 400). The Nepali government, which in 2005 signed an agreement with Qatar requiring Qatari employers to bear the entire cost of hiring workers, limits manpower companies in Nepal as well: They are not allowed to charge more than 70,000 Rs (669 USD) from Gulf-bound migrants, but due to the lack of control most workers pay double this amount (Rai 2015). Nepalese workers interviewed by Amnesty International in 2013 in Qatar typically owed around USD 1,150 when they arrived there, often borrowed at an interest rate of 36 per cent per annum, which means that they sometimes need two years or more to pay back loans of this size (Amnesty International 2013: 34f.).

According to a survey among Bangladeshi migrant workers in Saudi Arabia, most relied on multiple sources to fund their around 3,000 USD migration costs, an amount usually far beyond personal savings:

"selling land (27 per cent), mortgaging land (23 per cent), taking a loan (72 per cent), and disposing of other family assets such as livestock and jewelry (19 per cent). Only nine per cent of migrants used personal savings to meet the expenses of migration." (Rahman 2011: 401)

Moneylenders in Bangladesh often charge seven to ten per cent interest per month for migration loans, roughly 100 per cent per year. Taking into consideration that, if the interest is compounded, the debt will double in less than a year and triple in less than two years, this explains why the majority of households with a family member working in Saudi Arabia for a period of three years or longer were still saddled with sizeable debts (ibid.: 403). Comparing the average remuneration of 18,732 BDT (273 USD) per month that Bangladeshi workers in Saudi Arabia receive, their amounts of remittances, and their repayments of loans etc., the study found out that it takes Bangladeshi migrants on average 2.3 years to recover the financial costs of migration to Saudi Arabia (Rahman 2011: 404).

Especially for low-skilled and semi-skilled workers, the recruitment costs paid in advance often lead to forms of debt bondage, even though the debt is not directly owned to the employer or the recruiter – the latter described by Bales (2004: 121-123) in regard to contract work in Brazil as a contemporary form of "contract slavery". However, someone who arrives in the Gulf States heavily indebted will need to work for a significant time before he is able to pay the return flight home and/or to compensate a *kafil* for an NOC. Furthermore, he will probably endure unacceptable working conditions rather than returning home empty-handed. As shown in the case of Ann, mentioned above, decisions about the migration are often made at the household level.

As they are deeply intertwined with household livelihood strategies such as landholdings, school education for children, eradicating debts, and medical treatment for somebody in the family (Gardner 2014: 7), the remittances expected and needed by dependents in the country of origin comprise another force locking migrants in employment situations. This is not classical bonded labour, described in most definitions as work "against a loan of money, but the length and nature of this service is not defined and the labour does not reduce the origin debt" (Bales 2004: 116). Nevertheless, incurred debts at home, along with the difficulties involved in exiting a contract before its termination, bind migrant workers into exploitive employment conditions. Therefore, it could be described as a form of "neo bondage" as described by Breman (2008: 84-86) who stresses the huge diversity of bonded labour situations, both present and past, and demonstrated by examples in India that current practices of bondage are often a result of indebtedness and temporally restricted instead of previous forms of bonded labour which went on indefinitely or were even perpetuated in the next generation.

Figure 2: Labour Migrants in Dubai, 2014.

Source: Author's photo.

Sometimes there are additional costs after migrants' arrival in the Gulf States, as illustrates the case of Muhammad, a 42-year-old taxi driver from Bangladesh, who had to pay 1,360 USD for a six-month training program in order to receive a valid driving licence after his arrival in Dubai.[20] Compared to average monthly incomes in Bangladesh it is extremely difficult to save such sums in addition to the recruitment costs in advance. In 2014, for Bangladeshi garment workers the monthly minimum wage was 5,300 BDT (68 USD) and the best salaries 128 USD (Farhana /Syduzzaman/Shayekh Munir 2015: 572).

More skilled labour migrants with a higher income can also face difficulties in paying off recruitment debts and reimbursing a *kafil*, because living costs in the Arab Gulf States are high. The salary of Julie, a Cameroon nurse, for instance, who works twelve hours a day in a hospital in Dubai with one day off

---

20 Interview with Muhammad, Dubai, March 15, 2014.

per week, is, at 3,000 AED (720 USD), above average. However, the rent for her one-bedroom apartment in Dubai is also 3,000 AED. She therefore lives like many other migrant workers in so called "bed space", which means that she shares the bedroom with three other persons. Each one pays her share of the rent in order to keep enough of the income for other living costs, savings, or remittances.[21]

To provide a brief comparison of possible incomes and savings: Abdu from the Philippines, who has worked since three years in several malls in Dubai and recently became Assistant Sales Manager, earns 2,255 AED (614 USD) per month and pays around 790 AED (215 USD) for his "bed space" in a room he shares with two other Filipinos.[22] Amir from Kerala has been working in Doha for almost five years as a kind of freelance taxi driver for a huge taxi company. The company provides him and five other taxi drivers from Kerala with a room, pays his health insurance, and every two years also pays for a flight back to visit his wife and children in Kerala. He in turn rents a taxi from the company, for which he pays 264 QAR (73 USD) per day. Depending on numbers of passengers and traffic, in some months he is able to save around 1,500 QAR (412 USD), in others much less, or nothing at all.[23] Taxi drivers in Qatar who receive a basic salary from a company usually earn around 1,200 QAR per month, and like Abdu are provided with a "bed space" in a workers accommodation block, health insurance, and sometimes food. Cooking is often not allowed in the accommodation blocks. Aziz, who works as such a salaried taxi driver, usually saves between 282 QAR (77 USD) and 403 (111 USD) QAR, which he sends home to his family in Eritrea.[24]

On the other hand, high-skilled labour migrants in the GCC countries can secure substantial salaries, although there are great differences depending on the nationality of the migrant. According to the Gulf Business 2013 Salary Survey, the salary of a high-skilled "Western" expatriate working in the GCC in sectors such as real estate or finance is around 12,215 USD per month, that of an Arab expatriate around 10,556 USD per month, and that of an Asian expatriate 9,060 USD (Nagraj 2013). Therefore, companies in the private sector often prefer to employ Asians because they will accept lower salaries, as a Qatari Human Resource Officer explained in an interview with a newspaper:

---

21 Interview with Julie, Dubai, March 18, 2014.
22 Interview with Abduh, Dubai, March 12, 2014.
23 Interview with Amir, Doha, November 3, 2014.
24 Interview with Aziz, Doha, November 9, 2014.

"We cannot hire a European accountant for a monthly salary of QR 20,000 ($5,500) when we can get an Asian accountant for QR 5,000 ($1,370)." (Toumi 2011)

However, although high-skilled labour migrants are also bound to their employers by the regulations of the *kafala* system, in contrast to low-paid, low-skilled labour migrants, they do not fall victim to debt bondage incurred by their recruitment costs.

Diplomatic representatives of some sending countries try to monitor recruitment agencies, in both the sending and receiving countries. POLO, the Philippines Overseas Labour Office in Dubai, for example keeps a list of local recruitment agencies and blacklists those who mistreat their citizens. However, according to the head of POLO in Dubai, many Filipino migrants do not follow the prescribed procedure of applying with an agency back in their home country, but enter the Emirates with a visitors' or tourist visa. He estimates that this applies to around 70 per cent of the consulate's walk-in clients.[25] Some of them are in an irregular situation because they overstayed their visas, others found a *kafil* who agreed to arrange for employment by sending them for a "visa change" to Oman, Bahrain, or a nearby Iranian Island, and are now in regular employment.

However, some labour migrants choose to work in irregular employment situation as an advantageous alternative to restrictive employment regulations within the *kafala* system (cf. Damir-Geilsdorf/Pelican 2015).

LABOUR LAWS AND VIOLATIONS

All Arab Gulf States have labour laws that regulate contracts, maximum working hours, breaks, payment of overtime, safety regulations, annual leave, etc. Fines and penalties are imposed for the violation of labour laws, such as contract frauds or the withholding of wages, but there is a lack of control and enforcement. In order to crack down on the non-payment of salaries in the private sector, the UAE for example introduced a Wage Protection System in 2009, in the form of an electronic salary transfer that records wage payments. Although since its launch some thousand employers have been penalized,[26]

---

25 Interview with Delmer Cruz, Dubai, March 13, 2015.
26 For new measurements to combat labour law violations cf. United Arab Emirates, Ministry of Labour 2015a and 2015b.

several studies prove that in most Arab Gulf States withholding parts of workers' wages is still a common practice.

Also commonly reported are contract frauds in the recruitment process. Once the migrant worker arrives at the airport, the contract he has signed in his home country is substituted with a new contract, stipulating only half or two third of the originally promised salary. In a survey of more than 1,000 low-income labour migrants in Qatar, 21 per cent received their salary on time only "sometimes, rarely or never", and 20 per cent found they were paid a different salary from the one they had been promised prior to leaving their home country (Gardner et al. 2013: 9-10).[27] Jureidini (2014: 64) mentions in his research a company which lists a salary of QAR 1,000 (270 USD), but on their arrival gives workers only QAR 650 (175 USD) with the claim that QAR 350 (95 USD) of the listed amount was to cover food and accommodation. In another example from his research – according to Jureidini (ibid.) "an all too common practice" – a young man from Togo borrowed around 3,000 USD to pay an agent at home who promised him employment in Doha in a university's soccer team with a salary of 4,000 QAR (1,100 USD) per month. Once he arrived, he was placed in a labour supply agency specializing in security guards and sent to work in the French embassy in Doha with a salary of only 1,000 QAR (275 USD) per month, from which he must pay for his food, support his parents back home, and pay off his loan.

In particular low-income workers are at an increased risk of becoming victims of these forms of deception and abuse, since there are few avenues by which they can challenge such frauds. Indebted migrants who just arrived have little option but to accept the substitution of contracts at the airport. Companies seem to count on the fact that these workers are probably not able to afford their airfare in order to return home, and furthermore most probably will be reluctant to return without providing the expected financial support for their dependents.

Although laws of all GCC countries have for several years prohibited the withholding of migrants' passports, this practice still seems to be widespread. In the survey mentioned above, 90 per cent of the interviewed low-income labour migrants in Qatar said that their employers were in possession of their passports (ibid.). Longva (1999) showed, in her ethnographic fieldwork conducted in Kuwait in the 1980s and 1990s, that sponsors (employers) justified the confiscation of passports as a crime-preventing measure, with the argument that those who have committed an infraction will not be able to leave the country and escape prosecution. Today, the confiscation of passports in order to prevent

---

27 Cf. Amnesty International 2013.

employees from quitting their job or "running away" from problematic work conditions (Human Rights Watch 2014: 38-39; Gardner/Pessoa/Harkness 2014) is often explained as being a favor for their owners, with the claim that workers in labour camps otherwise would not find a secure place for the deposition of their papers.

According to labour laws in all GCC countries, migrant workers can file a lawsuit in case of labour law violations. Due to many practical obstacles, this remains a merely theoretical option, especially for low-qualified workers. They often come from rural areas, are illiterate, and speak only a little English or Arabic. Since the language used by governmental officials and courts is Arabic, they face many difficulties in submitting formal complaints to Ministries. Efforts like the "Workers [sic] Rights Book" (Al Ali 2009) for Qatari workers, published in English and Arabic by the National Human Rights Committee in Doha, with legal information about their rights, probably reach only a few of the workers. Furthermore, migrant workers in the GCC countries cannot rely on the help of trade unions or go on strike, as such actions are strictly forbidden, and punished by deportation. Trade unions are only allowed in Bahrain, Kuwait, and Oman, and there they do not include migrant workers (Khan/Harroff-Tavel 2011: 302). An additional obstacle to protesting against labour law violations is that the labour migrant will be exposed to a period without income until his case has been decided. Even if he wins a court case against an employer, the outcome will be the termination of the contract and hence the residence permit, which means that the worker will have to return home to his country of origin and start the costly recruitment process once again (Lori 2012: 16).

Some of the major sending countries such as India and the Philippines have appointed labour and welfare attachés as part of the embassy staff in the GCC country, and provide help for their citizens in irregular situations or labour disputes. However, the possibilities for them to intervene are limited. This is particularly the case for domestic workers, who are not covered by labour laws in most GCC countries, although some GCC states have been announcing changes for several years. While most sending countries have designed sample work contracts for domestic workers that state requirements such as regular working hours, a weekly day off, or the provision of a sim card, the fulfilment of these requirements can hardly be controlled. Ahmad for example, an Emirate employer, explains that he provided his two live-in maids with mobile phones and a sim-card, but only allows them to use the phones at the weekend, and in his presence. He justifies his control over their communication as a precaution to ensure that they do not use the mobile phone for immoral things, like "starting a love affair with the Bengali cleaner next door".[28] Studies show that obviously many housemaids are prohibited from leaving the house at all, or do not receive a bed from their sponsor but have to sleep on the floor next to the children of their *kafil* (Vlieger 2011; Amnesty International 2014).

(ILLEGAL) PROFITS IN RECRUITMENT PROCESSES

Some companies and individual sponsors in the Arab Gulf States have developed several strategies to subvert certain regulations of the *kafala* system in order to make an additional profit in recruitment processes. According to a human-resource officer (himself a migrant labourer from a Middle Eastern country) of a huge construction company in Doha which employs several thousand workers, the following practices are widespread.[29] Usually a company that wants to hire construction workers from Nepal contacts a local Qatari recruitment agency, and has to pay this agency around 5,000 QAR (1,375 USD) per worker in recruitment costs. Some companies in highly sought as employers by labourers from abroad can avoid these costs, and furthermore they are even (illegally) remunerated by Qatari recruitment agency with an amount of around 1,000 QAR (275 USD) for each recruited Nepali worker. The Qatari agency in turn covers its costs by charging a recruitment agency in Nepal, which passes on the charge to the workers. Thus, when hiring for example a stock of 200 workers, the *kafil* (the company) and his intermediaries can not only save recruitment costs of around 275,000 USD but also make an additional profit of 55,000 USD. As the human-resources officer in Qatar said, "there is the law, but reality is another thing". However, in his opinion "the biggest corruption starts at home, in Nepal or in the Philippines, they all pay hard currency". Companies that are well connected to governmental circles and do not have to fear legal prosecution also make additional profits by setting up fraudulent employment contracts and selling visas to workers without offering them employment. While the worker searches for employment on the black market and (illegally) works for somebody other than his *kafil*, the latter charges the workers for the maintenance and renewal of his visa, generating a profit for himself.[30] This can easily contribute to an additional income: In the case of 100 workers, for instance, each of whom pays around 3,000 QAR (824 USD) for a valid residence and working

---

28 Interview with Hasan, Dubai, March 16, 2014.
29 Interview with Ahmad, Doha, November 8, 2014.
30 Ibid.

permit, instead of its real cost of around 1,200 QAR (330 USD), the Qatari sponsor and his intermediaries can earn 180,000 QAR (49,450 USD).[31] A similar practice was observed by Crépeau, the Special Rapporteur of the human rights of migrants of the United Nations Human Rights Council, with the so-called "block visa". Some Qatari companies have access to this kind of visa, which entitles them to recruit a certain number of workers according to the company's assets and demand for workforce. Instead of employing workers, they sell the visa to the highest bidder (Crépeau 2015: 9).

These forms of illegal visa-trading obviously constitute a highly profitable business, and are widespread in various GCC countries. According to the research by Nasra Shah (2008: 9), in the UAE the prices for illegally traded visas seem to be higher than those in Qatar, but – as in Qatar – they depend on the migrants' countries of origin: In 2008, Indians had to spend on average 7,500 AED (2,042 USD) for a "free visa", and Iranians 15,000 AED (4,084 USD). While in 2004, the estimated number of workers sponsored by fictitious companies in the UAE was 27 per cent of the total workforce, the Labour Ministry in Saudi Arabia complained that around 70 per cent of the visas issued by the government were sold on the black market (ibid.). Both countries tried to crack down on this by instigating several measures, among them issuing bans on violating individual sponsors and companies, but as with other forms of labour law violation, there remains a serious lack of control.

A survey conducted in 2013 in Qatar found hundreds of workers without valid residence permits. In some cases, their employers had never given them a residence permit or the accompanying ID-card; in other cases their employers had failed to renew their expired permits (Amnesty International 2013: 36-37; 74). As the main reasons for these failures, managers of companies cited financial problems and a lack of cash flow, either due to slow government processes or due to the physical absence of the local sponsor, who is required to carry out the procedures. Another reason mentioned is that some companies transfer the sponsorship to subcontractors who do not complete the residence procedures. However, workers without valid papers find themselves in highly precarious situations. Despite the lack of access to provisions like medical treatment, they always have to fear police controls, and risk being assumed to have "absconded" from their employers, which will result in their deportation (Damir-Geilsdorf/Pelican 2015: 7).

Another strategy for increasing profit within the *kafala* system – this one legal – is to be a "passive sponsor" for a migrant worker who starts a business in

---

31 Ibid.

a GCC country and needs a national, either an individual or a company owned by at least by 51 per cent nationals, as a sponsor. Often, the latter has no interest in actively being involved in the business, but acts as "sleeping partner" or "passive sponsor", earning for his role as a pro forma business partner an additional income, which may be up to 3,000 USD per month. The dependent migrant business partner in turn risks that his pro forma business partner suddenly increases his share.[32]

Yet, rather than a simple narrative of local nationals exploiting foreign workers, main perpetrators of abuses are also often foreign nationals, local branches of multinational businesses, or diverse subcontractors (Amnesty International 2013: 8-9).

Conclusion

The chapter has shown that the *kafala* system exposes labour migrants to great risks and vulnerabilities, mainly because individual sponsors or sponsoring companies exercise wide-ranging control not only over their employment situation and their freedom to quit jobs or change employers, but also over their residence status and freedom to enter and exit the country. Taking into account these restrictions on personal freedom and mobility, the fact that migrant workers are criminalized and labelled as "absconders" or "runaways" when they leave their employers before the termination of their work contract, and requirements such as "exit permits" and "NOC"s from employers, accompanied by exploitative squalid working conditions, as has been frequently documented, some aspects of contract work under the *kafala* system could be considered as contemporary forms of unfree labour. However, unfree working arrangements are often defined by an involuntary entry into the relation (Barrientos/Kothari/ Philipps 2013: 1038-1039), whereas others suggest that contemporary forms of unfreedom arise from the inability to exit from working relations (Brass 2014: 575). These characteristics do not directly apply to contract labour in the GCC countries, since migrant workers come voluntarily, and at least theoretically have the option of canceling their contracts. Furthermore, many of them are able to save substantial sums during their stay.

At the same time, as discussed above, in particular low-skilled Asian migrant workers sometimes find themselves in employment or situations for which they did not voluntarily sign up at home. ILO Convention 29 from 1930 defines

---

32 Interview with Ahmad, Doha, November 8, 2014.

"forced or compulsory labour" as "all work or service which is exacted from any person under the menace of any penalty and for which the said person has not offered himself voluntarily". In a report of 2013, the ILO tried to break down legal definitions of unfree labour into "operational indicators", which can be summarized in the following three dimensions.

1) "Unfree recruitment", which means, in the description of the ILO, coercive as well as deceptive recruitment;
2) "Life and work under duress", with indications such as limited freedom, withholding of wages, forced overtime or task, and the retention of identity papers;
3) "Impossibility of leaving the employer" (Harroff-Tavel/Nasri 2013: 37). Some or all of these indications can definitely be applied to the employment of labour migrants in the GCC countries.

The highly precarious situations of migrant workers are not an unequivocal result of the *kafala* system, though. Rather, it is a result of widespread labour-law violations and illegal practices by sponsors, companies, recruitment agencies, sub-contractors etc., and the lack of control or enforcement of regulations also contributes to the precariousness. Especially low-skilled Asian migrant workers often face contract fraud, such as the substitution of their contracts when arriving at the airport, the withholding of wages, the confiscation of passports, or the requirement to work much longer hours than stated in the contract. Others find themselves in irregular situations due to their involvement with sponsors who were issued a "free visa" or " block visa", and the labourers now have to work illegally for somebody other than the original employer. As a study by Amnesty International (2013: 31) has shown, "employers have been able to use threats such as non-payment of wages, refusal to return passports and provide exit permits to leave the country and in some circumstances, physical threats in order to exact work from workers involuntarily". Since most low-skilled Asian migrant workers have heavily invested in their migration and incurred substantial debts, which sometimes take up to three years to pay back, they often have no other option but to accept exploitative working conditions and abuse.

Furthermore, migrants who want to return home before the termination of their contract have to pay their return cost, which otherwise would have been covered by their *kafil*, and which most migrants did not calculate in their investment for migration. As Derks has outlined in her study of bonded labour in Southeast Asia, the distinction between free and unfree should be considered as "gradual and contextual" (2010: 842). The same applies for coercion and being bonded. Since in contemporary contexts of migratory movements a range of actors have been able to profit from the aspirations, needs, labour, and earnings of migrants, they may cause migrants "to highly indebt themselves to finance their migration, to be transported, and treated as commodities and/or to face severe restrictions in their autonomy, as well as conditions of subordination and abuse – much like the coolies in colonial times" (ibid.: 843).

It is evident that the debts involved in the migration process incurred in the sending countries can lead especially low-paid labour migrants in the GCC countries not only into new forms of debt bondage, but also to the acceptance of employers' infringements of contracts, or contract frauds. The latter is also produced by the unequal power relationship between the *kafil* and the migrant worker, as well as migrant workers' very limited avenues for filing a legal case when they are abused or deceived. Moreover, the fact that labourers remain in situations of involuntary work is often due to other structural features in the *kafala* system such as the financial reimbursement of the *kafil* for a "no objection certificate" (NOC) in order to change employers or to leave the country. At the same time, the strong dependence of labour migrants on their *kafil*, because they entered the GCC with fixed contracts and are very limited in their ability to offer their workforce to the labour market, capitalizes on them, acting as an instrument by which migrant labour is controlled and cheapened.

References

"Abscond Reporting at Labour & Immigration – UAE", First Gate Business Services, July 12, 2016 (http://www.visaprocess.ae/beta/abscond-reporting-at-labour-immigration-uae/).
Al Ali, Hala (2009): Workers Rights Book, Doha: National Human Rights Committee in Doha, Qatar.
'Alam al-Mar'a, July 12, 2016 (http://www.womenw.co/f146/).
Al Sadafy, Muhammad (2012): "What to do when: Your housemaid in Dubai has absconded." In: Emirates 24/7, November 13 (http://www.emirates247.com/crime/local/what-to-do-when-your-housemaid-in-dubai-has-absconded-2012-11-13-1.482614).
Amnesty International (2014): 'My sleep is my break.' Exploitation of Migrant Domestic Workers in Qatar. MDE 22/004/2014, London: Amnesty International Ltd.

—— (2013): The Dark Side of Migration: Spotlight on Qatar's Construction Sector Ahead of the World Cup, MDE 22/010/2013, London: Amnesty International Publications.

Babar, Zahra (2013): "Migration Policies and Governance in the GCC: A Regional Perspective". In: Ali Rashid Al-Noaimi/Irena Omelaniuk (eds.), Labor Mobility. An Enabler for Sustainable Development, Doha: The Emirates Center for Strategic Studies and Research, pp. 121-142.

Baldwin-Edwards, Martin (2011): "Labour Immigration and Labour Markets in the GCC Countries: National Patterns and Trends", London: The London School of Economics and Political Science.

Bales, Kevin (2004 [2000]): New Slavery: A Reference Handbook. 2nd edition, Santa Barbara: ABC-CLIO inc.

Barrientos, Stephanie/Kothari, Umar/Phillips, Nicola (2013): "Dynamics of unfree labour in the contemporary global economy." In: The Journal of Development Studies 49, pp. 1037-1041.

Brass, Tom (2014): "Debating Capitalist Dynamics and Unfree Labor: A Missing Link." In: The Journal of Development Studies 50/4, pp. 570-584.

Breman, Jan (2008): "On Labour Bondage, Old and New." In: The Indian Journal of Labour Economics 51/1, pp. 83-90.

Crépeau, Françoise (2015): United Nations, General Assembly, Human Rights Council: Report of the Special Rapporteur on the human rights of migrants François Crépeau. Addendum: Mission to Qatar, April 23, 2014, A/HRC/26/35/Add.1, 9.

Damir-Geilsdorf, Sabine/Pelican, Michaela (2015): Between Regular and Irregular Employment. Subverting the kafala system in the GCC Countries. Paper for the Gulf Research Meeting 2015. Workshop No. 4: The Role of Legislation, Policies and Practices in Irregular Migration to the Gulf, Cambridge.

De Bel-Air, Françoise (2015a): "Demography, Migration, and the Labour Market in the UAE." In: Gulf Labour Markets and Migration (GLMM – EN) 7/2015.

—— (2015b): "The Socio-political Background and Stakes of 'Saudizing' the Workforce in Saudi Arabia: the Nitaqat policy." In: Gulf Labour Markets and Migration (GLMM – EN) 3/2015.

Derks, Annuska (2010): "Bonded Labour in Southeast Asia. Introduction." In: Asian Journal of Social Science 38, pp. 839-852.

Dusche, Michael (2011): "Kultureller Wandel durch Migration: Der neue Islam in Bangladesh, Sri Lanka, Gujarat und Kashmir." In: Südasien-Chronik – South Asia-Chronicle 1/2011, pp. 41-68.

Errichiello, Gennaro (2012): "Foreign Workforce in the Arab Gulf States (1930-1950): Migration Patterns and Nationality Clause." In: *International Migration Review* 46/2, pp. 389-413.

Fargues, Philippe/De Bel-Air, Francoise (2015): "Migration to the Gulf States: The Political Economy of Exceptionalism." In: Diego Acosta Arcarazo/Anja Wiesbrock (eds.), Global Migration – Old Assumptions, New Dynamics, Santa Barbara: Praeger, pp. 139-166.

Farhana, Kaniz/Syduzzaman, Muhammad/Shayekh Munir, Muhammad (2015): "Present Status of Workers in ready-made Garments Industries in Bangladesh." In: Europea Scientific Journal 11/7, pp. 564-575.

Gardner, Andrew M. (2014): "Ethnography, Anthropology and Migration to the Arabian Peninsula: Themes from an Ethnographic Research Trajectory." In: Gulf Labour Markets and Migration 10/2014.

—— /Pessoa, Silvia/Harkness, Laura (2014): Labour Migrants and Access to Justice in Contemporary Qatar, London: LSE Middle East Center.

—— /Pessoa, Silvia/Diop, Abdoulaye/Al-Ghanim, Kaltham /Le Trung, Kien/ Harkness, Laura (2013). "A *Portrait* of *Low-Income* Migrants in Contemporary Qatar." In: Journal of Arabian Studies 3/1, pp. 1–17.

Government of Dubai (2014): "Sponsor a Maid or Nanny in Dubai", July 8 (http://www.dubai.ae/en/Lists/HowToGuide/DispForm.aspx?ID=45).

Harroff-Tavel, Hélène/Nasri, Alix (2013): Tricked and trapped: human trafficking in the Middle East, Beirut: International Labour Organization (ILO).

Hopper, Matthew S. (2013) "Debt and Slavery among Arabian Gulf Pearl Divers." In: Gwyn Campbell/Alessandro Stanziani (eds.), Bonded Labour and Debt in the Indian Ocean World, New York: Routledge, pp. 103-118.

Hukumat Dubai (2013): "Ijra'at kafalat khadima fi Dubai", February 11 (http://www.dubai.ae/ar/Lists/HowToGuide/DispForm.aspx?ID=45).

Hukumi. Hukumat Qatar al-iliktruniyya (2014): "Al-Iblagh ´an hurub al-´ummal bi-mitrash 2", August 13 (http://portal.www.gov.qa/wps/portal/mediacenter/news/individualnews/moi%20calls%20for%20use%20of%20metrash %202%20for%20complaints%20on%20absconding%20workers/!ut/p/a0/04_ Sj9CPykssy0xPLMnMz0vMAfGjzOIt_S2cDS0sDNwNDMwsDTyDDUKD TbzcDfwdDfWDU_PsU9Pzy_Ry8pMTc1JtU_P0C7IdFQEZoaLk/).

Human Rights Watch (2014): "'I Already Bought You' – Abuse and Exploitation of Female Migrant Domestic Workers in the United Arab Emirates", October 13 (http://www.refworld.org/docid/544a1b784.html).

al-Imarat al-'arabiyya al-mutahhida. Wizarat al-'amal (2010): "Qarar wizari raqm 1186" (http://www.mol.gov.ae/molwebsite/ar/labour-law/announcements.aspx#page=1).

al-Imarat al-'arabiyya al-mutahhida. Wizarat al-'amal (2016): "Qanun al-'amal", July 12, 2016 (http://www.mol.gov.ae/molwebsite/ar/labour-law/labour-law.aspx).

Jayan, Aarun (2012): "NRK remittance in 2011: 31.2% of Kerala GDP." In: The New Indian Express, July 17 (http://www.newindianexpress.com/nation/article569033.ece).

Jureidini, Ray (2014): "Migrant Labour Recruitment to Qatar." Report for Qatar Foundation Migrant Worker Welfare Initiative, Doha: Qatar Foundation.

"Khadimat haribat@maidescape", July 12, 2016 (https://twitter.com/maidsescape).

Khan, Azfar/Harroff-Tavel, Hélène (2011): "Reforming the Kafala: Challenges and Opportunities in Moving Forward." In: Asia and Pacific Migration Journal 20/3-4, pp. 293-313.

Knight, Kyle (2014): "The subtle wounds of Nepal's remittance boom." In: Al Jazeera, April 13 (http://www.aljazeera.com/indepth/features/2014/04/subtle-wounds-nepals-remittance-boom-201441144741533395.html).

Kovessy, Peter (2014): "Qatar officials propose changes to kafala system." In: Dohanews, May 14 (http://dohanews.co/qatar-officials-propose-changes-kafala-system/).

Longva, Anh Nga (1999): "Keeping Migrant Workers in Check: The Kafala System in the Gulf." In: Middle East Report 211, pp. 20-22.

—— (1997): Walls Build on Walls Built on Sand: Migration, Exclusion, and Society in Kuwait, Boulder: Westview.

Lori, Noora (2012): Temporary Workers or Permanent Migrants? The Kafala System and Contestations over Residency in the Arab Gulf States. Paper, Paris/Bruxelles: Centre Migrations et Citoyennetés/Institut Français des Relations Internationales.

Mauqi' Khadimat, July 12, 2016 (http://www.shrte.com/).

Miers, Suzanne (2003): Slavery in the Twentieth Century. The Evolution of a Global Problem, Walnut Creek: Altamira Press.

Ministry of Development Planning and Statistics (2015): "Qatar Monthly Statistics. Edition June 2015" (http://www.qsa.gov.qa/eng/publication/QatarMontlyStatistics/QATAR-MONTHLY-STATISTICS-JUNE-2015-Edition-17.pdf).

"Muqabil 3000 alaf Dirham – Dubay: Tajir bashar ya'rud khadima lil-bay' wa-l-shurta taqbid 'alayhi bi-kamin", In: 24, May 10, 2015 (http://bit.ly/1CGAOjk).

al-Muriki, Fahd (2014): "Mukhtassun: Iqrar al-ta'min didd hurub al-ummala sayadmun isti'ada 8 alaf Riyal ka-hadd aqsa lil-kafil." In: Al-Riyadh, Oct 15 (http://www.alriyadh.com/985063, accessed August 13, 2015).

Nagraj, Aarti (2013): "Revealed: GCC Asian Expats EARn 26% Less Than Western Peers." In: Gulf Business, March 4 (http://gulfbusiness.com/2013/03/revealed-gcc-asian-expats-earn-26-less-than-western-peers/#.VeGpe5d_Rj9).

Philip, Shaju (2014): "Kerala migration survey 2014: State's youth still fly abroad for livelihood." In: The Indian Express, September 17 (http://indianexpress.com/article/india/india-others/kerala-migration-survey-2014-states-youth-still-fly-abroad-for-livelhood/).

Perumal, Santosh V. (2014): "Surge in demand for labour camps as worker inflow increases." In: Gulf Times, September 2 (http://www.gulf-times.com/qatar/178/details/406580/surge-in-demand-for-labour-camps-as-worker-inflow-increases).

Rahman, Mizanur Md. (2011): "Emigration and the Family Economy: Bangladeshi Labor Migration to Saudi Arabia." In: Asian and Pacific Migration Journal 20/3-4, pp. 389-411.

Rai, Om Astha (2015): "Zero-cost migration." In: Nepali Times, June 28 (http://www.nepalitimes.com/blogs/thebrief/2015/06/28/zero-cost-migration).

"Runaway domestics cost families SR 1 billion", August 26, 2014 (http://www.arabnews.com/saudi-arabia/news/620891).

Seccombe, Ian J./Lawless, Richard (1986): "Foreign worker dependence in the Gulf and the international oil companies: 1910-50." In: International Migration Review XX/3, pp. 548-574.

Shah, Nasra M. (2014): "Recent amnesty programmes for irregular migrants in Kuwait and Saudi Arabia: some successes and failures." In: Migration Policy Centre; GLMM; Explanatory note; 09/2014.

—— (2010): "Building State Capacities for Managing Contract Worker Mobility. The Asia-GCC Context." International Organization for Migration (IOM), Geneva, Background Paper for WMO 2010.

—— (2008): Recent Labour Immigration Policies in the Oil-Rich Gulf. How Effective are they likely to be? ILO Asian Regional Programme on Governance of Labour Migration. Working Paper No. 3, Bangkok: International Labour Office.

Snoj, Jure (2013): "Population of Qatar by Nationalities." In: bq, December 18 (http://www.bqdoha.com/2013/12/population-qatar).

State of Qatar. Ministry of Interior (2014): "Qatar Announces Wide-Ranging Labour Market Reforms", May 14 (http://www.moi.gov.qa/site/english/news/2014/05/14/32204.html).

Toumi, Habib (2013): "Saudi Arabia: 58,615 foreigners abscond in one year". In: Gulf News, December 25 (http://gulfnews.com/news/gulf/saudi-arabia/saudi-arabia-58-615-foreigners-abscond-in-one-year-1.1270683).

—— (2011): "Nationality-based salary discrimination causing discontent." In: Gulf News, May 25 (http://gulfnews.com/news/gulf/qatar/nationality-based-salary-discrimination-causing-discontent-1.812640).

Al-Ufuq News (2015): "50 alf Riyal mukafa'a li-man yajid khadima haribat fil-Riyad", March 25 (http://www.alufuqnews.com/4752.html).

al-Umran, Salwa/al-Utaibi, Ghazil (2014): "Tajrim hurub al-khadimat yadmun haqq al-muwatin." In: Al-Riyadh, November 21 (http://www.alriyadh.com/1005643).

United Arab Emirates. Ministry of Labour (2015a): "Labour Ministry conducts 332,000 inspections to check labour violations." In: Al'Amal, April 2015, pp. 14-15.

—— (2015b): "23 fines for different violations." In: Al'Amal, April 2015, p. 11.

United Nations, Department of Economic and Social Affairs, Population Division (2016): "International Migration Report 2015: Highlights." In: Annex (ST/ESA/SER.A/375), pp. 28-32.

United Nations, Department of Economic and Social Affairs, Population Division (2015). Trends in International Migrant Stock: The 2015 Revision (United Nations database POP/DB/MIG/Stock/Rev.2015).

Vlieger, Antoinette (2011): Domestic workers in Saudi Arabia and the Emirates: Trafficking victims? Amsterdam Law School Research Paper No. 32, Amsterdam: University of Amsterdam.

Wizarat al-'amal. Al-Mamlaka al-'arabiyya al-sa'udiyya (2014): Al-Kitab al-ihsa'i al-sanawi 1434/1435h./2013m, Riyad.

Zahra, Maysa (2015): "Bahrain's Legal Framework of Migration." In: Gulf Labour Markets and Migration 01/2015.

—— (2014): "The Legal Framework of the Sponsorship System in Qatar, Saudi Arabia and Kuwait: A Comparative Examination." In: Gulf Labour Markets and Migration 07/2014.

1808080.com, July 12, 2016 (http://www.1808080.com/viewlisting.php?view=25493).

Re-presenting and Narrating Labour: Coolie Migration in the Caribbean

LILIANA GÓMEZ-POPESCU

> "Yet if we have become overly visible, contemporary hypervisibility traces its roots to the singularly modern belief in appropriating and desire to appropriate the world by means of the gaze. The modernization of cultures and societies was linked to an increasing seculari-zation of the invisible. [...] Their use of a visual rhetoric that defines scenarios, excludes or includes protagonists, and, most crucially, evokes pedagogies of the gaze allows us to glean signs of becoming, modes of *making visible* imagined modernities and communities."
> JAGUARIBE/LISSOVSKY 2009: 175-176

---

1   I wish to thank Michael Zeuske, Gesine Müller, Ulrike Lindner and Sabine Damir-Geilsdorf at the Global South Studies Center in Cologne for organizing this conference and for their enriching discussion, which helped me to sharpen my ideas and outline my argument. Without that impulse I might possibly have missed the importance of discussing imperial formations in the Caribbean in the light of labour and labour history, and particularly coolie labour migration, when examining the photographic and visual archives. I also thank the other participants for having challenged my questions from a necessarily entangled and global perspective.

Visibilizing the Unseen

Beatriz Jaguaribe underscores what is widely acknowledged: the modern belief in appropriating the world through the gaze, the selective nature of which both renders seen, and invisibilizes. Mostly framed as an imperialistic gaze and conceptualized as a hegemonic perspective, it is broadly recognized that photography is a part of a dominant discourse being employed as a modern, efficient means in the service of the State, industry, and the sciences, in the way it appropriates time and space, freezing them into a linear narrative. However, focusing on this *grand récit* of photography would miss the pictures' *petites contre-histoires,* or their potential alternative narrative: that of a reclamation.

I am interested in the following three aspects, in order to unfold a picture-series' embodied reclamation from the vantage point of post-colonial and emancipatory discussions (cf. Gómez 2011). The first two are: making visible; and voicing/narrating; these two articulations are inextricably intertwined. The third aspect relates to the enclave as a modern spatial figure corresponding to the capitalist production of the plantation economy, and I will examine it against the idea of imperial debris. Drawing upon a larger conceptual framework I will argue that the two articulations and the spatial figure relate to the question of the archive and its relation to the public and the private. In his well-known essay on the *mal d'archive,* Jacques Derrida once astutely observed:

"Nothing is less reliable, nothing is less clear today than the word 'archive.' [...] Nothing is more troubled and more troubling. The trouble with what is troubling here is undoubtedly what troubles and muddles our vision [...], what inhibits sight and knowledge, but also the trouble of troubled and troubling affairs [...], the trouble of secrets, of plots, of clandestineness, of half-private, half-public conjurations, always at the unstable limit between public and private, between the family, the society, and the State, between the family and an intimacy even more private than the family, between oneself and oneself." (Derrida 1995: 57)

This certainly becomes true when examining the United Fruit Company photographic archive, with its thousands of images depicting the wide range of the United Fruit Company's agricultural operations and, moreover, an expanding experimental capitalism. These archival images contour the imaginary of modernization, while they are situated at the "unstable limit between public and private, between the family, the society, and the State" (ibid.). Interestingly enough, as we are reminded by Derrida, "[...] the technical structure of the archiving archive also determines the structure of the archivable content even in its very coming into existence and in its relationship to the future. The archivization produces as much as it records the event." (ibid.: 17-18). As *consignation*, the archive seems to outline a figuration of what can be told and seen, of what can be voiced and visibilized, of what is to come.[2] Moreover, the archive seems to be a sort of *figurality* corresponding, I argue in the case of the United Fruit Company, to the plantation economy experienced in the Caribbean for a long time.

Let me expand this idea by turning to a photograph series that "produces as much as it records the event" (see figure 1). In the company's albums on Jamaica we find a picture series that shows a small group of children in front of and behind the labourers' barracks at Golden Grove. At first glance the pictures show the private space of what had become the company's spatial organization of labour. At a second glance they visually bear witness to the event of coolie migration and its aftermath in the Caribbean. Several rows of children are grouped in front of the barracks where the migrant labourers used to be detained. Seemingly, the pictures aim to make visible the infrastructure, and to 'document' the housing that the company upgraded in the course of their presence in the Caribbean. However, as a *figuration* of recording the past and the present, the archive makes visible the as-yet unseen or overlooked. For although the United Fruit Company employed coolie labourers or incorporated those from a previous coolie migration to the Caribbean, it did not mention the coolies (see figure 2).[3]

---

2   Derrida relates the idea of the archive to that of consignation as follows: "The archontic power, which also gathers the functions of unification, of identification, of classification, must be paired with what we will call the power of consignation. By consignation, we do not only mean, in the ordinary sense of the word, the act of assigning residence or of entrusting so as to put into reserve (to consign, to deposit), in a place and on a substrate, but here the act of consigning through gathering together signs. It is not only the traditional consignatio, that is, the written proof, but what all consignatio begins by presupposing. Consignation aims to coordinate a single corpus, in a system or a synchrony in which all the elements articulate the unity of an ideal configuration. In an archive, there should not be any absolute dissociation, any heterogeneity or secret which could separate (secernere), or partition, in an absolute manner. The archontic principle of the archive is also a principle of consignation, that is, of gathering together" (Derrida 1995: 10).

3   With regard to coolie labourers in the plantations of the United Fruit Company, we find the following description in a historical document: "On the plantations of the United Fruit Company in Guatemala, I counted up the following racial groups: American, English, German, Swiss, Italian, Hebrew, French, Canadian, Scotch. This

Figure 1: Type design of labourers' houses. Front view of barracks.

Source: United Fruit Company Photograph Collection, Baker Library, Harvard Business School; photographer unknown.

The pictures do not tell us about coolie migration explicitly because, seemingly, they aim to show something else: among the series of photographs, to which

> group comprised the petty company officials of administration and supervision. Among the labouring class were found natives of all the Central American States, Mexico, Columbia and Venezuela. Due to the [in]adequate local labour supply, the fruit companies have imported black labour from the islands of the West Indies and British Honduras. There are also come American negroes who went to the Tropics as railway construction men. The Jamaican negro predominates as he is the original 'banana man'. Coolies from Jamaica and French negroes from Martinique and Guadelupe add to the babble of tongues. In the small towns that spring up in the vicinity of the plantations, Chinese merchants are numerous and further complicate matters." (Williams 1925: 117-118)

these two pictures belong (see Fig. 1-2), we primarily witness a sort of technical language of 'documentation,' showing the different types of barracks and labourers' housing. The archival pictures, though, become a part of today's imperial debris. As leftovers, the pictorial remnants in this imperial debris constitute a part of the increasing "secularization of the invisible" (Jaguaribe/Lissovsky 2009: 175). As part of the United Fruit Company's archive, the photographs did not circulate at the time because they were carefully kept in photographic albums and inscribed into a private corporate image economy. Nor are they disseminated today. Yet, as pictures, which were taken in the contact zone of the Company's plantations, they produced and recorded the event of labour migration, while they simultaneously open the way for a potential alternative narrative about coolie labour, in the way they visibilize the unseen and unspoken.

Figure 2: Labourers' houses at Golden Grove

Source: United Fruit Company Photograph Collection, Baker Library, Harvard Business School; photographer unknown.

With regard to the business practices of the United Fruit Company, a company that quite efficiently established a world market for tropical fruits, and the expansion of experimental capitalism into the Caribbean, coolie migration was never really brought up as a subject in its own right. Only recently has it started to be voiced or made seen, configuring a visibilization of the violent modernization of the societies and cultures of the Caribbean. The writer Khal Torabully offers us *coolitude*, a cultural concept, which raises awareness of a cultural experience that has been overlooked, related to indentured and forced labour, which continues to the present day, bound to the economic and legal situations of the coolies (cf. Müller/Abel, this volume). The concept focuses on the transfer of knowledge between colonial empires and work regimes worldwide. Furthermore, it raises awareness of a pluricultural configuration of the Caribbean, which the pictures conceal in order to produce a homogeneous space suitable for economic exploitation.

On the one hand, as images of utopia the pictures belong to the imaginary of economic expansion envisaged as a chronotope of the eternal transition towards modernity, a promise of modernization itself. On the other, as dystopian narratives they reflect the processes of modernization and what has been called a world/colonial system that is accompanied by the constant production of cycles of marginality. This seems important as it sheds new light on bonded labour intersecting here with post-colonial studies and labour history. This is also underscored by Ann Laura Stoler, who critically stimulates a new framing of the study of the Empire, and encourages us not only to look at the colonial legacy, but also at the imperial debris, its ruins, and the processes of ruination, which continue to exert their influence today as a post-colonial presence. She underlines that it is important thus to disrupt the

"[...] facile distinction between political history and poetic form, urging us to think differently about both the language we use to capture the tenacious hold of imperial effects and their tangible if elusive forms. [...] to track the uneven temporal sedimentation in which imperial formations leave their marks. [...] to ask how empire's ruins contour and carve through the psychic and material space in which people live and what compounded layers of imperial debris do to them." (Stoler 2013: 2)

Adopting voicing/narrating and making visible as epistemic practices, I wish to explore the "uneven temporal sedimentation" and, further, "the psychic and material space", in order to discuss the idea of imperial debris in the light of a series of archival photographs. Moreover, I argue that the concept of coolitude and the idea of imperial debris may serve to define a new conceptual framework for discussing the migrant labour we witness as the emergence of a modern political space that has reproduced and expanded the Empire right up to the present day. Scrutinizing two photograph series that depict the coolie migration in the Caribbean by examining the visual field gives rise to a series of questions: What do the images visibilize? How is labour represented and narrated? Do the photographs register the coolie experience? How should the imperial visual leftovers be conceptualized in terms of environmental degradation and ecological ruins? How do these images depict the imperial contours and "psychic and material space in which people live" both at the time and in the present day?

RE-PRESENTING LABOUR

As the archive seems to determine "the structure of the archivable content even in its very coming into existence and in its relationship to the future", in accordance with Derrida (1995: 17-18), the photographs depicting the Caribbean and the modern plantation economy at a threshold of experimentation involving diverse, modern capitalist labour forms contour a particular kind of spatial production by representing labour. Following this, in another, earlier image series in a photographic album from circa 1890, we find, among others, a few pictures that visually bear witness to the coolie presence in the Caribbean.[4] It is noteworthy here that they determine the major theme or *leitmotif*, so to speak, of the way plantation economy is represented as a discourse of landscape. This discourse is also mirrored in the United Fruit Company photographs in the way the violent environmental transformations resulting from the plantation economy are not depicted, or only visualized as a peaceful transformation of the land into an improved agricultural landscape. Moreover, the photographs configure a projection and a desire for this transformation. It is this overall visual theme of framing the plantation economy as landscape that determines the exceptional value of many of these kinds of photographs, which form an important visual archive of the Caribbean.

For example, Figure 3 shows a river (most likely the Demerara river) with splendid giant water lilies of the species *Victoria regia*, discovered by the German explorer Sir Robert Schomburgk in the northern South American region,

---

4   Mrs. Lilian Horsford Farlow was the wife of William G. Farlow, an American botanist, and gave this photograph album to the Widener Library at Harvard University in 1927. She was a member of the the Massachusetts Society of the Colonial Dames of America (1909-1910).

in the former British colony that is, today, Guyana, which at that time mainly produced a particular cane sugar, also known as Demerara sugar. At a second glance, we notice a small group of people, labourers, at the left-hand margin of the photograph, who merge into the impression of plentiful and magical nature. They seem, from their traditional clothing, to be of Indian origin, and may be coolie labourers. Three young coolie women or girls sit on a small base with two water jugs and a basket in front of them. However, what the picture shows is primarily a vision of nature that frames the plantation economy as landscape, showing the typical contours of sugar plantation monoculture, viewed here to the left and right of the river. It carefully conceals the previously necessary clearing of a vast area of virgin tropical rainforest, making it a 'reversed image' of what is later perceived as environmental degradation and imperial debris. When embracing the visual, Stoler points out, it becomes urgent to become aware of the invisibilities in the visual field of this debris, which we far too easily assume within a given image (2013: 3).

Figure 3: Demerara. Victoria Regia

Source: Photographer unknown, photographs and clippings of the West Indies, ca. 1890, Houghton Library, Harvard University.

Another picture from that same photographic album from the West Indies shows, as inscribed in the caption, "Coolies on Shipboard. Recently arrived" (see Figure 4). It is certainly one of those rare pictures representing the shipment and circulation of Indian coolies, here male labourers including two or three young boys, many of them in their traditional clothing, exhausted after a long middle passage on the journey to the Caribbean. The labourers gaze at the photographer, and the archival picture renders seen coolie labourers arriving at Demerara. Is this a scene of deportation? Does this picture belong to a visual economy that conceals or remembers the coolie experience, as it configures a new working regime and is a sign of a global becoming? Does this image belong to the visual archive that may give glimpses into the psychic and material space? Does its visual rhetoric include the coolie, in the way it reflects modes of making visible the imagined modernities and communities?

Figure 4: Demerara. Coolies on Shipboard. Recently arrived.

Source: Photographer unknown, photographs and clippings of the West Indies, ca. 1890, Houghton Library, Harvard University.

In the next picture (Figure 5) another process is rendered seen: at first glance we perceive a visual rhetoric that frames and represents landscape here as the main protagonist, peacefully orchestrated in the picture. But the caption, "immigration depot", clearly refers to another embedded discourse here: that of the modern spatial organization of the circulation of labourers. Moreover, the caption characterizes a newly introduced vocabulary that mirrors the modern belief in organizing space through labour. Likewise, architecture as media correlates with the novel procedure for organizing large-scale immigration, which the American continent has experienced ever since as an incomparably global labour diaspora that forms part of the imperial genealogies of the present.

The immigration depot as architecture and as material practice belongs to what Stoler has called "residual or reactivated imperial practices" (2013: 4), which we can witness today in its material and visual leftovers, in images, texts, words, bodies and artifacts, such as spaces, landscapes, and other residual repositories of meaning.

Figure 5: Demerara. Immigration Depot.

Source: Photographer unknown, photographs and clippings of the West Indies, ca. 1890, Houghton Library, Harvard University

Yet, as Stoler has put it, we are still "wrestling with the task of seeing, with acts of violation for which there are no photographs able to document bodily exposures and intrusions of space" (2013: 3). So it is that migration and labour are the primordial experience and focus in both Khal Torabully's poems and

Marina Carter's historical study, forming what is referred to with the concept of coolitude, when they observe:

"As more and more Indians migrated, their identification and control became a time-consuming task. Immigration Departments, headed by Protectors of Immigrants, increasingly became the depositories of registers, and the headquarters of a bureaucracy that policed the indentured and time-expired labourers, rather than a nerve-centre where grievances could be investigated and redressed. The identification of Indians according to an immigration number, which was reproduced on all official documents, assumed a huge importance in their lives." (Carter/Torabully 2002: 125)

The novel vocabulary is noteworthy, as it mirrors the modern imaginary of flow and capitalistic spatial production, into which these photographic series are embodied in the way they re-present or make present again coolie migration in the Caribbean. Following this, both the captions and the photographs belong to and form a constitutive part of the bureaucratic culture of the colonial, and thus imperial, production of space.

Figure 6: Demerara. Coolies.

Source: Photographer unknown, photographs and clippings of the West Indies, ca. 1890, Houghton Library, Harvard University.

This becomes even more apparent in the following two portrait pictures of coolies in Demerara, as the caption indicates (see Figure 6). Following a rather conventional visual rhetoric, the images show labourers in an orchestrated and well-arranged scenario, representing them distinctly as coolies, marked as culturally 'other.' One picture shows a group of male labourers wearing traditional clothing, some with necklaces and distinctive headgear, bearing typical agricultural tools and other specific accessories, such as a traditional hookah, to sustain the ethnic distinction and otherness of the labourers. In this sense the image corresponds to an exotic fantasy allowing for a pedagogy of the imperial gaze.

Among the Indian coolie labourers, we can distinguish two apparently Chinese coolies, one of them wearing a traditional rural hat, the other exposing his long, thin hair plait. The image visually bears witness to the long experience of indentured labour in the Caribbean since the mid-19th century, mainly as labour immigration from China and India. How is labour represented here? Coming from a visual economy that we perceive today in its visual leftovers as imperial debris, the picture imagines the cultural 'other' as a constitutive part of the reproduction, thus sustaining the modern economic regime of the plantation economy. At the level of pictorial language, the image mirrors a familiar and more conventional genre of labour representation that seems to dissolve any individual trait in favor of a stereotypical representation of the body, which becomes the embodiment of otherness.

The discourse of labour thus visually economizes the very idea of human resources and the human body, explicitly inscribed into the images' economy. As a picture from a photographic album on the plantation economy of the West Indies, a rather generic but characteristic form of storage and representation of that time, the image within this economy of display, situated at the "unstable limit between the private and the public" (Derrida 1995: 57), turns out to be the very imperial residue of our present time. I argue that the photographic album, so commonly used and materially fabricated, predominantly configures a hegemonic gaze, in that it corresponds to an imperial formation and the plantation economy, in the way it evolves the discourse of plantation, whose modern imaginary is consonant with landscape and labour. So the culturally violent act of indentured labour is never explicitly represented. Yet, it is always present in the archival visual and textual documents, and even seems to be the very condition of their existence. As violence is not re-presented and possibly even not archivable, today we may only relate to these imperial formations in the form of a visual leftover or residue. That is, to conceive of the archive as an epistemic figure, in the way it structures the "archivable content" and "in its relationship to the future" (Derrida 1995: 17-18). As Stoler remarks, these imperial formations have left "their bold-faces or subtle traces [...] which contemporary inequities work their way through", and which we perceive with regard to the archive (2013: 3).

Figure 7: Demerara. Coolies.

Source: Photographer unknown, photographs and clippings of the West Indies, ca. 1890, Houghton Library, Harvard University.

The following picture (Figure 7) shows another group of coolie labourers in an image the genre of which we are familiar with: that of a portrait depicting the ethnic and cultural 'other' with its distinct cultural and religious marks of difference, visually represented in the image. It depicts a group of female Indian coolie labourers, carefully arranged in rows, squatting, sitting, and standing. The photograph shows them in their traditional clothing with their jewelry and ornaments as distinctive markers of their pluricultural and diverse ethnic backgrounds. As a group portrait, it also shows male Indian coolie labourers with archetypal traditional headgear (such as a tarboosh) that seem to represent four different ethnic, religious, and cultural groups that were brought to the West Indies, among them seemingly Hindus, Sikhs, and Muslims, representing the great linguistic and cultural diversity of India. This image certainly discloses an imaginary of modern labour circulation marked by ethnic, religious, and cultural traits, highly hierarchized: the making of a global labour diaspora yet to come. Circumscribing the cultural depth of the concept of coolitude, Marina Carter pays a special attention to the fact that:

"If their mother-tongues functioned as a means of more perfect expression for overseas Indians, their native languages could also be a source of comfort and cultural sustenance. It was not uncommon for migrants to carry with them manuscript copies of their sacred texts; the literate among them would read aloud stories from the Ramayana [and the Qur'an] and other religious epics to their fellow labourers. [...] 'of all the religious books, the Ramayana has come closest to becoming the central text of overseas Hinduism. It was immensely popular among the contract and especially the indentured labourers in places as far apart as Fiji, Trinidad, South Africa, Suriname, Guyana and Malaysia... its central theme of exile, suffering, struggle and eventual return resonated with the experiences of the Hindu migrants, especially but not exclusively those of the indentured labourers." (Carter 2002: 128-129)

Interestingly, she further underlines that the "Ramayana gave them conceptual tools to make sense of their predicaments, articulated their fears, and showed them how to cope with these" (ibid.: 129). Female coolie labourers were brought along with the male since the very first British experiments with coolie indentured labour. Even children, including infants, were shipped to the Caribbean, though the mortality rate on the way was especially high among them. Notwithstanding this, their reproductive force became a part of an economy of labour in the transition from a slavery-bonded labour regime to a salary-based one, in which indentured labour was a new form of paid labour, although its slavery-like characteristics could never be totally abolished. This also seems to have been important for the imperial formation of a modern and global plantation economy and what would soon replace it. For example, labour in the plantation economy was already represented in 19th century paintings and lithographs, having defined a new genre, visually partaking in the transformation of landscape into peaceful and productive agricultural land (cf. Casid 2005).

Even though manifested and imagined as an aspect of peaceful environmental transformation, labour as a violent regime, as part of the plantation economy, was never represented as such. Instead, its cruelty and violence were invisibilized. This certainly becomes true regarding these photographic series where labour is *not* directly represented. Rather, labour seems to be naturalized and subordinated to a plantation economy, in the way the photographs conceal the violence of the environmental changes of the man-made monocultural landscape. So it is that the photographic series of this album makes of the plantation economy and labour a major but hidden *leitmotif* whose representational form corresponds to that of landscape, strikingly beautiful and with a visually appealing aesthetic language. Yet, the pictures cunningly invisibilize the omnipresent violence of plantation labour, which makes them imperial debris.

Besides this visual concealment of the hegemonic gaze, the pictures are visual 'documents' of coolie migration in the Caribbean. In the way they are situated as archival images at the "unstable limit between public and private" (Derrida 1995: 57), and because of their quintessential relationship to the future, they also open the way for an alternative historiography that contours the coolie as protagonist. Accordingly, a future reclamation and reception of the photographs as signs of becoming might emerge. In the way the photographs belong to a larger visual archive of the Caribbean, we may recognize today the long imperial genealogy of environmental degradation and forceful asymmetrical global migration, which has still not been reversed. I have argued that the series of photographs evolve 'landscape' in the light of the process of transforming land into a viable aesthetic, economic, and political space, through the circulation of commodities and bodies. Moreover, these photographs may help to disclose the embodied imperial genealogies of labour as an ecological media history, mirrored in the landscapes and flow of people, still present today.

NARRATING COOLIE MIGRATION

The second perspective centers on the epistemic practices of voicing/narrating, which I relate to uneven temporal sedimentation as an articulation of psychic and material space. Revealingly, the anthropologist E. Valentine Daniel focuses on the embodied violence of colonial capitalism when he conceives of indentured or forced labour as the core of the plantation economy:

"What nineteenth-century colonialism did to more than thirty million human beings by turning them into coolies, the massive contribution of labour to colonial capitalism that was made possible by this transmogrification, and the positive role colonialism and the plantation economy played in the making of a modern nation-state amounts to but half of the story. The other half lies in the violence wreaked on the land and the people by the political economy of colonialism in general and, in particular, by the plantation economy – one of colonial capitalism's most productive enterprises of the nineteenth century and the first half of the twentieth." (Daniel 2013: 70-71)

I wish to further discuss the question of the re-presentation of labour, and more specifically that of the indentured labour of coolie migrants in the Caribbean following the coolie perspective: how they voice and narrate their own experiences and survival within the imperial debris. Furthermore, I wish to speculate about the divergent but intersecting perspectives: firstly, that of visual representations of the coolie in the form of the photographs, and secondly, that of coolie voices retelling and remembering the coolie experience across many generations, articulating it as an intimate collective as well as subjective knowledge, by adopting aesthetic forms, such as epic songs, that shape today's post-colonial presence. In forming an archive, both perspectives seem to be entangled in the way they disclose "the unexpected capacity of objects to fade out of focus as they 'remain peripheral to our vision' and yet potent in marking partitioned lives" (Stoler 2013: 5).

Figure 8: Trinidad. Coolie.

Source: Photographer unknown, photographs and clippings of the West Indies, ca. 1890, Houghton Library, Harvard University

The photographic album of the plantation economy in the West Indies, or the few United Fruit Company photographs depicting coolie migration in the Caribbean, are objects that have faded out of sight, as they do not circulate, and have rarely been seen by latter-day 'coolie' generations. As *objets trouvés*, though, the pictures are visual leftovers that are important repositories of meaning. Moreover, as visual leftovers they are bound to the political as they confer on the archive the potential figuration of future meaning and reclamation.

For example, the final picture (Figure 8) shows a studio portrait of a girl in front of a setting of typical accessories of that time, a remnant of a Roman column at the left side of the picture and a studio curtain whose motif is not very clearly discernible. Much has been written about the economy of this type of popular, 19th century studio portrait. It reflects a typical motif portraying the house and plantation workers that became a part of a household or plantation 'inventory.' In the form of the popular *carte-de-visite*, this used to circulate widely outside the private image economy, defined by a personal or private photographic album. In this sense the imagery certainly belongs to a hegemonic discourse or the discourse of plantation, as Jill Casid (2005) coined the term.

However, I hesitate to conceive of this as the only one. Rather, I wish to argue for conceiving of this type of picture as an object that has, indeed, faded out of sight, but may be able to renew its meaning in the way it embodies the potential to circulate back and be re-appropriated by subsequent coolie generations. Despite the fact that the picture belongs to an image economy that emerges from a primarily hierarchical representational order, as an historical 'document' it seems to outline the Coolie as a protagonist and historical agent, allowing us to glean "signs of becoming" and the modes of making visible imagined modernities and communities. Following this, the picture narrates coolie migration, while it alludes to an imperial genealogy that the cultural concept of coolitude tries to critically uncover. Embodying an externalized view, it nevertheless recovers an internalized experience. As an *objet trouvé* it asks for the future reception of the image by later coolie generations. In this sense, the picture becomes a visual leftover of a situation allowing for different future uses, as images *per se* are poly-semiotic; it articulates the tangibility of a colonial past and a post-colonial presence. Moreover, pictures as material objects embody the complex semantic situations of the imperial experience.

I wish to relate these observations to the second perspective, that of the articulation of coolie voices in the epics and lyrics, with which Khal Torabully restores the figure of the coolie in order to imagine an end to discrimination and racism, when he notes that "l'apocalypse [...] révelera le martyre nègre, le martyre créole, et la prophétie annoncera la fin de la discrimination sociale et l'émergence de l'identité créole, grace a la dignité reconquise" (Carter/Torabully 2002: 5). He suggests that in narrative practices the coolie experience is recovered and dignity regained in the way they make available the complex semantic situations of humiliations and violations culturally, environmentally, and humanly committed.

So it is that the anthropologist E. Valentine Daniel, personally sharing the experience of plantation labour through his family history, opts for the form of an *epic* to retell and reflect upon the present history, recounting the Coolie experience in South Asia, namely that of the Tamil minorities of South Indian origin in today's Sri Lanka, former Ceylon. He gives shape to his experience in the form of a hybrid poem, bearing the title *The Coolie. An Unfinished Epic*, by adopting an experimental ethnography and an oral history as major truthful non-linear narratives. But he also integrates written historical records about coffee, rubber, and tea plantations within the lyrical form. With the first stanzas he retells and remembers the experience of the generation and the idea of time, so deeply embodied in the plantation, tangible to us in our very post-colonial presence. Moreover, he opens to an archive that is, in the words of Derrida, truly situated "at the unstable limit between public and private, between the family, the society, and the State, between the family and an intimacy even more private than the family, between oneself and oneself" (Derrida 1995: 57):

Generations and Time

"When I leave this island," said Rukku, "a single
witness will still remain to tell of the observed
and the absorbed of the shedders of blood mingled

"with blood shed. Mother earth here has been quite reserved,
abashed to confess that she, soaked in venal crude,
puddles her own clay to create out of this sludge,

"coolies as us, over and over again. Lewd
our senses, our ways rude, so deemed by all who judge
and miss our dialect's pulchritude. Eternal

"returnees, requisite detritus. Judge not lest
you too be judged for having seen but not witnessed
harm infernal, unlike Ramu, who has lived our every test."
[...]
All prattle ceased. Her whispers, transformed into song
Pierced the rising mist as light would a veil of tears.
Place held time still. "Time," said Adhi "is neither long

"nor short. Length, could not its unchanging measure be.
Some times are gaugeable, as a repast's vaunted
Flavors are, in x lumens of intensity."

[...]
Chronicles keep now and then apart and airtight;

they declare time long or short. In heritage,
now becomes then and then becomes now. Five, eight or ten
hereafters reporting to this blend, may somehow

incinder the sum, causing the now into then
to collapse and effervesce, celebrate or mourn
and thereby time's space-analog vitiate. But

never always, nor forever. Its gift to burn
makes time a tree. For in the rings of its clean-cut
wound reposes the past's presence in synchrony.
[...]
(Daniel 2013: 75-78)

What both Daniel and Torabully make explicit is that narrating the coolie experience corresponds to the aesthetic forms of remembrance and transmogrification of global migration and indentured labour. Moreover, narrating as epistemic practice is entangled with perceiving and articulating time and space, so meaningful to the experience of migration, revealed in particular in the "unfinished" epic by Daniel. Further, the epic as well as the pictures, I argue, reflect the shifting time-space experience: they are imperial debris of repetition and cultural transformation materialized in language, belief, and rhyme. As a contestation to modernity, narrating-as-voicing becomes here the primordial form of resistance. Likewise, this contestation is embodied in the photographic series that subverts the discourse of plantation being the *raison d'être* of its production, haunting "our 'true' reality as a specter of what might have happened, conferring on our reality the status of extreme fragility and contingency, [that] implicitly clashes with the predominant 'linear' narrative forms of [historiography]" (Zizek 2005: 39).[5]

---

5 As observed elsewhere by the philosopher Slavoj Zizek: "This perception of our reality as one of the possible – often even not the most probable – outcomes of an

In her study, Marina Carter observes that

"[m]inorities in Creole societies, overseas Indians took refuge in the language and culture of a homeland, which became more and more mythical as the notion of returns faded. Paradoxically, as fast as Indians became part of a Caribbean or Pacific or African landscape, they sought to distinguish themselves." (Carter 2002: 130)

As "images of a continuing exile," she conceives, mobility in time and space becomes a major theme that predominantly resonates in the unfinished epic by Daniel. Once overseas,

"the indentured labourer plunged ever further into diaspora, wandering further and further afield. From Reunion, Tamil workers re-migrated to Mauritius; from Mauritius, labourers were engaged for Natal, and there was cross-migration between the Indian Ocean, Caribbean and even the later Pacific Ocean Indian diasporas." (Carter/Torabully 2002: 131)

This remarkably continuous mobility and movement, as submerged and yet invisible landscapes, re-surfaces as images in these pictures that allow for a reading of an alternative narrative beyond the discourse of plantation economy. Moreover, it is this mobility in time and space that allows migrating labourers to adopt new identities and to de-essentialize them. It is this very mobility in time and space, materialized in the cultural changes of language, word, and rhyme, that resonates with this poem and transcends a linear historiography, while expressing something that we as humankind all share: "Chronicles keep now and then apart and airtight;/ they declare time long or short. In heritage,/ now becomes then and then becomes now [...]" (Daniel 2013: 77).

In the psychic and material space the epic narrative makes tangible a very modern time-space experience, which we share as migrant labourers of a globalized future world: "never always, nor forever. Its gift to burn/ makes time a tree. For in the rings of its clean-cut/ wound reposes the past's presence in synchrony" (ibid.: 78). These narratives thus become performative acts, in which time and space, as of resistance and memory, are contested in the way they make

---

'open' situation, this notion that other possible outcomes are not simply canceled out but continue to haunt our 'true' reality as a specter of what might have happened, conferring on our reality the status of extreme fragility and contingency, implicitly clashes with the predominant 'linear' narrative forms of our literature and film." (2005: 39).

situations semantically available as alternative. This is because they emerge from an open situation by configuring an archive that is situated at the "unstable limit between public and private, between the family, the society, and the State" (Derrida 1995: 57) continually shifting this fragile equilibrium of time-space relations: Narrative practices challenge the boundaries of the public and the private, and their inter-relationship. They may further reclaim the once private and make it public. Accordingly, what is reclaimed is the very idea of the *common* articulated with coolitude and with regard to the indentured modern form of labour whose experience is shared with humankind. I wish to argue at this point that the archive thus becomes a potential and powerful lieu of reclamation of the common, in the way it configures a potential voicing and renders seen the excluded at the unstable limit between the public and the private.

IMPERIAL DEBRIS: THE ENCLAVE

There is another articulation with regard to the imperial debris, which I wish to discuss as the modern spatial figure of the enclave. Imperial ruins are leftover material infrastructures that we witness today – in this case – as fragments of the structures of a plantation economy in the Caribbean. Interestingly, Stoler remarks that

"such infrastructures of large and small scale bear what captivated Walter Benjamin, the 'marks and wounds of the history of human violence'. It is these spatially assigned 'traces of violence', more than the 'deadening of affects' to which we turn." (Stoler 2013: 22)

By focusing on the materiality of debris, she suggests, the "logic of the concrete" may be unlocked, as "ruins can be marginalized structures that continue to inform social modes of organization but that cease to function in ways they once did" (ibid.: 22). Adopting this perspective, I argue that the spatial figure of the enclave reflects the materiality of the imperial debris, in the way it materially corresponds to the organization of a modern plantation economy, being shaped by the transition from slavery into a post-slavery labour regime at the heart of colonial and corporate capitalism. Stoler astutely asks: "What happens when island enclaves […] become repositories of vulnerabilities that are likely to last longer than the political structures that produced them?" (ibid.: 22).

In the context of modern spatial production the enclave can certainly be conceived of as a special figuration of the organizing of space and time on the plantation. Moreover, I argue for conceiving of it as an epistemic figure when it comes to describing the formation of a modern political space. As has been acknowledged, environmental changes in the Caribbean correspond to the rise of corporate colonialism at the turn of the 19th century, which reproduces and reorganizes the previous relations of labour and 'race'. Accordingly, the functional-technological enclave emerges as a type of new spatial phenomenon of a territorial organization, that is, a space that is characterized by transnational economic expansion. Likewise, the enclave as a figure describes the socio-economic space of the plantation developed in the Caribbean through slavery. In the alliance between labour control and racial hierarchy, we identify the foundations of the formation of this modern political space, to which the enclave corresponds as both a spatial and an epistemic figure.

I wish to expand this argument. One of the key categories that describe the modern economic expansion is that of 'race', as noted by scholars including Ann Laura Stoler, Étienne Balibar, and Immanuel Wallerstein. This is also relevant for the hierarchical and hegemonic organization and production of space constitutive of the emergent corporate colonialism: As visual technology, 'race' participates in the spatial order of the enclaves, plantation and company towns. Corporate colonialism's production of space is based on, as pointed out by Balibar and Wallerstein, "a variable combination of a continuous external exclusion and an internal marginalization" (Balibar/Wallerstein 1990: 55). With regard to the photographic archive, many pictures flamboyantly evidence the material organization of the agro-urban enclaves and the plantation, and 'document' the environmental transformation of space that makes effective a new corporate social and labour hierarchy.

Thus the photographic album corresponds to a discourse of labour constitutive of racial lines. 'Race', as Deborah Poole (1997) has remarked, is a visual technology here, in that this technology reiterates a racial hierarchy, both as an external exclusion and an internal marginalization, that enhances the idea of modern productivity and discipline through labour. The enclave as a modern spatial and epistemic figure correlates with this hierarchy. Today, as imperial debris, it remains a leftover structure, though it becomes a part of the

"new de-formations and new forms of debris [that] work on matter and mind to eat through people's resources and resiliences as they embolden new political actors with indignant refusal, forging unanticipated, entangled, and empowered alliances." (Stoler 2013: 29)

So it is that at the level of psychic space the photographs materialize a visual imaginary that correlates with the enclave as raw material and epistemic figures of this space, carving out the contours of the modern political space.

In terms of territorial organization the emergence of this modern space is accompanied by a politics of the enclave that seems to characterize even the first half of the twentieth century. More generally, the enclave is defined as a principle of sovereignty, and is a closed area. This is certainly true for the island enclaves as a constitutive part of modern corporate colonialism. Moreover, with the implementation of the labour camp, spatial segregation is reproduced, reified and perfected. In this process, I argue, the enclave became the privileged form of an imperial formation, which corresponded to designations such as "plantation", "camp", "labour camp", etc. I wish to remind you, at this point, that the functional-modern enclave reflects the changing economic value of the workforce, experienced after the abolition of slavery. Moreover, it reflects the practices of hierarchy and difference, the inclusion and exclusion of labourers, and thus becomes an important spatial figure of a new ordering of the territory in the discourse of plantation. Accordingly, the enclave as labour camp seems, I argue, to be the paradigm of the modern political space. This reading of the paradigm leads us conceive of the enclave, which had generally been studied from the economic perspective as a place of direct foreign investment, as a phenomenon of modernization. With regard to an imperial and modern spatial formation, photography played an important role in modern social regulation, where spatial order converges with the discourse of race, and materializes as violent discrimination. Race as a visual technology, as the photographs reflect, seems to participate effectively in the spatial ordering of the enclave. Likewise, this as-such-configured visual archive provokes reflection on the enclave and the discourse of race as corresponding parts of the expansion of a corporate colonialism. In other words, as interlocked components they form a regime that works on social regulation through a hierarchical spatial order.

Interestingly, as Ann Stoler (1995) has demonstrated in another study, the exclusive policies of colonialism are demarcated not only by external limits, but also by internal frontiers that specify internal conformity and order within colonial societies; the categories of colonizers and colonized are underwritten by a racial difference that is also constructed in terms of gender. Above all, the company towns and plantations were centers of dominant masculine cultures, to which female labourers only visibly entered much later, as domestic servants, plantation labourers, or for the maintenance and serving of the plantation infrastructure. In this sense, the album photographs undeniably reproduce the plantation-as-discourse. As media of technology they articulate and reify the intimate racial fantasies and fears of racial intermixing. In this way, coolie labourers as well as other labourers on the plantations and in the company towns, as depicted in the photographic series of the United Fruit Company, are represented as being a constitutive part of the enclave or labour camp. Yet, the pictures are cultural documents, which reverberate with the imperial debris, which, as material leftovers, remain a powerful historical source embodied in the landscapes today.

In this sense, both the United Fruit Company photographic series, which bears witness to the coolie presence, and the photographic albums of the plantation economy of the French and Dutch Caribbean colonies of 1890 imagine and visibilize the coolie labourer as a part of the economy of the enclave, while they reiterate the discourse of labour. At the same time they open up to a future and potential reclamation to be articulated by generations to come, because they *render seen,* and in so doing, continue to *make visible.* Interestingly, Carter points out in her study that

"as overseas Indians became permanent settlers, they recreated the sacred topography of their homelands, constructing sites of worship and places where gatherings of their co-religionists could be held. Moving out of the estates and into towns and villages, status was defined less by a superior position in the plantation hierarchy than by one's attendance at spiritual and cultural functions of one's peers." (Carter 2002: 129)

This observation seems important, as it may help to conceive of the enclave rather as a porous spatial entity than as a hermetic and strictly closed space. And yet, the enclave as an epistemic figure responds to a hierarchical ordering of space through labour.

However, the pictures clearly conceal the violence of the spatial segregation and any traces of eventual violent incidents or arbitrary physical aggression by white employees against coolie labourers. This becomes evident most notably in the spatial hierarchy the great majority of the pictures depict, representing the development of different types of housing in accordance with the varying segments of labour. Further, this hierarchy is embodied in the photographic archive's own order, at least with regard to the United Fruit Company's photographs, in the way the pictures are arranged to mirror the fantasy of technological progress. The pictures in this sense camouflage violence and eventually obscure labour, on which this spatial hierarchy is founded, and make them disappear altogether by visually underpinning a discourse of technicality and modern production – that is, the discourse of plantation.

POSTSCRIPT

In a related context the literary critic Edward Said once observed:

"[...] how the production of a particular kind of nature and space under historical capitalism is essential to the unequal development of a landscape that integrates poverty with wealth, industrial urbanization with agricultural diminishment. The culmination of this process is imperialism which achieves the domination, classification, and universal commodification of space, under the aegis of the metropolitan center. Its cultural analogue is commercial geography, whose perspectives [...] justified imperialism as the result of 'natural' fertility or infertility, of available sea lanes, of permanently differentiated zones, territories, climates, and peoples. [...] Thus is accomplished 'the universality of capitalism', which is 'the differentiation of national space according to the territorial division of labour'." (Said 1988: 12)

This perspective, focusing on labour and indentured labour from within the imperial genealogies of the present, allows for a working "through the less perceptible affects of imperial interventions and their settling into the social and material ecologies in which people live and survive" (Stoler 2013: 4). As Stoler further underscores, this means "to look at 'imperial formations' rather than at empire per se [...] to register the ongoing quality of processes of decimation, displacement, and reclamation" (ibid.: 8). This observation seems important to me because it opens up to the potential for readdressing the question of empowerment and agency. In this sense, visual leftovers, such as these two photographic series, ask for reclamation by generations to come in order to overcome discrimination and racism.

This kind of potential and powerful renewed reception of visual leftovers seems to avoid the reproduction of fixed structures that come along with an exclusive focusing on Empire, Capitalism, or Plantation. It allows an avoidance of the reiteration of the same metanarratives by causing fissures and fractures that open the way for *petites contre-histoires* or alternative semantics, such as those provoked by *The Coolie. An Unfinished Epic*, and oppose well-known discourses, which inhibit "sight and knowledge, but also the trouble of troubled and troubling affairs", as framed by Derrida with the *mal d'archive* (1995: 57). In this sense, vis-à-vis these visual leftovers, reading the archive means to read it 'against the grain' in order to allow the materialized and concrete fragments of the imperial debris to speak. So it is that the cultural concept of coolitude, that of articulating the experience of modern labour, becomes meaningful as it allows a raising of awareness of the modern political space and its global forms of "a continuous external exclusion and an internal marginalization" (Balibar/ Wallerstein 1990: 55). Furthermore, the concept of *coolitude* allows for and reclaims the *common* beyond ethnic or racial lines, because it speaks out against global and modern bonded labour as a *conditio sine qua non* of the degradation of environments and personhoods.

REFERENCES

Balibar, Étienne/Wallerstein, Immanuel (1990): Rasse – Klasse – Nation. Ambivalente Identitäten, Hamburg: Argument.
Carter, Marina/Torabully, Khal (2002): Coolitude. An Anthology of the Indian Labour Diaspora, London: Anthem Press.
Casid, Jill (2005): Sowing Empire: Landscape and colonization, Minneapolis: University of Minnesota Press.
Daniel, E. Valentine (2013): "The Coolie. An Unfinished Epic." In: Ann Laura Stoler (ed.), Imperial Debris: On Ruins and Ruination, Durham: Duke University Press, pp. 67-114.
Derrida, Jacques (1995): "Archive Fever: A Freudian Impression." In: Diacritics 25/2, pp. 9-63.
Gómez, Liliana (2011): "Un caso de archivo fotográfico: economía visual de la circulación de mercancías, cuerpos y memorias." In: Liliana Gómez/Gesine Müller (eds.), Relaciones caribeñas. Entrecruzamientos de dos siglos/Relations caribéennes. Entrecroisements de deux siècles, Frankfurt am Main: Peter Lang, pp. 109-131.
Jaguaribe, Beatriz/Lissovsky, Maurício (2009): "The Visible and the Invisibles: Photography and Social Imaginaries in Brazil." In: Public Culture 21/1, pp. 175–209.
Poole, Deborah (1997): Vision, Race, and Modernity: A Visual Economy of the Andean Image World, Princeton: Princeton University Press.
Said, Edward (1988): Yeats and Decolonization, Derry: Field Day.
Stoler, Ann Laura (2013): "Introduction." In: Anne Laura Stoler (ed.), Imperial Debris: On Ruins and Ruination, Durham: Duke University Press, pp. 1-35.
—— (1995): Race and the Education of Desire: Foucault's History of Sexuality and the Colonial Order, Durham: Duke University Press.
Williams, John (1925): The Rise of the Banana Industry and its Influence on Caribbean Countries. (Unpublished)

Zizek, Slavoj (2005): "Everything You Always Wanted to Know from Schelling." In: Jason Wirth (ed.), Schelling Now: Contemporary Readings, Bloomington: Indiana University Press, pp. 31-44.

Cultural Forms of Representation of 'Coolies': Khal Torabully and his Concept of Coolitude

GESINE MÜLLER AND JOHANNA ABEL

CREOLISATION AND *COOLITUDE*[1]

Cultural studies attempt to systematically conceptualise a "conviviality in peace and difference" in a wide variety of spaces around the world that have taken on a greater role since the beginning of the twenty-first century (Ette 2010: 169-170, 183). They have been developed in response to the failure of the label 'multiculturalism', or as a rejection of the essentialist concept of identity. For a number of obvious reasons, they are currently the subject of intense debates among intellectuals of the Caribbean and its diasporas (Müller 2012: 255-264). This literature-rich region, which is especially well suited to "literatures without permanent residence" (Ette 2005: 123–156), has also evolved in recent decades into one of the most privileged spaces of theory formation. Theories of *Négritude, Créolité, relationnalité* – in this chronological order – have attempted to take stock of conviviality in the Caribbean and its diaspora, and from there to develop universal categories, as Édouard Glissant (1999) did in *Poétique de la relation*, and as Benitez Rojo (1998) did in *La isla que se repite*. Here the question has been raised repeatedly as to how ethnic difference can be conceptualised without falling into essentialisms. In keeping with the critique of multiculturalism articulated by leading English-language intellectuals like Arjun Appadurai (2009) or Paul Gilroy (2004), Walter Mignolo (2000: 241-242) has expressed deep criticism of the discourse around creoleness:

---

[1] Cf. Müller/Abel 2015; translation by Bill Martin.

"Creoles, Caribbeanness, and Creoleness are still categories that overlap but which belong to different levels. Being or defining oneself as Creole means identifying a group of people, differentiating them from others. Thus, to say that 'neither Europeans, nor Africans, nor Asians, we proclaim ourselves Creoles' (Bernabé 2002 [1989]: 75) is an identification in relation to a territory, and to the historical processes that created that territory." [2]

In what way can this criticism be countered? Glissant (1996:15; [French quotation translated by Bill Martin][3]) called his alternative model "creolisation", which is:

"[...] an encounter between cultural elements from completely different places, which have really become creolized, really merged and got jumbled together to produce an absolutely unforeseeable, absolutely new thing, which is Creole reality [...] The creolization that is taking place in [the Caribbean], and the creolization spreading to other parts of the Americas, is the same one everywhere around the world. The thesis I will defend before you is that the world is becoming creolized, that is to say, that the cultures of the world today are frantically and utterly knowingly coming into contact with each other, changing through this exchange, through irredeemable conflicts and merciless wars, but also through advances in moral conscience and in hope [...]."

---

2   "Criollos, caribeanidad y criollidad son todavía categorías que se soplan pero que pertenecen a diferentes niveles. Ser o definirse a uno mismo como criollo significa identificarse con un grupo de gente y diferenciarse de otro. Así, decir que 'ni europeos, ni africanos, nos proclamamos criollos' [Bernabé et al. 2002 [1989]: 75] es identificarse en relación con un territorio y con los procesos históricos que crearon ese territorio." (Mignolo 2003: 197)

3   "Ce qui se passe dans la Caraïbe pendant trois siècles, c'est littéralement ceci: une rencontre d'éléments culturels venus d'horizons absolument divers et qui réellement se créolisent, qui réellement s'imbriquent et se confondent l'un dans l'autre pour donner quelque chose d'absolument imprévisible, d'absolutment nouveau et qui est la réalité créole [...] la créolisation qui se fait dans la Néo-Amérique, et la créolisation qui gagne les autres Amériques, est la même qui opère dans le monde entier. Le thèse que je défendrai auprès de vous est que le monde se créolise, c'est-à-dire que les cultures du monde mises en contact de manière foudroyante et absolument consciente aujourd'hui les unes avec les autres se changent en s'échangeant à travers des heurts irrémissibles, des guerres sans pitié mais aussi des avancées de conscience et d'espoir qui permettent de dire [...]." (Glissant 1996: 15)

Over the last few years, in addition to Édouard Glissant, more and more voices around the world have engaged with the theoretical concepts coming out of the Caribbean (Müller/Ueckmann 2013: 7). A prominent role in this new dispensation has been played by Khal Torabully, a Mauritian poet, filmmaker, and cultural theorist (Cf. Bragard 2008) who with his concept of *coolitude* both builds on Glissant's work and at the same time critiques its omission of an Indian point of view. Regardless of whether they ended up on islands in the Indian Ocean or in the Caribbean, indentured labourers from the Indian subcontinent – who were recruited from 1830 on as an alternative to slaves – created a worldwide Indian diaspora that demonstrated its own unique mechanisms of acculturation and transculturation. After all, this "population with an autochthonous culture" consisted of people who were both "creole *and* Indian" (Glissant 2005: 41; italics in the original).

KHAL TORABULLY

Born in Port Louis, Mauritius, in 1956, and based today in France, Torabully launched his *coolitude* project in the 1980s. It constitutes a poetic and poetological attempt to develop, on the basis of including those who have historically been excluded, a vision and a revision of both historical and current globalisation processes and desires to give speech to all those living subjects who, due to their miserable circumstances, have been forced to hire themselves out as wage- and contract labourers (Ette 2012: 291).

Torabully's *coolitude* manifesto not only honoured the *coolies* – who came primarily from India, but also from China and other countries – with a literary memorial and a space of memory, as it were; it also developed for them a poetics of global migration, which he had first given voice to in his 1992 book *Cale d'Etoiles – Coolitude* (Ship-Hold of Stars – Coolitude):

"Coolitude, to lay the first stone of my memory of all memories, my language of all tongues, that part unknown which numberless bodies and histories have often cast in my self, my genes and my islands [...]. Here is my love song to our travels and our sea, the odyssey which my seafaring people have never written [...]. As I know my crew will firmly dissolve frontiers to widen the country of Man." (Quoted in Carter/Torabully 2002: 219-220)

What is crucial for Torabully is that he deals not only with the memory of certain forms of barbarous exploitation, but also with a relationality that is both historical and constitutive of the space of intersecting movements of migration:

> You from Goa, Pondicherry, Chandernagore
> Cocan, Delhi, Surat, London, Shanghai
> Lorient, Saint-Malo, people of all the ships
> Who took me towards another me, my ship-hold of stars
> Is my travel plan, my space and vision of an ocean which
> We all had to cross, even if we do not
> See the stars from the same angle.
>
> In saying coolie, I am also speaking of every navigator without
> A ship's register, every man who has gone towards the horizons
> Of his dreams, whatever the ship he had to board.
> For when one crosses the ocean to be born
> Elsewhere, the sailor of the one-way voyage likes to plunge back
> Into his history, his legends, and his dreams.
> Even during his absence of memory.
> (Torabully 1992; quoted in Carter/Torabully 2002: 226)[4]

Significantly, Torabully makes a point of never defining the concept of "coolie" in terms of exclusion. Furthermore, it is used much more in a figurative sense and illuminates specific phenomena of a globalisation "from below", a globalisation of migrants who traverse the sea in search of work. By means of lyrical condensation, a worldwide network emerges of all those "travellers", the objects of an extreme exploitation, who connect the islands and cities of India, China and Oceania with the colonial ports of Europe (Ette 2012: 293).

---

4 "Vous de Goa, de Pondicheri, de Chandernagor, de Cocane, de Delhi, de Surat, de Londres, de Shangai, de Lorient, de Saint-Malo, peuples de tous les bateaux qui m'emmenèrent vers un autre moi, ma cale d'étoiles est mon plan de voyage, mon aire, ma vision de l'océan que nous traversons tous, bien que nous ne vissions pas les étoiles du même angle. En disant coolie, je dis aussi tout navigateur sans registre de bord; je dis tout homme parti vers l'horizon de son rêve, quel que soit le bateau qu'il accosta ou dût accoster. Car quand on franchit l'océan pour naître ailleurs, le marin d'un voyage sans retour aime replonger dans ses histoires, ses légendes, et ses rêves. Le temps d'une absence de mémoire." (Torabully 1992: 89)

COOLITUDE

Torabully's inclusion of the ethnic complexity of post-abolitionist societies in the Caribbean and in the Indian Ocean allows one to grasp the process of creolisation in a less essentialising manner. With his concept of *coolitude*, he advances Franco-Caribbean models of archipelagic creoleness, such as *Négritude*, *Créolité*, *Antillanité* and creolisation, as well as the concepts of *Indianité* and *Indienocéanisme* (Carter/Torabully 2002: 5-7, 16). The concept of *coolitude* is not predicated by geographical affiliation or ethnic origin, but by the economic and legal situation of the coolies – contract labourers who made their way not only from India and China, but also from Europe and Africa to various archipelagic regions like the Caribbean, the Indian Ocean, and the Pacific. With his mosaic model of combined identities, Torabully introduces social status as a theoretically crucial factor in creolisation (Abel 2013: 65–81).

In his foundational works of poetry *Cale d'Étoile, Coolitude* (1992) and *Chair Corail, Fragments coolies* (1999), Torabully implemented the theoretical premises of *coolitude* for the first time. However, international reception and coverage were first achieved with the 2002 publication of the major work *Coolitude: An Anthology of the Indian Labour Diaspora*, co-written with the historian Marina Carter. This work is an anthology in more ways than one. It brings together Khal Torabully's own poetry on the global Indian labour diaspora with a literary anthology of prose and poetry by Indian diaspora authors from the mid-18th century onwards. It focuses above all on the Indian Ocean and Oceania, with works from Mauritius (from 1843 on) and Fiji, Java, and Goa (1860–1870); but it also includes writings from the Americas: from Trinidad, Guyana, Surinam, Guadeloupe, and Martinique (from 1846 onwards). Beyond that, it includes a study of the theory of *coolitude* and its poetics. Formally, *Coolitude* combines a historical anthology in the strict sense with a workbook of brief definitions and a theoretical exploration of *coolitude* in the form of interviews conducted by the authors.

This hybrid book offers both academic interpretations and artistic access to the world of the Indian diaspora by narrating the "essence, or the essences" (ibid.: 148) of the Indian colonial diaspora and by deconstructing traditional views of the British Empire.

The introduction sheds light on the theoretical genesis of the concept by presenting theories of creolisation and relationality produced by Glissant, Deleuze and Guattari, Confiant, Chamoiseau and Bernabé, Benoist, and many others. The second chapter presents the development of one of the key themes of *coolitude*, the "coolie odyssey" – the stigmatised overseas journey from the Indian subcontinent. Chapter three and four are devoted to cultural-theoretical aspects of the perception of coolies by others, as well as their threefold stigmatisation and experience of surviving indenture. According to Carter and Torabully (2002: 187-188), three dispositifs of othering embedded the coolie in victimhood: first, as a mirror to the "oriental mystery"; second, as a "barbarian [...] invader"; and third, as "an ambassador of exoticism and sensuality". Chapter five deals with the "coolie heritage" and considers the politics of memory of the Indian diaspora in the nineteenth and twentieth centuries.

Before the anthology reaches its final chapter, "Revoicing the Coolie", and the concluding selection of Torabully's poetry and critical prose, it goes into a long interview between Carter and Torabully titled "Some Theoretical Premises of Coolitude". The first part of their conversation illuminates the relationship between Césaire, *Négritude*, and *coolitude* (ibid.: 143–159). Part two examines "Elements of the Coolie's 'Memory'" (ibid.: 160–165). In part three, the authors consider aesthetics and literature (ibid.: 165–189); while part four addresses "Tradition, Society and Indianness". In the fifth part – "Some Literary Characteristics of Coolitude" (ibid.: 195–213) – purely poetological features are defined.

The Belgian theorist Véronique Bragard, whose 2008 book *Transoceanic Dialogues: Coolitude in Caribbean and Indian Ocean Literature* has advanced the theoretical reception of *coolitude*, points elsewhere to an important poetological feature of *coolitude* – namely, that it is "not based on Coolie as such but relies on the nightmare transoceanic journey of Coolies as both a historic migration and as a metonymy of cultural encounters" (Bragard 1998, cited in Carter/Torabully 2002: 15). The literary focus is thus fixed on the overseas journey as a phenomenon that both destroys identity and continually reconstructs it. The journey comes to be understood as a *coupure* [cut], displacing the loss of home from the centre of diasporic identity. Thus on an abstact level, the journey is generally linked to a repressed meta-memory of diasporic island identities that would establish ties, or rather produce so-called *hommes-ponts* – "human bridges" – who in turn might serve as interpreters of world cultures in their respective island microcosms (Turcotte/Brabant 1983, cited in Carter/Torabully 2002: 216).

Torabully's special contribution to the figure of the transoceanic journey refers to a poetics of "Indian elements" (Carter/Torabully 2002: 148). The trauma of crossing the ocean takes on a particular significance in the Indian framework since it rests on the key role of the *Kala Pani* myth. The taboo of *Kala Pani*, "the black water" or "Dark Seas", refers to the levelling of caste differences in the liminal space of the ship. These psychosocial dimensions of the transoceanic trauma are taken up in the language of *coolitude* and shape its particular aesthetic.

CORAL

A further aesthetic element resulting from the focus on the transoceanic journey is the search for maritime symbols. The central image of *coolitude* is thus the metaphor of coral, the *chair corail* (coral flesh), which stands for hybrid relationalities in island cultures: "No longer the Hindu man from Calcutta / But coral flesh from the Indies" (Carter/Torabully 2002: 223).

The coral metaphor is not unlike *Créolité*'s images of mangroves and rhizomes, but it is framed transoceanically. As a symbol of the fluidity of relationships and influences, it uses the characteristics of coral as a hybrid being of rock and animal that occurs only in the sea, primarily in the tropics. Coral thus stands for an archipelagic thinking à la Glissant, a *pensée de l'ambigu*, and for a permeability by different currents. The characteristic spiral formations, the corals' *circomvolutions*, suggest visualisations of fractal logic in the processes of creolisation. Not just theoretically, but aesthetically, too, *coolitude* demonstrates its affiliation with Glissant and the *Créolité* writers, who likewise viewed diaspora identities "as not static or fixed but rather as 'subject to the continuous play of history, culture and power'" (Stuart Hall 1993, cited in Carter/Torabully 2002: 11).

The coral can be observed in its living habitat, unlike the rhizome, which exists underground. Beyond that, it allows for a composite rather than just an erratic collectivity, one that grows, palimpsest-like, through layering, condensation and sedimentation, but that nevertheless retains the egalitarian aspect of its conjunctions and openness to being traversed by all currents. The coral is in its very nature a hybrid, for it is born of the symbiosis of a phytoplankton and a zooplankton. It is the perfect metaphor for diversity. It is simultaneously a root, a polyp, and a splitting; it is fluid in form, both pliant and hard, dead and alive; and beyond that, it has many colours. Although it is rooted, it dispatches the greatest migration on the planet, a migration of plankton that, if seen from the moon, would be as clearly visible as the Great Barrier Reef (which UNESCO has designated a World Heritage site). This coral archipelago is quite simply the most extensive living sculpture on the planet (Torabully 2012: 70; cited in Ette 2012: 295).

Aside from its "marine spirit" (Carter/Torabully 2002: 158), *coolitude* also entails more static moments of visualisation that hearken back not to three-dimensional dynamic structures but to two-dimensional composite models, such as the mosaic, in which Indian-Creole tiles complete the overall picture of creolisation without the idea of fusion being privileged. Torabully refigures these composite parts of the mosaic for the third dimension as individual roots of the rhizome (ibid.: 152). The idea of stone, of something fixed, does not simply disappear in the coral metaphor, however, but continues to index the fundamental significance of Aimé Césaire for the development of *coolitude*. Torabully's invocation of *Négritude* and what may be understood as its inheritor, *Antillanité*, is essential for understanding how the theory of *coolitude* is framed. His deep empathy with the founder of the *Négritude* movement and the 1997 interview he conducted with him in Fort-de-France, Martinique – in which the legacy of that movement and its continuation in *coolitude* were discussed – are two of the foundational myths of this concept of creolisation.

Négritude and *coolitude* are connected by two ideas: the reconciliation of the "descendants of the oppressed" (ibid.: 172), which supports efforts to come to grips with the historical tensions between the legacy of the Atlantic slave trade and that of the coolie in Creole societies, and the idea of conceptual negotiation and/or redefinition.

The model of *coolitude* represents a possibility for overcoming the theoretical limits of *Négritude*, which with its calls for and recognition of a specifically black identity disregards the ethnic complexity of post-slavery creolised societies. Carter and Torabully argue throughout their book that *coolitude* is not an Indian version of *Négritude*. For one, it is not based on ethnic or essentialist categories (ibid.: 150, 153). Second, their focus is on the overseas voyage, not on exile or the myth of origins – instead, identity is dissolved in permeability. *Négritude* and *coolitude* share in the discursive reallocation of stigmatised colonial alterities. They diverge from each other, however, when it comes to recognising the cultural influence that the global migration of indentured labourers from India has had on modern societies – regardless of whether that influence has been extensive, as in Mauritius, Trinidad, Guyana, and Fiji, or more limited, as in Guadeloupe, Martinique, or Eastern and Southern Africa.

Coolitude indexes a conception of space that not only emphasises an internal archipelagic relationality of heterogeneous communications between islands and archipelagos, but also points to the dynamics of an external relationality (Ette 2012: 40). In this way *coolitude* becomes a case study of a history of space which is always simultaneously a history of movement. The forced deportations of enslaved persons, such as Indian indentured labourers, shows that the connection between internal and external relationalities is necessary for understanding spaces in their entirety.

REFERENCES

Abel, Johanna (2013): "Orientalische Dopplungen in der Karibik: Coolitude als inklusives Kreolitätsmodell und seine dissoziativen Dimensionen." In: Gesine Müller/ Natascha Ueckmann (eds.), Kreolisierung revisited: Debatten um ein weltweites Kulturkonzept, Bielefeld: transcript, pp. 65-81.

Appadurai, Arjun (2009): Die Geographie des Zorns, Frankfurt: Suhrkamp.

Benítez Rojo, Antonio (1998): La isla que se repite, Barcelona: Casiopea.

Bernabé, Jean/Chamoiseau, Patrick/Confiant, Raphaël (2002 [1989]): Éloge de la Créolité, Paris: Gallimard.

Bragard, Véronique (2008): Transoceanic Dialogues: Coolitude in Caribbean and Indian Ocean Literatures, Frankfurt am Main/Berlin/New York: Peter Lang.

—— (1998): "Gendered Voyages into Coolitude: the Shaping of the Indo-Caribbean Women's Literary Consciousness." In: Kunapipi: Journal of Postcolonial Writing 20/1, pp. 99-111.

Carter, Marina/Torabully, Khal (2002): Coolitude: An Anthology of the Indian Labour Diaspora, London: Anthem Press.

Ette, Ottmar (2012): TransArea: Eine literarische Globalisierungsgeschichte, Berlin/Boston: Walter de Gruyter.

—— (2010): ZusammenLebensWissen: List, Last und Lust literarischer Konvivenz im globalen Maßstab, Berlin: Kadmos.

—— (2005): ZwischenWeltenSchreiben: Literaturen ohne festen Wohnsitz, Berlin: Kadmos.

Gilroy, Paul (2004): After Empire: Melancholia or convivial culture?, London: Routledge.

Glissant, Édouard (2005): Kultur und Identität: Ansätze zu einer Poetik der Vielheit, Heidelberg: Wunderhorn.

—— (1999): Poétique de la relation, Paris: Gallimard.

—— (1996): Introduction à une poetique du divers, Paris: Gallimard.

Hall, Stuart (1993): "Cultural Identity and Diaspora." In: Patrick Williams/ Laura Chrisman (eds.), Colonial Discourse and Postcolonial Theory: A Reader, London: Routledge, pp. 392-403.

Mignolo, Walter (2003): Historias Locales/Diseños Globales. Colonialidad, conocimientos subalternos y pensamiento fronterizo, Madrid: Akal.

—— (2000): Local Histories, Global Designs: Coloniality, Subaltern Knowledges and Border Thinking, Princeton: Princeton UP.
Müller, Gesine/Abel, Johanna (2015): "Korallen: Migration und Transozeanität. Khal Torabully/Indian Diaspora." In: Jörg Dünne/Andreas Mahler (eds.), Handbuch Literatur und Raum, Berlin: De Gruyter, pp. 505-514.
—— /Ueckmann, Natascha (eds.) (2013): Kreolisierung revisited: Debatten um ein weltweites Kulturkonzept, Bielefeld: transcript.
—— (2012): Die koloniale Karibik: Transferprozesse in hispanophonen und frankophonen Literaturen, Berlin/Boston: Walter de Gruyter.
Torabully, Khal (2012): "Quand les Indes rencontrent les imaginaires du monde." In: Ottman Ette/Gesine Müller (eds.), Worldwide. Archipels de la mondialisation. Archipiélagos de la globalización, Madrid: Iberoamericana/ Vervuert, pp. 63-72.
—— (1999): Chair corail, fragments coolies, Petit-Bourg, Guadeloupe: Ibis Rouge.
—— (1992): Cale d'étoiles, Coolitude, Sainte-Marie, Réunion: Azalées.
Turcotte, Paul/Brabant, Claude (1983): "Ile Maurice: Nuvo Sime." In: Peuples Noirs/Peuples Africains 31, pp. 100-106.

Authors

Abel, Johanna, research fellow in the project *Iconic Presence. Images in Religions* at the Center for Literary and Cultural Research (Berlin, Germany). PhD in Romance Studies on the narrativization of body knowledge in 19th-century travel accounts by European women writers on the Hispanic Caribbean. Her monograph was published in 2015 as *Transatlantisches KörperDenken: Reisende Autorinnen des 19. Jahrhunderts in der hispanophonen Karibik* (Berlin: tranvía).

Damir-Geilsdorf, Sabine, professor of Islamic Studies at the University of Cologne, Germany. Her areas of research include political Islam, transformations of religious concepts, reform Islam, Salafism in Germany, popular cultur in the Middle East. She is the author of *Die ‚nakba' erinnern. Palästinensische Narrative des ersten arabisch-israelischen Kriegs 1948.* (Göttigen: Reichert, 2008) and *Herrschaft und Gesellschaft. Der islamistische Wegbereiter Sayyid Qutb und seine Rezeption* (Würzburg: Ergon, 2003).

Gómez-Popescu, Liliana, associate professor at the University of Zurich and and director of the research project *Transcultural Workspaces* at the University of St. Gallen, Switzerland. Her main research fields are Ibero-American literatures and cultures. She edited the Special Issue "History through Photography" *Estudios Interdisciplinarios de América Latina y el Caribe* (2015, 26: 2), with Carlos Rincón, and is the author of *Lo Urbano. Teorías culturales y políticas de la ciudad en América Latina* (Pittsburgh 2014).

Hutson, Alaine, professor of history at Huston-Tillotson University (Austin, Texas), with a research focus on African and Middle East history, in particular slavery and gender in Islamic societies. Her main publications include "Enslavement and Manumission of Africans and Yemenis in Saudi Arabia, 1926-

1938" in *Critique: Critical Middle Eastern Studies*, and "African Sufi Women and Ritual Change" in the *Journal of Ritual Studies*.

Lindner, Ulrike, professor of modern history at the University of Cologne, Germany. Areas of research include European colonialism in Africa, comparative imperial history and social policy in late colonial Africa. She is the author of *Koloniale Begegnungen: Deutschland und Großbritannien als Imperialmächte in Afrika* (Frankfurt a.M.: Campus, 2014) and of "The Transfer of European Social Policy Concepts to Tropical Africa, 1900-50: The Example of Maternal and Child Welfare" in *The Journal of Global History* (2014).

Müller, Gesine, professor of Romance Studies at the University of Cologne, Germany. Her areas of research include literatures of French and Spanish Romanticism, Latin American contemporary literature, Latin American culture theory, literatures of the Caribbean, literary transfer processes and transcultural studies. Her current research includes the ERC-funded project "Reading Global: Constructions of World Literature and Latin America". She is the author of *Die koloniale Karibik. Transferprozesse in frankophonen und hispanophonen Literaturen* (Berlin: De Gruyter).

Tappe, Oliver, Senior Researcher at the Global South Studies Center, University of Cologne. His main field of research is the historical anthropology of upland Southeast Asia. He is co-editor of the volume *Interactions with a Violent Past* (with Vatthana Pholsena, National University of Singapore Press, 2013), and editor of the special issue "Frictions and Fictions – Intercultural Encounters and Frontier Imaginaries in Upland Southeast Asia" in *The Asia Pacific Journal of Anthropology* (2015).

Van Rossum, Matthias, Senior Researcher at the International Institute of Social History (IISH) in Amsterdam. NWO Veni Research Grant (2016-2019) for the research project *Between local debts and global markets* on the history of slavery and slave trade in early modern (Dutch) Asia. He published Dutch monographs on the history of slavery in Asia (*Kleurrijke Tragiek*, 2015), on Asian and Europeans sailors working for the Dutch East India Company (*Werkers van de wereld*, 2014) and on sailors' unions and interracial relations on the Dutch merchant fleet in the 20th century (*Hand aan Hand*, 2009).

Zeuske, Michael, professor of Latin American history at the University of Cologne. His recent publications include *Amistad. A Hidden Network of Slavers* *and Merchants* (translated by Steven Rendall), Princeton: Markus Wiener Publishers, 2014, *Handbuch Geschichte der Sklaverei. Eine Globalgeschichte von den Anfängen bis heute* (Berlin/Boston: De Gruyter, paperback edition 2016), and *Sklavenhändler, Negreros und Atlantikkreolen. Eine Weltgeschichte des Sklavenhandels im atlantischen Raum* (Berlin/Boston: De Gruyter Oldenbourg, 2015).